The Androgyne in Early German Romanticism

Stanford German Studies

Edited by the Department of German Studies
Stanford University, California

Herausgegeben vom Institut für Germanistik
der Universität Stanford, Kalifornien

Vol. 18

PETER LANG
Bern · Frankfurt am Main · New York

Sara Friedrichsmeyer

The Androgyne
in Early German Romanticism

Friedrich Schlegel, Novalis
and the Metaphysics of Love

PETER LANG
Bern · Frankfurt am Main · New York

CIP-Kurztitelaufnahme der Deutschen Bibliothek

Friedrichsmeyer, Sara:
The Androgyne in Early German Romanticism:
Friedrich Schlegel, Novalis and the Metaphysics
of Love / Sara Friedrichsmeyer. – Bern; Frankfurt
am Main; New York: Lang, 1983.
(Stanford German Studies; Vol. 18)
ISBN 3-261-04993-6

NE: GT

© Verlag Peter Lang AG, Bern 1983
Nachfolger des Verlages der
Herbert Lang & Cie AG, Bern
Alle Rechte vorbehalten.
Nachdruck oder Vervielfältigung, auch auszugsweise, in allen Formen
wie Mikrofilm, Xerographie, Mikrofiche, Mikrocard, Offset verboten.

Druck: Lang Druck AG, Liebefeld/Bern

ACKNOWLEDGEMENTS

I would like to record my gratitude to Professor E.P. Harris, Professor Les Chard, and especially Professor Helga Slessarev, all of whom read the manuscript in various stages; their valuable suggestions have helped to shape the present work. I remain grateful to Professor Renée Lang, who introduced me to the concept of androgyny. The University of Cincinnati has provided funding at different stages of my work for which I am also thankful. To my family, again I say thank you; their interest and support have meant much to me.

TABLE OF CONTENTS

Introduction 7

Chapter One 9
Metamorphoses of the Androgynous Ideal

Chapter Two 39
The Romantic Appropriation of the Androgyne

Chapter Three 63
Novalis' Unfinished Novels: Androgynous Wholeness for the Golden Age

Chapter Four 91
Hymnen an die Nacht: The Saving Graces of "Christ and Sophie"

Chapter Five 109
Friedrich Schlegel's Greek Period: The Androgyne as a Model for Equality

Chapter Six 131
Friedrich Schlegel's Romanticism: Embracing Metaphysics

Conclusion 169
The Early German Romantic Androgyne in Retrospect

Bibliography 177

Index of Names 187

INTRODUCTION

An androgyne is, most simply defined, precisely what its etymology implies: a combination of masculine and feminine. Since there have been few physiological manifestations of the word -- biological hermaphrodism in all ages has been extremely rare -- the concept of an androgynous entity has originated in the imagination. As a consequence, the androgyne has appeared in a multiplicity of guises, each of which mirrors and thus helps to define the culture into which it has been adapted. In primitive times it was a prevalent expression of the divine. In later ages it has served as a model for human perfection -- be it biological or spiritual -- and even as a paradigm for understanding the all too obvious tensions within the world of nature. More recently some contemporary feminists have attempted to offer the word and the concept it infers as a guide to psychological wholeness and as a model for human rather than sexually determined behavior. Controversy has often accompanied the concept; but despite its less than universal acceptance, the fusion of male and female into a single entity has remained for centuries a quintessential ideal of perfection.

All assessments of early German Romanticism stress the movement's attempt at wholeness, both for the individual and for the universe. Given their unprecedented awareness of history, the early Romantics dismissed previous orientations as too categorical and strove in their own literature and philosophy to embrace the most dichotomous principles. Throughout history the non-rational has often exerted its sway when an age has become exceedingly rational; in similar fashion, the Romantics, reacting to their historical predecessors, recognized the benefits of including a non-rational, even mystical element into their definition of self-fulfillment; this wholeness they also wished for their world. Filled with hope salvaged from both the Enlightenment and Christian traditions, these intrepid poets and philosophers were convinced that by their synthesizing efforts they could inaugurate a renewed Western tradition. It is true that their optimism did not long endure; following the defeat at Jena, it yielded after 1806 to an increased nationalism or to Catholic fervor. Any remaining enthusiasm was extinguished even more forcefully in the wake of Schopenhauer's philosophy. But for the short time of its primacy, the early German Romantic movement and the thinkers who gave it life were imbued with a surety in the perfectibility of the world and of their own role within that framework.

Throughout the literature of the period, one of the most consistent expressions of the harmony its writers desired was love. Love has always been a primary unitive force, but for the Jena Romantics it transcended the bounds of the individual union to encompass the entire universe. Critics have recognized the importance of love to the Romantics' vision, but it has not been widely understood that the impetus for their encomium of that union was the ancient dream of androgynous perfection. In typical early Romantic thinking, not only the human being but the entire world was divided into opposites to which sexual designations were applied. Not only in their literature, but in their literary theory, their philosophy, their religion and their natural science, wholeness was believed to result from a synthesis of those antipodal forces. Their premise that a perfected human being was the necessary preliminary stage for a harmonious world thus ensured that heterosexual love would become the prototypical synthesis of all polarities and the singular most important medium for effecting the restoration of universal accord.

The androgyne is important in much of the literature of the Romantic age, but in the works of Novalis and the early Friedrich Schlegel it is the major image for perfection. Although Schlegel at the beginning of his career attempted a rather modern interpretation of bisexual totality, his views changed when he became immersed in the Romantic movement. After the mid 1790's he used the androgyne as did Novalis and others. I have attempted here to survey the historical development of the ideal of bisexual perfection up to the time of its resurgence in the Romantic era, emphasizing those currents which were to prove significant for German Romanticism. I have also attempted to analyze the reasons for the prevalence of the model in the literature and philosophy of the period. To demonstrate the Romantic conviction that the synthesis of sexual polarities could change the world, I have chosen to discuss selected works of Schlegel and Novalis.

Chapter One

METAMORPHOSES OF THE ANDROGYNOUS IDEAL

The longing for totality and its ensuing harmony, which in its extreme form is a desire for perfection on earth, has been experienced in many ages. Variously articulated as a desire for oneness with God, as a compulsion for unity with nature, or as the need for the "back to the womb" security of which contemporary psychologists speak, this yearning has also been expressed as a penchant for the completion accompanying the union of male and female. The latter vision of totality has inspired a concept which symbolizes the union of sexual opposites and which has been alternately termed the hermaphroditic, the bisexual, or the androgynous ideal. Frequently controversial, yet discernible as the structuring principle in many religions and myths, this understanding of perfection has resurfaced at various times throughout recorded history, manifesting itself in varying modes to reflect the needs of dissimilar cultures.

Most creation myths tell of a world which came into existence following the break-up of a primordial unity into two opposing principles. These resulting polarities have been construed by diverse cultures in a number of ways, among them light and dark, good and evil, earth and sky, or man and woman. The imperfections so obvious in this world were then easily attributed to the tensions between the oppositions; consequently, efforts at recombination to regain pristine wholeness became the goal of many religions. This threefold scheme is, in fact, the core of most forms of worship: 1) a vision of original harmony; 2) cognizance of a split, or in Christian terminology, the "fall;" 3) attempts at recapturing the bliss associated with a primal condition.[1] Those who have studied religions and myths as reflections

---

1 See for example Mircea Eliade's *Patterns in Comparative Religion*, trans. Rosemary Sheed (New York: New American Library, 1958), p. 419.

of the human soul – among them C. G. Jung, Mircea Eliade and Joseph Campbell[2] – trace this longing for indivisibility, regardless of the form, to a search for the primeval unity we sense in our, to use Jung's formulation, "collective unconscious."

Attesting to the frequency with which early cultures gave sexual designations to the all-encompassing polarities thought to structure their world is the pervasiveness of the primordial divine androgyne, an imaginary entity whose simultaneous existence as male and female or whose incorporation of male and female attributes confirmed its totality. The great pantheon of early gods and goddesses also included other less primordial deities who, perhaps in emulation of the supposed original being, exhibited similar characteristics. In fact, instances abound. From cultures as diverse as those of the early Scandinavians and Germans to those of the Egyptians and Iranians, the divine androgyne was a potent religious force. Babylonian bisexual gods, some critics believe, were so much in evidence that they were even perceived as a direct threat to the developing Hebrew faith. Eastern tradition contains numerous dual-sexed divinities, many of whom have not been obscured throughout the ages and who operate on a fairly sophisticated level even today. The Hindu tradition, including that of the Upanishads and the Puranas, posits a supreme bisexual being who separated into male and female; the Buddhist religion sustains a belief in primary opposites within a totality. One of the oldest expressions of the harmonious union possible between the masculine and feminine principles is found in Taoism, the ancient Chinese attempt at explaining life. Tao is the ultimate force and is composed of the Yang, or male principle representing life and light, and the Yin, the female principle consisting of death and darkness. Signifying what are thought to be the archetypal poles of nature, they thus appear to be irreconcilable opposites

---

2   C.G. Jung, *Symbols of Transformation*, in *The Collected Works of Carl G. Jung*, trans. R.F.C. Hull, 2nd ed., Bollingen Series XX, vol. 5 (Princeton: Princeton University Press, 1967); Jung's works are cited in this study according to the second edition. Eliade, *Comparative Religion*; Joseph Campbell, *The Masks of God: Occidental Mythology* (New York: Viking, 1964).

but are, in fact, defined only through a creative relationship with one another.[3]

The impact of this particular version of perfection can also be noted in variations. Many great goddesses, for example Cybele and Isis, created without consort and were thus assumed to have united within themselves both masculine and feminine powers. In addition to single entities, numerous cosmogonies paid tribute to divine couples; in the highly developed religions of India, for instance, the deity is often represented as Siva-Kali. A further mutation of the original ideal is manifested in the single divinity whose appellation, Father and Mother, is an apparent allusion to completeness.[4]

Western tradition recognizes Dionysus as the best known of the bisexual deities; fragments attributed to Aeschylus (Fragment 61) and Euripides (*The Bacchae*), in addition to several well-preserved statues, attest to his duality. This definition of his essence, however, is often pointedly ignored. Even though a concept of the Dionysian was central to their thought, Winckelmann, Hölderlin and Nietzsche, for example, overlooked or tacitly circumvented this component of the god's being. To more contemporary investigators, the true nature of Dionysus seems equally elusive. Even Robert Graves, experienced as he is at interpreting myths, touches only slightly and then indirectly on the bisexuality latent in the Dionysus legends. Nowhere does he credit this divinity with great powers emanating from a bisexual nature, but instead explains his twofold essence as the result of con-

---

[3] A world map indicating the areas in which the phenomenon has been documented is appended in Hermann Baumann's *Das doppelte Geschlecht: Ethnologische Studien zur Bisexualität in Ritus und Mythos* (Berlin: Reimer, 1955), p. 352. Taoism, with reference to androgyny, is discussed by June Singer in *Androgyny: Towards a New Theory of Sexuality* (Garden City, New York: Anchor/Doubleday, 1976), pp. 192-207; further discussion of the androgyne in Taoism as well as in the thinking of the Upanishads and Puranas can be found in Alan Watts' *The Two Hands of God: The Myths of Polarity* (New York: Collier, 1969), pp. 75, 80, 45-66; for a general discussion see Joseph Campbell's *The Masks of God: Primitive Mythology* (New York: Viking, 1959).

[4] Several examples of this phenomenon can be found in Alfred Bertholet's *Das Geschlecht der Gottheit* (Tübingen: Mohr, 1934), p. 19.

fusion during the transition from a matriarchy to a patriarchy.[5] Others, including James Frazer, who are also recognized for their investigations of early religions are only slightly more objective.[6]

Despite the relative lack of attention the phenomenon has drawn, classical antiquity did boast several bisexual deities, all originally symbols of extraordinary power and integration. The bearded Aphrodite and Hermaphroditus, himself the offspring of Hermes and Aphrodite, provide testimony as imposing as the statue of the six-breasted Dionysus. That bisexual divinities were ideals and not concrete representations of a living reality is evident from records of the Greeks' horror at the birth of a child with physical signs of hermaphrodism; such a child was thought to be the punishment of a supreme being and left to die.[7] The best analysis of the bisexual absolute in the classical world has been offered by Marie Delcourt, whose study, *Hermaphrodite: Myths and Rites of the Bisexual Figure in Classical Antiquity*, represents an attempt to rescue the concept of the androgyne from its many detractors throughout history. She traces the development of Dionysus, for example, from the virile and very potent dual-sexed divine being of the earliest representations, to the often effeminate or even asexual youth of Hellenistic interpretation whose sexual ambiguity reflected only a lack of power. Her explication of the evolving myth: when the Greeks no longer understood the deep religious needs which were met by the deity's double nature, they invented other legends to explain the phenomenon.[8] Guiding the interpretations and artistic efforts of subsequent

---

5   Robert Graves, *The Greek Myths*, vol. 1 (New York: Braziller, 1959), p. 73. When elaborating on the birth and maturation of Dionysus, he points out only that the god was raised as a girl to protect him from Hera, pp. 55-56, and that Dionysus was usually depicted as an effeminate long-haired youth, p. 263.
6   James Frazer, *The Golden Bough: A Study in Magic and Religion*, vol. 1 (New York: Macmillan, 1940), pp. 385-392.
7   Mircea Eliade, *Mephistopheles and the Androgyne: Studies in Religious Myth and Symbol*, trans. J. M. Cohen (New York: Sheed and Ward, 1965), p. 100.
8   Marie Delcourt, *Hermaphrodite: Myths and Rites of the Bisexual Figure in Classical Antiquity*, trans. Jennifer Nicholson (London: Studio Books, 1961), p. 25.

generations were frequently the later versions. Thus Winckelmann, for example, saw only the visual representations of Dionysus sculpted during the Hellenistic age and fell victim, perhaps for reasons also explained by his own psychological make-up, to the fallacious conclusion that the models for the idealized statues were beautiful eunuchs. In turn, such portrayals continued to obscure the original intent of the twofold deity and contributed to a devaluation of the androgyne, reducing it to an equation with abnormal sexuality.

Rarely content to let the absolute remain an undifferentiated spirit, human beings have throughout the ages tenaciously attempted its anthropomorphization; once ascribed human qualities, the divine has then quite consistently been seen as a model for emulation. Many means have thus been devised to approach or attain the original perfection of an allegedly bisexual deity. Primitive societies often contented themselves with an orgiastic togetherness in which all distinctions were supposedly obliterated. In some of the more complex systems, disciplined and even ascetic methods of contemplation were prescribed as the means for spiritually transcending all antipathies. Other, more concrete strategies for imitating a double-sexed being are attested to in the records of ancient rites, such as those stipulating the exchange of costume.[9] Also fairly wide-spread were initiatory androgynization rituals performed at the onset of puberty or before the wedding night. One of the more determined of these attempts was the primitive Australian practice of subincision, whereby a male's penis was slit on the underside to give him an experience approximating menstruation as well as the semblance of a vagina.[10] All can be seen as manifestations of a phenomenon described by Eliade: "In short, from time to time man feels the need to return -- if only for an instant -- to the state of perfect humanity in which the sexes exist side by side as they coexist with all other qualities, and all the other attributes, in the Divinity."[11]

Although there can be little doubt of the frequent primitive insistence on androgynous absolutes, numerous differences must be

---

9 Delcourt, pp. 1-16; Eliade, *Mephistopheles and the Androgyne*, pp. 112-114.
10 Joseph Campbell, *Primitive Mythology*, pp. 102-103.
11 Eliade, *Comparative Religion*, p. 424.

acknowledged, both in the descriptions of the deities, themselves, and in the religious practices which they have engendered. Campbell concedes the dissimilar interpretations as well as the varying levels of sophistication on which the ideal has been expressed; nevertheless, he believes that the legends of a powerful, bisexual divinity worthy of emulation have been derived from a single common tradition. The myths and rites surrounding the divine androgyne represent to him humanity's efforts to bring its "individual life into concord with the whole," an attempt employing imagery "so marvelously constant" that we may "wonder whether it may not simply be coeval with the human mind."[12] Campbell has, in fact, been credited with identifying the androgynous impulse throughout mythology.[13] While conceding disparities, Eliade also stresses the similarity between the various manifestations of the myth, arguing that all the disparate treatments affirm the *coincidentia oppositorum* in the very nature of the divinity. This paradox of a divine reality in which all contraries were reconciled or transcended is, according to Eliade, one of the most elementary ways in which primitive man expressed the difference between himself and an absolute being.[14] Heraclitus said it succinctly: "God is day night, winter summer, war peace, satiety hunger: all the opposites, this is the meaning."[15] Even the Christian god, it can be noted, is perceived as being at once benevolent and terrible, creative and destructive, jealous and loving.

That the apprehension of the deity as one containing all opposites came so often to be expressed in terms of bisexuality can be partially explained by the simplicity of the model. Regardless of whether or not they are manifestations of an archetypal pattern, as Eliade and Campbell infer, sexual polarities are among the most obvious antipathies and can be understood on many levels, often without abstraction. In the numerous adaptations of the androgyne

---

12 Campbell, *Primitive Mythology*, p. 109.
13 Carolyn G. Heilbrun, *Toward a Recognition of Androgyny* (New York: Harper and Row, 1973), p. 176 n. 8.
14 Eliade, *Comparative Religion*, p. 419.
15 G.S. Kirk and J.E. Raven, *The Presocratic Philosophers* (Cambridge: Cambridge University Press, 1957), p. 191.

one constant must be stressed: it has survived as a representation of an ideal and has only rarely been deemed a ready model for physical emulation. History records few, if any, attempts either at establishing a concrete divine androgyne in history, or at biological imitation with the production of an anatomical hermaphrodite.

There is no way of ascertaining the time during which the androgyne first took hold of humanity's imagination, although its multitudinous elaborations attest to its longevity. Its first important documentation in Western philosophy is found in Plato's *Symposium*, that dialog written around 385 B.C. which reports the earlier speeches of various ancients trying to explain the mystery of love. After several other opinions have been advanced, Aristophanes comes forward with a unique explanation:

> In the first place there were three sexes, not, as with us, two, male and female; the third partook of the nature of both the others and has vanished, though its name survives. The hermaphrodite was a distinct sex in form as well as in name, with the characteristics of both male and female, but now the name alone remains, and that solely as a term of abuse.[16]

Each of the three types of beings, Aristophanes announces, was spherical and ran by rolling; but each had a different origin. The males were descended from the sun, the females from the earth, and the hermaphrodites from the moon, alleged to contain both sun and earth. Arrogant and powerful because of their wholeness, these creatures challenged the gods, who responded by splitting each sphere in two. Thus divided, each was relegated to a life spent in search of its missing half. Lacking a means of reproduction, these beings soon began to die out. As Aristophanes reports it, Zeus came to the rescue:

> By moving their genitals to the front, as they are now, Zeus made it possible for reproduction to take place by the intercourse of the male with the female. His object in making this change was twofold; if male coupled with female, children might be begotten and the race thus continued, but if male coupled with male, at any rate the desire for intercourse would be satisfied. . . . It is from this distant epoch, then, that we may date the innate love which human beings feel for one another, the love which restores us to our ancient

---

16 Plato, *The Symposium*, trans. W. Hamilton (Harmondsworth, Middlesex: Penguin, 1951), p. 59.

state by attempting to weld two beings into one and to heal the wounds which humanity suffered.[17]

This is not the place to discuss Plato's purpose or tone, which is admittedly ironic and playful, or even his explicit justification of homosexuality. A cautionary word is also in order: the tale set forth in the *Symposium* should not be read as Plato's serious contribution to the genesis myth, nor should it be interpreted as a reflection of the existence, at some earlier time, of spherical human beings. Choosing a poet rather than a philosopher as the mouthpiece for this particular explication of love was perhaps Plato's signal of distance.[18] Whereas a poet can relate a myth or vision as an ideal not bound to concrete reality, a philosopher, on the contrary, expounds truth in terms of what he or she perceives to be that reality. However, despite its less than solemn intent, the story presented in the *Symposium* remains a testimony to the ubiquity of the myth of the androgyne and marks a significant turning point in its history. No longer merely an ideal according to which early cultures could visualize their supreme beings, or the impetus for a divine model requiring ritualized emulation, the androgyne was now imbedded in the very course of human life. Personal happiness and fulfillment were to be gained only by a return to an androgynous condition. For the first time this goal was deemed attainable through love, a force unambiguously equated with sexual drive. Through Plato's recounting, the ideal of the androgyne was channeled into the currents of Western intellectual history, many of which would later exert a significant influence on German Romanticism.

The Hebraic tradition also bears the mark, if less overtly, of the ancient myth of an androgynous deity. That there are two differing accounts of creation in Genesis has long been ignored or rationalized by the majority of Biblical scholars; recent exegesis, however, has

---

17 Plato, pp. 61-62.
18 Aristophanes was the author of *Lysistrata*, a drama which questioned sexual stereotypes; perhaps this is another reason why he was chosen to advance this particular theory of love.

recognized that the two accounts were written by different people perhaps far apart in time.[19] Genesis 1:26-27 records:

> Then God said, "Let us make man in our image, after our likeness; and let them have dominion over the fish of the sea . . . and over all the earth. . . . So God created man in his own image, in the image of God created he him; male and female he created them.

With this version – which can legitimately be interpreted to imply an androgynous divine being, although the formulation "our image" is usually construed as a reference to God and the angels – is to be contrasted the older account of the creation in Genesis 2:21-22:

> So the Lord God caused a deep sleep to fall upon the man, and while he slept took one of his ribs and closed up its place with flesh; and the rib, which the Lord God had taken from man he made into a woman and brought her to the man.

This latter version is generally known as the creation account and has been used to justify the relatively inferior position of female to male, although it has been the basis for an androgynous tradition as well.[20]

Critics have identified in the Old Testament a misogynist strain based on an equation of woman with temptress.[21] Following that Hebraic tradition the Christian church, in turn, has also undervalued the role of women and sought to deny sexuality; indeed its Catholic form has idealized celibacy and enshrined virginity. Given their masculist bias, the writers of the Bible quite naturally insisted upon a male god. Questioning the validity of the older Genesis 2 account, Theodore Reik in *The Creation of Woman* suggests that its author,

---

19 An interesting discussion of these two versions is presented by Theodore Reik in *The Creation of Woman* (New York: Mc Graw-Hill, 1973), pp. 17-23.
20 See discussions of Böhme, pp. 29-32, and Baader, pp. 58-60, below.
21 See for example James Frazer's *Folklore in the Old Testament* (New York: Macmillan, 1923); Mary Daly's *Beyond God the Father* (Boston: Beacon, 1973); and Reik. Also pertinent is Louis Ginzberg's retelling of the story of Adam's first wife Lilith who, because she insisted on equal treatment, was deposed in favor of a more docile Eve; see *The Legends of the Jews*, trans. Henrietta Szold, vol. 1 (Philadelphia: Jewish Publication Society of America, 1909), pp. 64-69.

influenced by his own culture and time, tried to obviate all references to a female deity.[22] Reik argues from the premise of a matriarchal reality which he felt the Israelites greatly feared. Whether or not the positing of such a social structure is necessary to explain the dogmatic insistence on a masculine deity is debatable. Regardless, the writer of the Genesis 2 version, presumably a product and also a perpetuator of the Hebraic emphasis on patriarchy, was only comfortable with a creation myth which saw woman created after man, and then only from his rib, to be his "help-meet." Despite this inflexibility, it can be surmised that another convention found its way into the first chapter of Genesis and perhaps even into the second, the authors of which unconsciously testified to the power of an androgynous absolute.

Only in the thinking of those adhering to less orthodox forms of Judaism and Christianity was an androgynous strain allowed to surface. In *Legends of the Jews,* Louis Ginzberg speaks of the prevalent belief in an original androgynous Adam within certain Judaic circles and emphasizes its relationship to the ideals formulated in Plato's *Symposium.*[23] Verification is provided in several *midrashim,* the early Jewish interpretations of Biblical texts. According to one of these, the *Bereshith Rabbah,* "When the Holy One, blessed be He, created Adam, He created him an hermaphrodite, for it is said, 'Male and Female created He them and called their name Adam.' "[24] Other versions hold that Adam and Eve were created back to back or even joined at the side and divided subsequently by God into the two sexes as we know them today.[25] According to one of its foremost interpreters, Gershom Scholem, Jewish mystical literature was composed largely by and for males.[26] Yet the *Zohar,* one of its most popular works, contains a clear description of the original deity with

---

22 Reik, p. 149.
23 Ginzberg, vol. 5, 1925, pp. 88-89.
24 *The Midrash Rabbah. Genesis,* trans. Harry Freedman, vol. 1 (London: Soncino, 1977), p. 54.
25 Eliade, *Mephistopheles and the Androgyne,* p. 104.
26 Gershom G. Scholem, *Major Trends in Jewish Mysticism,* 3rd ed. (New York: Schocken, 1954), p. 37.

a female counterpart, the Shekkinah, still intact. Identified sometimes as Israel, at others as the Queen and/or Bride of God, the Shekkinah was averred to have been separated from the masculine essence of the Almighty with the introduction of sin into the world; their eventual reunion would betoken a condition of earthly peace.[27] That the recombination is depicted as a return of the long-lost female to the waiting male, rather than, as in the *Symposium*, a reconciliation of equals, is a reflection of patriarchal attitudes according to which the male is the acknowledged norm and fulcrum.

The *Apocryphal New Testament* also contains quite specific references to an androgynous absolute. In one of the gospels attributed to the Egyptians is found the following: "When Salome asked when what she had inquired about would be known, the Lord said, 'When you have trampled on the garment of shame and when the two become one and the male with the female (is) neither male nor female.'" A different rendering states: "For the Lord himself, on being asked by some one when his kingdom should come, said: When the two shall be one and that which is without as that which is within, and the male with the female neither male nor female."[28] The discovery of the Gnostic texts in 1945 in upper Egypt has also proven a dependence on a bisexual deity during the time the New Testament was being written. Composed perhaps between 50-150 A.D. and already declared heresies by the second century, several of these works, as Elaine Pagels in *The Gnostic Gospels* has recently demonstrated, posit a dual-sexed absolute and document an attempt to reflect that sexual equality in a communal societal structure.[29] Wayne Meeks, another Biblical scholar, has also identified an an-

---

[27] Scholem offers a valuable discussion of such sexual symbolism within the general context of Jewish mysticism, pp. 205-243.
[28] Edgar Hennecke and Wilhelm Schneemelcher, ed., *New Testament Apocrypha*, trans. A. J. B. Higgins et al., vol. 1 (London: Lutterworth, 1963), pp. 168-169. Further examples are adduced in Eliade, *Mephistopheles and the Androgyne*, pp. 105-107.
[29] Elaine Pagels, *The Gnostic Gospels* (New York: Random, 1979), see especially pp. 48-69.

drogynous principle in several practices of the early Christian church before the entrenchment of the orthodoxy.[30]

Further references could be appended, but those already quoted suffice to show an irrefutably androgynous undercurrent within the Hebraic and Christian traditions which was rejected by the orthodox faith, in itself a reaction worthy of study. Although these persuasions developed without being substantially influenced by the androgynous ideal and instead in a distinctly patriarchal direction, there are thus reminders for all who care to be reminded that the tradition of a patriarchal God the Father was a conscious and not inevitable choice.

Paralleling the development of the Judeo-Christian religion can be detected another less well-defined mode of thought commonly referred to as Hermetism. Recognizing the apocryphal Hermes Trismegistus as its founder, Hermetic philosophy approaches religious salvation by mystical and non-rational means, usually through a process synthesizing variously designated polarities. Its doctrines are contained in the *Corpus Hermeticum*, compiled between 100 and 300 A.D., and are thought to have been formulated as an alternative to Greek Rationalism. Remaining true to its origins, Hermetism in its various forms has constituted an alternative to frequently more mainstream rational thought throughout the ages. In the first lines of the Emerald Table, attributed again spuriously to Hermes Trismegistus, is contained its basic axiom, *Quod superius sicut quod inferius.*[31] This equation of the macrocosm and the microcosm was the impetus

---

30 Wayne Meeks, "The Image of the Androgyne: Some Uses of a Symbol in Earliest Christianity," *History of Religions*, 13 (1974), 3, pp. 165-208.

31 The doctrines of Hermetism are collected in *Hermetica*, trans. and ed. Walter Scott, 4 vols. (Oxford: Clarendon, 1924-1936). A good discussion of both Hermes Trismegistus and Hermetic lore is available in Frances A. Yates' *Giordano Bruno and the Hermetic Tradition* (Chicago: University of Chicago Press, 1964), pp. 1-19. M.H. Abrams, in *Natural Supernaturalism: Tradition and Revolution in Romantic Literature* (New York: Norton, 1971), p. 146, introduces a discussion of Neoplatonism with a cautionary word about what can be called the Hermetic tradition. Its basic conceptual scheme, he says, is "recognizable in writings which range from positions near the lunatic fringe of thought to some of the most subtle attempts in our literature to assess man and his place in nature and in the historical process."

for all Hermetic practitioners, among them the Gnostics, the Kabbalists, the alchemists, and even many mystics. One of the first to deal with Hermetism, Father Festugière divided its doctrines into two categories, one of which so consistently decried the world as evil that its goal was to transport matter into the spiritual realm; a more optimistic branch practiced as astrology and alchemy, however, attempted to merge the two realms by bringing the spiritual to earth.[32]

Although the orthodox Christians and Jews rejected the various manifestations of Hermetism, they did not succeed in nullifying its influence. In fact, as has been recently affirmed, it is largely through the little recognized influence of Hermetic philosophy that original perfection in Western religions became synonymous with unity; the fall -- that is, evil or empirical reality -- with division; and heaven with regained unity.[33] In its oscillating course through history, Hermetism has also been the primary vehicle for the transmission of the androgynous ideal. The first book of the *Corpus Hermeticum*, the "Poimandres," gives clear expression to an androgynous divinity as well as to a similarly endowed first being. Creation is depicted as follows: "And the first Mind . . . being bisexual . . . gave birth to Man, a Being like to Himself." After a certain time "all living creatures, having till then been bisexual, were parted asunder . . . and so there came to be males . . . and likewise females." And the absolute being ordered them, "Increase and multiply."[34] Complicated imagery, to be sure, and worthy of comparison with the formulations in both the *Symposium* and the Bible, but an androgynous first principle who created humanity in its own image is clearly discernible.

Several theologians who have investigated the concept of androgynous perfection in the Christian tradition have corroborated its affinity with Hermetism. After identifying and examining the image

---

32 See the discussion in Yates, pp. 22-23, 44-49. Yates divides Hermetic literature into philosophical (creation account) and practical (alchemy, astrology) branches; while she is no doubt correct, her analysis does not detract from that of Festugière's whose divisions are more applicable for this study.
33 Abrams, pp. 145-154.
34 *Hermetica*, vol. 1, pp. 119-125.

in Christian theology, W. Schulze concluded several decades ago that the androgyne was not an inherently Christian pattern.[35] The prevalence of the ideal in Christian thinking was analyzed at about the same time by Ernst Ludwig Dietrich. Although these two studies do not refer to one another, Dietrich's provides an answer to the question implicit in Schulze's work by associating the androgyne with Hermetism.[36]

As the myth of the androgyne was interpreted by succeeding ages, a changing emphasis can be detected. That the majority of cosmogonic divinities had been imagined as bisexual has been explained as the primitive's attempt to express the awesome paradox of the divine who, by dint of its perfection, contained within itself all polarities. An important corollary was an intensified awareness of the distinction between humanity and an absolute being. Later thinkers, especially those practitioners of Hermetism determined to merge the spiritual and physical realms, were less concerned with articulating their conception of a transcendent deity and their lost paradise; their desire was instead to actualize the perfection of the divine on earth by overcoming in some way the incompatibility between themselves and their heavenly counterpart. As evidenced in the practices of medieval alchemy and mysticism, both of which were important for the Romantic movement,[37] the androgyne was readily adaptable to such strivings.

---

35 W. Schulze, *Das androgyne Ideal und der christliche Glaube* (Lahr-Dinglingen: St-Johannes, 1940).
36 Ernst Ludwig Dietrich, "Der Urmensch als Androgyn," *Zeitschrift für Kirchengeschichte*, 3. Folge IX, vol. 58 (1939), 3/4, pp. 297-345.
37 Ronald Gray, in *Goethe the Alchemist: A Study of Alchemical Symbolism in Goethe's Literary and Scientific Works* (Cambridge: Cambridge University Press, 1952), demonstrates the importance of alchemy primarily for Goethe but also for his entire age. Goethe was, says Gray, fascinated with the subject and performed his own alchemical experiments but felt he had to downplay his interest. Gray attributes Goethe's constant search for totality in large measure to this early study. Paul Kluckhohn, in *Die Auffassung der Liebe in der Literatur des 18. Jahrhunderts und in der deutschen Romantik*, 2nd ed. (Halle: Niemeyer, 1931), pp. 119-139, discusses the importance of mysticism for the Romantic view of love.

Most adepts throughout the history of alchemy firmly believed that because of a tension between opposites inherent in all matter, everything found on earth existed in an imperfect state. The same dictum propelling other branches of Hermetism -- "What is above is like that which is below" – was interpreted as a mandate to neutralize these polarous entities and thus regenerate the world. Following the history of alchemy is a formidable task, not merely because of the esoteric nature of the discipline itself, but also because the alchemists were frequently under attack and so insisted upon a great deal of secrecy to assure their own survival. Especially in the Christian world, where they were usually perceived as trying to become partners with God to create a universe more complete and perfect than that with which he could be credited, were these practitioners subjected to pressure. Their claims and aspirations were, after all, viewed as tantamount to blasphemy. Despite such difficulties, their art survived for centuries; even after being replaced by Newtonian science, alchemy remained an alternative for those dissatisfied with what they perceived to be a mechanical world view.[38]

Because they saw their work as a process of creating harmony out of the most extreme dissonances, the alchemists were fond of paradoxes; to this inclination as well as to their need for privacy can be traced their predilection for obtuse symbols, which in the alchemical treatises often seem to be plagued by a deliberate obscurity. Endeavoring to express the polarous forces in the world, it is conceivable that the alchemists discovered for themselves the tremendous potential of the sexual dichotomies; it is equally possible, however, that the Hermetic tradition influenced the selection. In any case, most descriptions of the alchemical *magnum opus* depend on sexual imagery, and it is here where the androgynous impulse is to be identified. In fact, after C. G. Jung's work, no serious discussion of

---

38 For an introduction to alchemy see Gray, pp. 1-37. Standard works dealing favorably with the subject include Herbert Silberer's *Problems of Mysticism and its Symbolism*, trans. Smith Ely Jelliffe (New York: Weiser, 1970); and A.E. Waite's *The Occult Sciences* (1891; rpt. Secaucus, N.J.: University Books, 1974).

alchemy could ignore its debt to an ideal of androgynous perfection.[39]

On the physical plane the combinatory *opus* of the alchemists was usually described as a search for a way to complete the transmutation of base metals into gold. Although there surely were alchemists who tenaciously searched for gold as a metal bereft of any spiritual connotations, the usual aim was a less tangible "gold" equated with human or cosmic perfection. To accomplish their purpose, the alchemists concentrated on the creation of what they called the philosopher's stone, often thought to be attainable by the proper combination of sulphur, as representative of the feminine or earthly pole, with salt, thought to embody the masculine or intellectual component of all matter. Bridging the two was mercury, which, because of its supposed ability to combine the feminine sulphur and the masculine salt, was often referred to as a hermaphrodite. The "gold," to stress its creation from the "marriage" between male and female elements, was also described not infrequently as the "hermaphroditical infant." Even the stone itself, that "noble tincture" never found naturally upon our imperfect world, was alluded to with similar imagery.[40] Developing Jung's insight, Erich Neumann has not only identified the circle, and thus the philosopher's stone, as the prototypical symbol of original wholeness, but has also recognized its androgynous essence.[41]

To determine the precise role of the alchemical androgyne is a difficult task, and one to which scholarship has not yet addressed itself. It may have functioned merely as a conventional formula for wholeness and thus have been intended, as Ronald Gray suggests, "to represent the unitive and universal nature of the Stone."[42] On the

---

39 See Jung's *Mysterium Coniunctionis*, vol. 14, 1970; and *Psychology and Alchemy*, vol. 12, 1968.
40 Evelyn Underhill, in *Mysticism: A Study in the Nature and Development of Man's Spiritual Consciousness*, 12th ed. (New York: Dutton, 1930), pp. 140-148, offers a summary of alchemical symbolism. Not all alchemists, it should be noted, agreed on the proper combination to produce the stone.
41 Erich Neumann, *The Origins and History of Human Consciousness*, trans. R.F.C. Hull (New York: Pantheon, 1954), pp. 8-11.
42 Gray, p. 34.

other hand, it is also possible that, for at least some of the adepts, the concept of androgynous wholeness had deeper import as a humanistic model for personal, psychic fulfillment. In either case, a cursory glance through various alchemical handbooks shows that for their compilers the sexual polarities were more than abstract labels. Many such manuscripts carry illustrations of the proposed hermaphrodite, envisioned, for example, as a male body with a female head or as a composite figure, male on the left and female on the right.[43] It would be absurd, of course, to suppose that the true alchemists were striving in even the remotest way to create an actual biological hermaphrodite. Regardless of what else they might have signified to the adepts, these visual oddities were primarily representations of an ideal; each depicted the polarous forces in nature which the alchemical *opus* was seeking to combine.

When practiced at the most spiritual level and only for the benefit of the soul, alchemy resembles mysticism, another vehicle for communing with an ultimate principle. In Christian terminology the goal of mysticism is union with God, the *unio mystica*; in nontheistic contexts it is a combination with some "other," often perceived as an opposing entity. Primarily a unitive, non-rational experience, mysticism may or may not be associated with organized religion. Although it forms the core of Hinduism and Buddhism, it is a less visible strand -- and frequently a disturbing one -- in Judaism, Islam and Christianity.[44] Angelius Silesius, to adduce one example among many, challenged the Christian church by ecstatically pronouncing his equality with God; he was, he declared, "as large as God" and God was as small as he.[45]

---

43 Many of these illustrations can be seen in Jung's *Psychology and Alchemy*.
44 Underhill is one of the definitive contributors to an understanding of mysticism. Her book is infused with the belief that mysticism is the active expression of a power latent in the whole human race -- the power of perceiving transcendental reality -- and that the mystic is someone who possesses more of this desire than do ordinary human beings, p. 73 for example. Other standard works include Walter T. Stace's *The Teachings of the Mystics* (New York: New American Library, 1960). The first chapter of his book provides an objective statement on the essence of mysticism.
45 Angelius Silesius, "Der cherubinische Wandersmann," in *Sämtliche poetische Werke*, ed. Hans Ludwig Held, 3rd ed., vol. 3 (München: Hanser, 1949), p. 8. Unless otherwise noted, the translations throughout this study are my own.

It seems fairly consonant with most discussions to state that, despite the differences, most mystic experiences can be grouped into two main categories. Many Christian mystics have declared God's utter transcendence based on their conception of a complete separation of the human and the divine; their journey was upward and outward and has been labeled by William James, one of the earliest to discuss the history of religions and religious phenomena, the experience of the "sick soul" crying out of despair to the far away perfection. Modern theology often prefers the doctrine of immanence favored by many Eastern religions and practiced by those whom James referred to as the "healthy minded." Such mystics feel the absolute to be implicit within both the self and the universe.[46] The goal of the latter -- and this is the form which found its way into Romanticism -- is for an ambiguously defined "center."[47]

Critics of mysticism, and there have always been many,[48] point to those adherents who in their penchant for intoxication remain isolated from the world. Those who evaluate mysticism more positively stress the experience of universal truth which the mystics must share in their attempt to mediate between essence and existence. Because the mystics, then, have tried to express in words an experience which they themselves repeatedly described as "ineffable" -- William James considered ineffability one of the few constants of genuine mysticism[49] -- they were compelled to seek symbols, images, rhythmic patterns and, inevitably, paradoxes to convey their visions. The Romantic conception of a symbol as a means for conveying the inexpressible and Goethe's definition of a symbol as an idea which, though articulated in all languages, remains nevertheless inexpressible, may both have received common impetus from mystic writings. For

---

46 William James, *The Varieties of Religious Experience* (New York: Longmans, Green and Co., 1912), pp. 78-165.
47 For a discussion of the importance of the "center" see Jung's "Commentary on 'The Secret of the Golden Flower,' " in *Alchemical Studies*, vol. 13, 1967, pp. 1-55.
48 See for example the assessment by John Passmore in *The Perfectibility of Man* (London: Duckworth, 1970), pp. 304-327.
49 James, p. 380.

although the roots of the appreciation for symbols lie in the Western acceptance of Platonic forms, it is equally feasible to credit the dilemma inherent in mysticism with a refocusing of attention on the genuine symbol and away from the medieval allegory.

The myriad accounts of the mystic experience appear subsumable into four major symbols – those of nature, pilgrim, saint and lover. Symbolism of the latter variety, in which the ancient ideal of the androgyne may be glimpsed, was primarily used by those to whom mysticism was above all else a personal relationship with an "other."[50] It was especially pervasive among Christian mystics familiar not only with the sexual imagery in Hermetic writings, but also with that in the Bible. The popularity of the sexual symbol in mysticism has traditionally been attributed to the erotic elements of the Song of Songs, a work often interpreted as an allegory of spiritual life. Although less acclaimed, another potent impetus to the mystics' acceptance of such physical imagery is a variation of androgynous union which has accompanied both Judaism and Christianity since their beginnings. Both Testaments contain books essentially devoted to portraying the end of all things in time, specifically Daniel and Revelations; a similar intent was marginally influential in other books, such as Isaiah. Throughout these works, numerous images were adapted to depict the final days, many of which involved unions of opposites, a preference traceable perhaps to Hermetism. Quite common were the transcended antipathies between lion and lamb, for example, or that between sexual oppositions, the latter an image which M.H. Abrams has identified as the Biblical "apocalyptic marriage."[51] The earliest form of this Biblical convention, according to Abrams, can be traced to the perception of marriage as a covenant; by extension such a union soon referred to a covenant between the Lord and Israel. Within this framework Isaiah, for example, rejoices about the future of Jerusalem. The land, he promises, will be called "Married" because the Lord is pleased; and "as the bridegroom rejoices over the bride," so shall God rejoice over Jerusalem (Isaiah 62: 4-5).

---

50 Underhill discusses these symbols, pp. 125-148.
51 Abrams, pp. 37-46. I am indebted to Professor Abrams for the following discussion of this convention.

So consistently adhered to was this imagery that Israel, in her deviations from the faith, was even castigated as an adulteress, as for example in Hosea 2-4. In the New Testament can be seen a variant of this image representing a further transfer of God's metaphoric union with Israel to a future coupling between Christ and the New Jerusalem, his bride. The resulting union was to be the signal for the millennium. One such articulation of the end of the world appears in the Revelations of John (21:9-10):

> Then there came one of the seven angels ... saying, Come, I will show you the Bride, the wife of the Lamb. And ... he carried me away to a great, high mountain, and showed me the holy city Jerusalem coming down out of heaven from God.

So widely accepted was the perception of Christ as a bridegroom that his words on the cross, *"consummatum est,"* were in some circles understood as constituting an erotic consummation between him and his followers. A sermon attributed to Augustine includes the following:

> Like a bridegroom Christ went forth from His chamber. ... He came to the marriage bed of the cross, and there, in mounting it, He consummated his marriage. And when He perceived the sighs of the creature, He lovingly gave himself up to the torment in the place of His bride ... and He joined the woman to Himself for ever.[52]

Whether enunciated as a oneness with the New Jerusalem or with a group of the faithful, the conjugal union of Christ with his partner was also susceptible to metamorphosis; as adapted by many mystics, it expressed the very personal union of the soul, traditionally viewed as passive and therefore feminine, with Christ. Thus St. Bernard could explain in his sermons on the Song of Songs the potentially troublesome line, "Let Him kiss me with the kiss of His mouth," with reference to the soul waiting for union with the Savior. "Who speaks? The bride. ... The soul thirsting for God," he instructed his listeners.[53] To female mystics familiar with the metaphor which called every nun the bride of Christ, describing their own ecstasies as

---

[52] Quoted in Abrams, p. 45.
[53] *Saint Bernard on the Love of God*, trans. Rev. Terence L. Connolly (Techny, Ill.: Mission Press, 1943), p. 67.

a marriage between themselves and Christ or God was a simple extension. Bearing strong witness to this convention in Germany are the works of Mechthild von Magdeburg.[54] It can be noted that even today every Catholic nun wears a wedding ring to signify her union with Christ. The predominance of sexual imagery in both mystical and alchemical writings has rendered both vulnerable to what sympathetic interpreters insist is exaggerated misinterpretation. Such controversy, and it will continue, brings cognizance of the very precarious boundary between the real and ideal applications of the myth of androgynous perfection.

One of the most important links in the evolution and further transmission of the androgynous ideal was the Protestant mystic, Jakob Böhme. Greatly influenced by the alchemist and medical practitioner Paracelsus, who had flavored Hermetism with Christian perspectives and who had entertained a notion of humanity's twofold nature,[55] Böhme brought to Christianity the contours of the Hermetic tradition. In his investigation of Böhme's thought, *The Mystic Will*, H.H. Brinton indicates the extent of his subject's debt to alchemy: "Boehme did more than borrow a large part of his vocabulary from alchemy, he took over the alchemistic world-view which he developed into a philosophic system."[56] Assessed by another critic as one of the most important shapers and transmitters of a mode of thinking which joined the ideas of Neoplatonism and Kabbalism to those of Christianity,[57] Böhme is to be credited with incorporating the androgyne into the process of Christian salvation.

Postulating the need for self-knowledge as the primary drivingforce within the universe, Böhme justified the fallen world as the manifestation of an undifferentiated first principle, the necessary mirror through which the supreme being could attain consciousness.

---

54 Note particularly her work *Das fliessende Licht der Gottheit*, ed. Margot Schmidt (Einsiedeln: Benzig, 1955).
55 Paracelsus, *The Hermetic and Alchemical Writings of Paracelsus*, ed. and trans. A.E. Waite, vol. 1 (London: Elliot, 1894), p. 161.
56 Howard H. Brinton, *The Mystic Will: Based on a Study of the Philosophy of Jacob Boehme* (London: Allen and Unwin, 1931), p. 81.
57 Kluckhohn, *Die Auffassung der Liebe*, p. 121.

As the first principle, in Böhme's idiom the *Ungrund*, was deemed androgynous, "a masculine virgin, neither woman nor man,"[58] so too from the Biblical account of Eve's creation out of Adam's rib did Böhme deduce Adam's originally dual-sexed condition. As envisioned by the theosophist in *Mysterium Magnum*, his commentary to Genesis, Adam was "male and female, with both divine heavenly tinctures;" in him neither the fire (male) nor the light (female) was to dominate, for "they should stand in equal weight . . . in God" (V, 89). Drawing on legends inherent in various strains associated with Hermetism, such as early forms of Jewish mysticism and Christian Gnosticism, he called Adam's feminine half Sophia, the Virgin or Heavenly Wisdom.[59] Adam, however, was not content. Paralleling the creator, this first human desired self-awareness, a condition possible only with the separation of the divine Virgin from the masculine essence. Because of Adam's need to "know" the female within him, or the "worldly spirit of lust within him," as Böhme also referred to it (III, 118), God separated the sexes, giving them "bestial members [*thierische Glieder*] for propagation" (V,95). This was to the theosophist the first fall. But reminiscent of the same event in the *Symposium*, the separation carried with it the incentive for eventual recombination. As the Almighty's goal was an eventual reunion with an "other," Adam and with him all of humanity would find a final androgynous perfection in the reunion with a sexual opposite. For, according to Böhme, although God had divided Adam, "yet it is one thing: only the property of the tincture was divided" (I, 108). As elucidated in *Beschreibung der Drei Principien Göttlichen Wesens*, the Virgin departed into the heavenly ether "and waits there for all the children of Adam" until they are ready to "receive her for their bride again" (III, 118).

---

58 Jakob Böhme, "Mysterium Magnum," in *Sämmtliche Werke*, ed. K.W. Schiebler, vol. 5 (Leipzig: Barth, 1922), p. 140. Future references to Böhme's work will be cited according to this edition of his collected works and will be referred to in the text by volume and page number.
59 A similar linkage of the feminine with wisdom can be extracted from Proverbs 8 and permeates the apocryphal Wisdom of Solomon, see especially chapters 7 and 8.

Because the eating of the apple and the consequent ejection of the first human pair from Paradise constituted for Böhme only the second fall, a distinct priority is given to a metaphysics of sex rather than to a metaphysics of morality; human life was to be spent retracing the steps to original unity. Only through Christ and love, Böhme stressed, was this a possibility. Christian alchemists had long referred to the philosopher's stone which could purify matter as the "indwelling Christ." In Böhme's adaptation, an individual could be "transmuted" into androgynous perfection simply by loving Christ, the second androgynous being on earth. Like Adam and his progenitor, Christ was a "masculine virgin" (V, 103) containing the Heavenly Virgin Sophia within. As had others before him, Böhme interpreted Christ's words on the cross, "*consummatum est,*" to signal a final merging of the sexes, now within an individual (V, 101). As detailed in his works, Christ offered redemption specifically because to the man he was a "bride," to the woman a "bridegroom." By loving Christ, each man and woman would thus be reunited with the counterpart which had previously been lost (VI, 197).

That Böhme could so effectively impose an androgynous configuration upon the story of the fall from grace is partially due to a structural correlation between the two myths. As in many religions, salvation in Christianity is viewed as the result of a triadic progression, beginning with the perfection of the Garden of Eden. The second stage is the fall into evil, and the third and culminating phase calls for a return to the heavenly paradise. The myth of the androgyne exhibits a parallel pattern: original androgynous perfection is followed by the fall into diversity, that is, into separate sexes, which in turn will yield to a regained oneness.

Propelled by the need in Hermetic philosophy for a physical corollary, Böhme declared Christ's representative on earth to be the partner in each marriage; thus the marital union became the key to spiritual salvation. This mandate also provided a justification for sexual desire, the "divine inclination;" for the division of the tincture had left in each a longing for its partner, so that humanity "continually seeks the Virgin, its playmate [*Gespielin*]." From this yearning for wholeness "comes the great desire of the masculine and feminine sex . . . to copulate, for one sex continually supposes that the other has the Virgin" (III, 127). Uncomfortable with the erotic consequences of his creed, Böhme took care to label connubial love an inferior substitute for the divine union it represented. Sophia, for example, was repeatedly eulogized as Adam's true wife; conjugal relations, on the other hand, were consistently deprecated with labels such as "whoredom" (VI, 197) and decried for effecting "bestial propagation [*viehische Fortpflanzung*]" (III, 119).

Although never accepted by the orthodoxy -- indeed much of Böhme's work was produced only after he had been forbidden from further writing -- Böhme's theosophy and with it the ideal of androgynous perfection had a far-reaching effect on subsequent generations. Because of his encomium of poetic imagination, Böhme has been recognized as important for early German Romanticism.[60] Böhme's belief that the creation of the world had only been possible because the first principle had imagined it was interpreted by the Romantics as philosophical proof that the perfect world of which they dreamed could be created through their own works of art. But few literary critics have seen a Romantic translation of Böhme's commitment to androgynous wholeness. In *Adam: Der Mythus vom Urmenschen*, however, Ernst Benz offers a valuable discussion of Böhme's theosophy and chronicles the perpetuation of his particular view of redemption through European thinking into the nineteenth century. The mysticism of the Scandinavian Immanuel Swedenborg, Radical English Protestantism, Russian mysticism of the seventeenth and eighteenth centuries, and even the thinking of Louis Claude de Saint-Martin in revolutionary France, according to Benz, were all indebted to Böhme's legacy.[61]

In Germany, although censored for a time, Böhme's works were available after 1682 when J.G. Gichtel published them in their first complete German edition. Soon they became the inspiration and

---

60 See for example Edgar Ederheimer's *Jakob Boehme und die Romantiker* (Heidelberg: Winter, 1904); and Carl Paschek's *Der Einfluß Jacob Böhmes auf das Werk Friedrich von Hardenbergs*, Diss. Bonn, 1967 (Bonn: Rheinische Friedrich-Wilhelms-Universität, 1967).
61 Ernst Benz, *Adam: Der Mythus vom Urmenschen* (München: Otto-Wilhelm-Barth, 1955).

major doctrinal focus for certain groups, later associated with Pietism, which were seeking an alternative to what was judged the mechanistic religion of Rationalism. Never a monolithic movement, Pietism thrived instead in various strains, some closer to the orthodox church than others but all united in their opposition to the Enlightenment. Because of its insistence on individual salvation, Pietism has recently been evaluated by Friedrich Wilhelm Kantzenbach as a continuation of and the most important theological development within Christianity since the Reformation.[62] Not all Pietists acknowledged Böhme's importance. Although those who did maintained his vision of humanity's androgynous beginning and end, their greatest interest was in the androgynous Savior, the Christ in whom the Virgin Sophia had returned to earth.

Gichtel, a forerunner of Pietism, had dedicated his Böhme edition to the "lovers of Theo-Sophiae" and introduced the work with the phrase "Jesus-Sophia!" Soon after he completed it, he published a commentary interpreting Böhme's teachings. With a devotion to the Heavenly Virgin Sophia verging on fanaticism, Gichtel insisted that Böhme intended a strict prohibition against marriage. Salvation, he decreed, would come only through love for the androgynous Christ: "For Jesus is a virgin to men and a *man* to women; he is the true and complete Adam with both tinctures."[63] More closely linked with Pietism, Gottfried Arnold, like Gichtel, recorded his devotion to Sophia in many poems and referred quite readily to her centrality in his visions. His poetry, however, as that

---

62 Friedrich Wilhelm Kantzenbach, *Orthodoxie und Pietismus*, Evangelische Enzyklopädie, No. 11/12 (Gütersloh: Mohn, 1966), pp. 130-134. On Pietism see also Martin Schmidt's *Wiedergeburt und neuer Mensch* (Witton: Luther, 1969); and Albrecht Ritschl's *Geschichte des Pietismus in der lutherischen Kirche des 17. und 18. Jahrhunderts*, 3 vols. (Bonn: Marcus, 1880-1886). Ritschl's work is still referred to in most studies of Pietism, although critics recognize his negative bias and the influence of that position on subsequent discussions. For a discussion of Pietism's influence on Romanticism see Kluckhohn's *Die Auffassung der Liebe*, pp. 119-150, 176-198.
63 Johann Georg Gichtel, *Theosophia Practica*, vol. 3 (Leyden, 1722), p. 1949. The dedication to Böhme's works is found in *Theosophia Revelata*, vol. 1 ([Holland], 1715), no page number.

of other Pietists in which an androgynous vein is discernible, has only a spurious claim to literary value. Though best known for his *Unparteiische Kirchen- und Ketzerhistorie*, a popular work read avidly by many including the young Goethe, Arnold was also respected for a work entitled *Das Geheimnis der göttlichen Sophia*. With its focus on the feminine "inner bride" lost to man through the fall, the work is clearly indebted to Böhme. Arnold's writings also indicate that the ambivalence surrounding Böhme's explanation of the fall from grace -- a philosophical need to "know" oneself which is alternately described as a sexual desire for the female within -- has been overcome. Here, as in the works of most Pietists, sexual desire alone is held responsible for bringing evil, that is, division, into the world. In one representative poem Arnold's Adam laments having fallen "through his own desire" and having consequently lost the inner "bride" who had been given to him as the "aim [*Ziel*]" of his love. As his desire "turned outwards from within," God took Sophia "out of" him and returned with her to heaven. And thus, he concludes, "paradise was no more."[64] Although for a time strongly opposed to earthly marriage, Arnold later argued its value as a "measure against whoredom."[65] His own marriage ended his friendship with Gichtel.

To enunciate a philosophy compatible with both the Bible and with natural science was the life-long goal of Friedrich Christoph Oetinger, one of the leaders of Pietism in Württemberg. Veering from Newtonian perspectives, he found instead an inspiration in the nature mysticism of Böhme; his influence remained strong even after his death in 1782. A more original thinker than either Gichtel or Arnold, and less obsessive as well, Oetinger's vision of salvation was nevertheless derivative. Convinced of humanity's twofold origin, he worked assiduously to demonstrate the viability of Böhme's dependence on the androgyne in the process of redemption. Finding verification in literal renderings of verses such as Galatians 3:28 in which Paul

---

64 Gottfried Arnold, *Das Geheimnis der göttlichen Sophia*, part 2 (1700; facsimile rpt. Stuttgart: Frommann, 1963), pp. 55-56.
65 Gottfried Arnold, *Das eheliche und unverehelichte Leben der ersten Christen* (Frankfurt: Fritschen, 1702), p. 163. St. Paul's views on marriage were also influential for Arnold's later opinions.

declares that in Christ there shall be "neither male nor female," Oetinger believed all angels to be bisexual. Saved through love of the androgynous Christ, human beings would attain even on earth a state he equated with an absence of sexuality; he often described that condition, however, in psychological rather than physical terms. Union with Christ, he announced in *Über Jakob Boehmes Adamsspekulation*, would grant a male the "feminine gentleness" he lacked and would provide a female with the "masculine vigor and strength" she required for wholeness. In defense of his admittedly controversial views, he added a qualification: "The time will come when this will be better understood."[66]

Less directly influenced by Böhme, Count Nikolaus Ludwig von Zinzendorf incorporated into his theological speculations a more favorable attitude toward marriage than was found in the works of many of Böhme's ascetic followers, but one which nevertheless proscribed eroticism. Remembered today chiefly as the founder of the Herrnhut Brotherhood and as a composer of Protestant hymns, Zinzendorf hailed marriage as the creation of one entity out of two, the earthly catalyst for granting each partner a partaking of the androgynous Savior.[67] So visual was his conception of the Redeemer that he even alluded to Christ's wound as his vulva, a phenomenon largely responsible for the train in Pietist thinking referred to as the theology of the wound (*Wundentheologie*).[68] Referring to himself as Christ's earthly representative, he wrote to his wife on their twenty-fifth wedding anniversary of his desire to "present" her to Christ, her true "husband," and further commented upon his own life "with your and his children."[69]

Although the resurgence of an androgynous ideal in eighteenth century Germany was largely due to its role in Pietism, other trans-

---

66 Friedrich Christoph Oetinger, *Über Jakob Boehmes Adamsspekulation* (1776; rpt. Stuttgart, 1849), pp. 498, 128.
67 See for example his poem "Eigene Hochzeit-Gedanken" reprinted in *Das Zeitalter des Pietismus*, ed. Martin Schmidt and Wilhelm Jannasch (Bremen: Schünemann, 1965), pp. 300-304.
68 See the discussion on Zinzendorf in Martin Schmidt's *Pietismus* (Stuttgart: Kohlhammer, 1972), pp. 93-108; see also Kantzenbach, pp. 201-202.
69 Zinzendorf, "Aus den Homilien über die Wundenlitenai," in *Das Zeitalter des Pietismus*, p. 363.

mitters of Böhme's theosophy which had already helped to shape Pietist thinking continued to play a role in legitimizing the concept. Böhme's focus on androgynous completion was also made known through the Berleburg Bible, a scriptural exegesis done in the second quarter of the eighteenth century and based on the interpretations of numerous mystics including those of the Silesian shoemaker, Böhme. Though rejected by the orthodox church, this work was very popular among the Pietists; Heinrich Jung-Stilling, among others, praised it frequently.[70] Swedenborg's teachings were also widely read in Germany in the 1770's. Believing, like Böhme, in earthly marriage as the representative of humanity's mystic union with the androgynous Christ, Swedenborg nevertheless viewed conjugal union more favorably than did many Pietists. In *Conjugial Love*, Swedenborg declares that humans were created with an instinct towards union with a member of the opposite sex without which each would remain a divided or half human being.[71] In the 1770's, however, Rationalism held sway in Germany and the Swedish mystic was attacked by more conventional figures, not the least of them Kant, who dogmatically declared him the "archfantasist [*Erzphantast*] among all fantasists."[72] It has been suggested that Kant's strong and even emotional rejection of Swedenborg's works did not have its intended effect and instead only heightened public curiosity; the works of the Swedish mystic were then read, if in secret, ever more widely.[73] Unambiguous in his own appreciation of Swedenborg's works, Oetinger applauded him as a scientist and prophet and helped to acquaint many of his own contemporaries with the Swede's thinking, among them Lavater, Jung-Stilling, Goethe and Novalis. Although less important, a French

---

70 See discussion in Benz' *Adam*, pp. 135-150.
71 Emanuel Swedenborg, *Conjugial Love*, trans. Samuel M. Warren (New York: Swedenborg Foundation, 1928), p. 43. In contrast to purely sexual love, marital love was for Swedenborg so powerful that it would continue after death, pp. 55-69.
72 See Ernst Benz' "Immanuel Swedenborg als geistiger Wegbahner des deutschen Idealismus und der deutschen Romantik," *Deutsche Vierteljahrsschrift für Literaturwissenschaft und Geistesgeschichte*, 19 (1941), 1, p. 9.
73 Benz, "Immanuel Swedenborg."

translation of Böhme's theosophy, done by Saint-Martin and retranslated into German by Matthias Claudius in 1782, also helped to spread the doctrine of androgynous redemption. Studied and even improved later by G.H. Schubert and other students of Schelling, this translation also helped to put the concept of marriage into philosophical language.

Although the Romantics did not discover Böhme directly until after 1798 when Tieck recommended his works, his theosophy and with it his acclaim for androgynous perfection were thus accessible to their entire generation long before. Indeed, because his theosophy was adapted by so many thinkers in the late 1700's, Benz has labeled the philosophy of German Idealism a Böhme Renaissance.[74] More recently, Marshall Brown has redirected attention to Böhme's thinking as instrumental for the "shape" of German Romanticism.[75] Pietism, frequently dismissed as a radical offshoot of Protestantism, played a significant role in transmitting the theosophist's beliefs; in the Romantics' adaptation of the androgynous ideal, it also proved a dominant influence. It was not merely intellectual curiosity which led the Romantic thinkers to Pietism; indeed many writers and philosophers of the late eighteenth century – Schelling, Schleiermacher, Novalis, Hölderlin, Schiller, Hegel and Kant among them – grew up in Pietist environments.

Thus has the androgynous ideal appeared in a multiplicity of guises from prehistory to the Romantic age. Serving both as a description of primal perfection and as a model for future wholeness, it has resurfaced in various eras, mirroring the needs of the cultures into which it has been adapted. Perhaps it has been so malleable because it is delimited by nothing in reality; its expression must therefore be a product of the imagination. By the time the Romantics encountered the concept, the androgyne had been incorporated into theosophy, philosophy and the natural sciences; had they been accepted disciplines, anthropology and psychology would also have been affected. In these various modes of thought the androgyne found common favor as an ideal for human perfection, the secular attainment of which was, by all accounts, the goal of the early German Romantics.

---

74   Benz, *Adam*, p. 23.
75   Marshall Brown, *The Shape of German Romanticism* (London: Cornell University Press, 1979).

Chapter Two

THE ROMANTIC APPROPRIATION OF THE ANDROGYNE

Although the androgynous ideal can be clearly identified in several of the religious and intellectual currents which helped to define Germany before 1800, it had relatively little impact on German literature during those centuries. Echoes can be discerned in the medieval *Tristan*,[1] but Gottfried's encomium of androgynous love remained a solitary phenomenon in German letters until the end of the eighteenth century when the early Romantics recognized its potential. Almost another century passed before critical attention was directed to this resurgence; although these analyses stirred a slight controversy at the time, they garnered little approbation. Ricarda Huch, the first to identify the model in Romantic literature, interpreted its prevalence as corroboration of her thesis that the Jena Romantics were among the first to recognize the need for psychological wholeness.[2] Fritz Giese devoted an entire book to his investigation of androgyny in that movement, a concept which he, too, saw as originating in the psychological desire for totality. More a documentation than an analysis, his work did adduce evidence demonstrating not only the existence of a strong wave of the androgynous ideal in early German Romanticism, but also an awareness on the part of several of the artists that they were writing and thinking within a very old tradition.[3]

---

1   To my knowledge, no critic has offered such an interpretation.
2   Ricarda Huch, *Die Romantik I: Blütezeit der Romantik*, 13th ed. (Leipzig: Haessel, 1924), pp. 116-149, 247-275. Huch makes the mistake, however, of accepting the same traditional stereotypes as did the Romantics and therefore applauds their recognition of the need to combine the "feminine" unconscious with the "masculine" conscious mind.
3   Fritz Giese, *Der romantische Charakter I: Die Entwicklung des Androgynenproblems in der Frühromantik* (Langensalza: Wendt and Klauwell, 1919). Giese's work is valuable today primarily as a source for documenting the androgyne in Romanticism.

Few major critics reacted to these studies, although those who did -- Oskar Walzel and Paul Kluckhohn among them -- were rather insistent in their refutations.[4] Stemming primarily from their inflexible definition of the androgyne as an anatomical composite, their intransigence influenced subsequent study; although contemporary critics are beginning to discuss once again the impact of this ideal in the thinking of the Romantics,[5] standard references on German Romanticism do not acknowledge the concept. Indeed, critics in general have allotted to the androgyne no role in the German cultural tradition which culminated in the Romantic movement. To ignore its presence in German culture around 1800, however, is not only to disregard its impact on Romantic literature and philosophy or to overlook its importance in Pietism and in the thinking of others influenced by Böhme, but also to ignore evidence that a principle of bisexual totality was intellectually accepted during the time for its role in the myths and religions of other cultures. Providing the initial impetus for this line of investigation was Winckelmann's eulogy of the hermaphrodites of antiquity. His studies, in turn, lent credence to the assorted androgynous deities which were gaining recognition through the influx of Oriental religions and thought. Such influences helped to create an intellectual matrix for further examination of double-sexed entities. Testifying to this interest are investigations such as those of Friedrich Creuzer and K.A. Böttiger, who explored its origin in myth and religion; and that of Friedrich Welcker, who assessed its influence in art.[6] Although some of the

---

4   Oskar Walzel, "Ricarda Huchs Romantik," in *Vom Geistesleben alter und neuer Zeit* (Leipzig: Insel, 1922), pp. 337-365. Walzel's attack is directed as much against Huch as a woman and against what he considers her intuitive methodology as against her ideas; he warns: "Be careful of the brain power of a woman who with such energy strings her material on a chain!", p. 359. See also Kluckhohn's *Die Auffassung der Liebe*, pp. 354-355, 520 n. 1, 550-551.
5   See for example A. J. L. Busst's "The Image of the Androgyne in the Nineteenth Century," in *Romantic Mythologies*, ed. Ian Fletcher (London: Routledge and Paul, 1967), pp. 1-95; and Richard Exner's "Androgynie und Preussischer Staat. Themen, Probleme und das Beispiel Heinrich von Kleist," *Aurora*, 39 (1979), pp. 51-78.
6   See Giese, pp. 41-59, for a discussion of these studies.

actual studies were published too late to have had an immediate effect upon the early Romantics, all bear witness to the renewed interest in the phenomenon of bisexual totality in the years around 1800.

To be sure, these influences and investigations were there for others to develop as well. Only in early German Romanticism, however, did the androgyne emerge as a quintessential ideal of wholeness. That only the Romantics in Jena incorporated the androgyne so thoroughly into their ideology is, as will be demonstrated, a measure of its compatibility with their philosophy. Because of the various traditions which it sought to combine and which were perceived as embodying dichotomous principles, their philosophy rendered them supremely susceptible to a construct which by definition eliminated boundaries.

Much has been written on the contribution of both the Neoplatonic and Judeo-Christian traditions to the development of Romantic philosophy. Each was an attempt to explain what Morse Peckham has articulated as the disparity between orientation – the order an individual perceives or wants to perceive in the world in order to structure value into his or her society – and the unavoidable experience of randomness in the world.[7] A spirit or ideal world beyond the confines of empirical comprehension was thus posited by both traditions to explain the ineluctable presence of evil and to unequivocally limit it to the physical realm. It was Plato who first assumed an intangible world of forms, but it was Plotinus who later revived Plato's doctrines and translated that world of forms into a world of spirit. Thus redefined, this philosophy was interwoven with Christian dogma to the extent that it is quite legitimate to speak of Neoplatonized Christianity. Among other legacies, these modes of thought are to be held accountable for the firmly entrenched dualistic world view which appeared so ominous to the Romantics and to the overcoming of which their own philosophy was addressed.

Quantitatively less has been written about the subtle yet potent impact of the Hermetic tradition which transmitted to the Romantics the primary impetus for harmonizing the spiritual and physical worlds.

---

7   Morse Peckham, "Towards a Theory of Romanticism: II. Reconsiderations," in *The Triumph of Romanticism* (Columbia, S.C.: University of South Carolina Press, 1970), p. 28.

Often dismissed as fostering an arcane and primitive science of the occult -- and its detractors point to such allegedly obscurantist practices as magic, alchemy, astrology, metempsychosis and the Rosicrucian Order -- Hermetism, as was demonstrated earlier, is more correctly regarded as a religious philosophy inciting and directing its adherents to rise above the illusions of empirical reality to a realm of the divine on earth. Its basic intuition of the world as composed of and fueled by a vast system of polarities, in obvious analogy to sexual reproduction and consequently laden with androgynous symbolism, provided an intellectually acceptable schema for explaining the universe until replaced by Newtonian science, and even later for those dissatisfied with the idea of a mechanistic world. Its underlying tenets remained intact long enough to contribute to the early Romantics an incentive for defying the extremism they recognized in previous orientations; in contrast to their predecessors' advocacy of either rational or non-rational avenues to truth, the early Romantics saw the potential for earthly perfection only in their synthesis. In the Pietist view of history -- itself an amalgam of Christian and Hermetic principles -- they found not only a structure for these dreams, but also assurance that their lofty goals could be actualized.

One of the most impelling assumptions in Pietism was that of an imminent apocalypse, an idea which often accompanied Hermetic thinking. Although this concept had resurfaced intermittently in Christian circles, the frame had altered over the centuries. To the early Christians persecuted by the Romans, the apocalypse, often conveyed through the motif of a marriage between Christ and the New Jerusalem, had been primarily a promise of material and physical well-being. In accordance with their own priorities, the Pietist translation of the end of the world embraced instead the finality of spiritual fulfillment. Although it never achieved the status of orthodox dogma, the apocalypse did become a preoccupation in eighteenth century Germany. So thorough was this orientation that even Kant in 1794 addressed himself to the problem in an essay, "Das Ende aller Dinge." In a tribute to Pietist eschatology, if not to its imagery, Hans-Joachim Mähl in *Die Idee des goldenen Zeitalters im Werk des Novalis* assesses Christian millennial thinking as one of five factors contributing to the Romantic dream of a Golden Age.[8] Abrams has also certified the influence of such Christian anticipations on the structure of Romantic thought.[9] But whereas Abrams appraises the religious pattern as the primary structural model for Romantic ideology, Mähl relativizes its uniqueness by discussing it as merely one of five factors and, in fact, credits the literary idyll as more influential. Within the limited circumference he allots to the Christian model, however, Mähl values the Pietist contribution to Romantic chiliasm. Others, notably Benz, have established the Romantic proclivity for eschatological speculation as specifically indebted to Pietism. In his study of Johann Albrecht Bengel, the founder of Pietism in Württemberg whose works many of the Romantics studied and admired, Benz credits Bengel as the direct impulse to such thinking not only in Pietism but throughout German Idealism.[10]

The Pietists constructed no theories of history, but the eschatologically oriented view of history first associated with the Enlightenment, its philosophical chiliasm, was indebted to the Pietist legacy. The physical world contained the capacity for perfection and was even at the present engaged in an almost perceptible evolution towards that goal. This was the core of the Enlightenment philosophy of history, as adumbrated in Germany by Lessing and Kant, and even

---

8 Hans-Joachim Mähl, *Die Idee des goldenen Zeitalters im Werk des Novalis* (Heidelberg: Winter, 1965), pp. 232-245. The other four factors are 1) the ancient myth of the Golden Age; 2) Arcadian dream worlds known to Romantics as idylls; 3) a belief in a world monarchy and concommitant world peace; 4) a conception of the utopian state, p. 1.

9 Abrams articulates his "recurrent" though not exclusive concern to be with "the secularization of inherited theological ideas and ways of thinking" in both Germany and England, where a history of political and theological radicalism "fostered collateral developments of response" to the French Revolution, p. 12.

10 Ernst Benz, "Johann Albrecht Bengel und die Philosophie des deutschen Idealismus," *Deutsche Vierteljahrsschrift für Literaturwissenschaft und Geistesgeschichte*, 27 (1953), 4, pp. 528-554. Mähl, in "Novalis und Plotin," in *Novalis*, ed. Gerhard Schulz (Darmstadt: Wissenschaftliche Buchgesellschaft, 1970), pp. 357-423, establishes Bengel's influence on Novalis.

by others only marginally identifiable with Enlightenment thought such as Herder and Schiller.[11] Schiller, himself reared in Pietist surroundings, was among the first to give artistic form to the Pietist and Enlightenment historical schema when he posited progress not in a return to Arcadia but in a reaching out for Elysium.[12] Although the Romantic secularization of the end point remained more aligned with the spiritual promise of Pietism than with the future of moral perfection espoused during the Enlightenment, its utopian vision clearly paralleled the pattern of history articulated during the Age of Reason.

Entwined within this view of progress was the equation between an original condition and unconscious harmony which Rousseau had so convincingly advanced. Unable to transcend this idea, Enlightenment philosophers in their attempts at a consistent theodicy had insisted upon the necessity of their disjointed present as a propellant for a higher degree of perfection than had been possible in the "unconscious" original state. In 1786 in *Mutmaßlicher Anfang der Menschengeschichte*, Kant gave this idea a rational articulation by imputing even the fall from grace to man's reasoning capabilities. Although not widely recognized, Böhme's voice also contributed to this rationalization. Attempting to explain why a perfect God had found it expedient to create a world, Böhme had been forced to posit a will to consciousness within the *Ungrund*, the first principle. Although associated with evil and separation, the fallen world was nevertheless understood as the mirror through which the Almighty could fathom its totality. For Kant, too, evil was thus a necessity,

---

11 A summary of these philosophies of history can be found in Arthur O. Lovejoy's "Herder and the Enlightenment Philosophy of History," in *Essays in the History of Ideas* (Baltimore: Johns Hopkins University Press, 1948), pp. 166-182. See also Lewis White Beck's introduction to *On History: Immanuel Kant* (New York: Bobbs-Merrill, 1963), pp. vii-xxvi. The influence of Christian thinking on this view of history is documented in Ernest Tuveson's *Millennium and Utopia: A Study in the Background of the Idea of Progress* (Berkeley: University of California Press, 1949).
12 Friedrich Schiller, "Über naive und sentimentalische Dichtung," in *Schillers Werke: Nationalausgabe*, ed. Benno von Wiese, vol. 20 (Weimar: Böhlaus, 1962), p. 472.

because the reunion between God and his creation which would inevitably follow would be more meaningful for its inclusion of consciousness.[13] Long known as the "paradox of the fortunate fall," this justification of evil was accepted by the Romantics along with the additional philosophical underpinnings it had so recently acquired.[14]

The quintessential paradigm of the Romantics' frame of mind can thus be assessed as a longing for the rebirth they believed would follow the union of polarities roughly corresponding to the spiritual wholeness posited in the past and the rational empiricism of their present. The various programs they enunciated for bringing about a revivified world have certain common denominators: 1) the apprehension of a long ago, serenely unified and total world; 2) the experience of a disjointed present and a plan for its dissolution; 3) the reestablishment of lost primal harmony, albeit on a higher level. This triadic pattern for regaining original perfection was common to thinkers of the age from Kant to Hegel. To Friedrich Schlegel the dream would be realized by an artistic fusion of what he analyzed as the natural and objective glories in earlier art and culture with the subjective and often excessively conscious perspective of his own time.[15] Schiller had hoped for the same with different terminology when he proposed a combination of the "naive" and "sentimental," and Goethe would later apotheosize the union in the marriage of Helen and Faust. Hölderlin in his extremely personal way yearned for the day when the ancient gods would return; using the analogy of the marionette, Kleist lamented man's lost innocence and harmony through consciousness and voiced hope for their eventual reclamation. Novalis, too, longed for a Golden Age in which the spiritual and physical would merge in their original splendor. The

---

13 Immanuel Kant, "Mutmaßlicher Anfang der Menschengeschichte," in *Werke*, ed. Ernst Cassirer, vol. 4 (Berlin: Cassirer, 1922), pp. 325-342.
14 The theological origins of this rationalization are discussed by Lovejoy in "Milton and the Paradox of the Fortunate Fall," in *Essays in the History of Ideas*, pp. 277-295.
15 Schlegel used the words "subjective" and "objective" to mean "of the subject" and "of the object."

adaptations of this triad also differ beyond the form; the distinctions are apparent first and foremost in the degree to which the various writers believed the third stage possible. Schiller, Fichte and to some extent Friedrich Schlegel, for example, maintained their footing in rationalist thinking and were resigned to the tensions of separateness. Others, especially Novalis, thought perfection not only attainable but imminent.

These renewal efforts can also be subsumed under a pattern which Abrams has detailed in his study of Romantic ideology in Germany and England. The title *Natural Supernaturalism* is borrowed from Carlyle and reflects, as Abrams emphasizes, the concern of the age to secularize inherited theological ideas as well as to naturalize the supernatural.[16] Specifically, it is the inherent Biblical structure of paradise, paradise lost, and paradise regained which Abrams cites as exerting control over the Romantic vision. In its secularized form, this structure can nowhere be more aptly applied than to the dreams of the early German Romantics whose personal and historical ambitions for wholeness were conditioned by the lure of the paradisiacal "Eden" before the "fall."

It becomes obvious that this tripartite pattern is the common property of the androgynous ideal, mythologized long before the Biblical model was established, but created out of the same psychic need for totality. Recognizing the myth as a tenet of Hermetism, Abrams lauds it as the "major pictorial medium for embodying and sustaining the doctrine that perfection is identical with simple unity and that the cosmic course is from the One and the Good into evil and multiplicity and back to the One."[17] It is understandable then that, corresponding to the degree with which the Christian doctrines of an age have been tinged with or influenced by Hermetism, the androgyne has been a frequent though unapplauded Christian image of indefectibility. Böhme's theosophy as well as Pietism with its mystic bent, always considered a fringe movement within Protestantism, provides obvious documentation. Such Hermetically shaped Christianity strongly affected the German Romantics, perhaps most

---

16 Abrams, pp. 12, 68.
17 Abrams, p. 155.

conspicuously in the triadic scaffold which they impressed upon history, but just as indelibly in their choice of the androgyne as a symbol for progress and ultimate perfection. It was an image by which such consummate wholeness, embracing all polarities and admitting of no distinctions, could be expressed.

Helping to establish the androgyne as a symbol of perfection was the early Romantic understanding of nature. The eighteenth century saw the currency of many theories of nature, so that to try to define *the* Romantic attitude to the natural world would prove an elusive undertaking. Although Fichte and those in his train espoused the rationalist's disregard for physical phenomena, there were others for whom nature subsumed its previous Hermetic definition. To earlier generations, the parallel thought to exist between the macro- and microcosms had indicated a unified man and nature as the complement to God. Influenced by such suppositions, eighteenth century figures often assumed, as Ernest Tuveson has demonstrated, that God's plan for humanity was synonymous with his plan for nature.[18] To many Romantics, such thinking dictated that organic nature be seen as a model for human behavior, that its struggles and processes be assigned a role in the development of the individual. The ideal of the androgyne could thus only gain philosophical credibility through Schelling's *Naturphilosophie* which intellectually credited the natural world as an inclusive system within which all polarities exist and must exist. Further, it was only by dint of the tension inherent in these polarities, which he even labeled male and female, that a dynamics of progress could be maintained. In his very influential *Von der Weltseele* (1798), for example, the principles according to which he defined his philosophy of nature were Weight [*Schwere*], associated with the female and the real, and Light [*Licht*], termed the male and the ideal.[19] Long recognized as

---

18 Tuveson, especially pp. 113-152.
19 The principles are named in the subtitle, "Development of the First Axioms of the Philosophy of Nature According to the Principles of Weight [*Schwere*] and Light [*Licht*];" associations of those principles with the sexual polarities are clearly stated within the work: "Von der Weltseele," in *Sämmtliche Werke*, ed. K.F.A. Schelling, Abt. 1, vol. 6 (Stuttgart: Cotta, 1860), pp. 406-418. Future references to Schelling's works will be cited according to this

indebted to Böhme, Schelling's philosophy has recently been correctly assessed as a refined version, but nevertheless a resurfacing, of the Hermetic view of the universe, a view which Cartesian and Newtonian science had all but obliterated.[20]

In the service of their commitment to bringing the divine to earth, the Romantics further adapted the theory equating the macro- and microcosms. Again according to Schelling, although human beings and nature were parallel in many ways and although the processes of the natural world could serve as a model for man, the two were not equal. While man enjoyed an elevated status as *microtheos* in his works, nature, Schelling asserted, was merely engaged in the evolutionary process toward the absolute. Thus, in that age of secular promise, humanity gradually replaced God as nature's antipode. Böhme's influence can again be discerned in this attitude. His earlier works, especially *Aurora* which was the most frequently read in Germany before 1800, have been criticized for an incipient pantheism; his later works, however, heralded the split between humanity and nature which so plagued the Romantics. Influenced by Renaissance thinking enough to set humanity above the rest of creation, Böhme in *Mysterium Magnum* definitively acclaimed man the microcosm of the world (V, 9-11). It was, after all, as God's image that Adam had been inspired to the self-revelation which had resulted in the breakup of bisexual totality.

Believing in man's godlike status, the Romantics therefore focused their aspirations on the individual within whom the all-important synthesis of polarities was to be forged, in whom the

---

edition of his collected works. The sexual opposition throughout nature is a theme of "Erster Entwurf eines Systems der Naturphilosophie," Abt. 1, vol. 3, 1858, pp. 44-54. He claimed nature as the structural model for human development in "Allgemeine Deduktion des dynamischen Processes," Abt. 1, vol. 4, 1859, pp. 75-78. Schelling's early view of nature is also presented in "Ideen zu einer Philosophie der Natur," Abt. 1, vol. 2, 1857.

20 Abrams, p. 171. For further comparison of Schelling's system with that of Böhme see Robert F. Brown's *The Later Philosophy of Schelling: The Influence of Boehme on the Works of 1809-1815* (Lewisburg: Bucknell University Press, 1977). Schelling's main study of Böhme occurred after the Jena group had disbanded, but Brown documents his earlier contact with the theosophist's ideas as well.

divine could be brought to earth. Other influences also contributed to their lack of attention to or interest in collective action. Partially because of the failure of the French Revolution, but also following the German tradition of political non-engagement – and W.H. Bruford records Mdme. de Staël's amazement that even Goethe, Schiller and Wieland did not read newspapers[21] – the early Romantics did not set their goals in the political arena. Influenced as well by the Pietist emphasis on individual salvation, their belief in inevitable historical progress found a structural analogue in their philosophy of individual self-improvement in the pursuit of higher stages of humanity. In this way, by a concentration on the perfection or *Bildung* of the individual, they felt they could effect a change in the world, a view which was not seriously challenged until Marx did so half a century later. Accordingly, a pattern involving recombination of the sexual dichotomies, so flexible that their forerunners had used it to signal the end of the physical world or even to denote a personal mystic experience of oneness with the divine, held great appeal. Concretized in heterosexual love, it represented a method of recapturing an original condition which could be initiated by human effort.

Never in doubt of their rationality, the early Romantics characterized themselves as alienated from their non-rational and spiritual powers. Individual wholeness, they were convinced, would only follow from the synthesizing, in a true Hermetic revival, of humanity's physical and spiritual essences. Friedrich Schlegel's call for a new mythology can be understood as his proposal for incorporating into everyday reality the spiritual and non-rational. Goethe was revered by the early Romantics because his own scientific pursuits, in contrast to those more strictly associated with Newtonian science, involved a methodology combining both reason and intuition. Likewise, the pseudoscientific investigations of Ritter and Schubert found devotees among their Romantic contemporaries because of their utilization of

---

21 W. H. Bruford, *Culture and Society in Classical Weimar: 1775-1806* (Cambridge: Cambridge University Press, 1962), p. 393. On this tradition itself and its consequences see Bruford's *The German Tradition of Self-Cultivation* (Cambridge: Cambridge University Press, 1975).

comparable methods. Many of the early Romantic thinkers and poets strove to enhance their own carefully preserved reasoning faculties by following all avenues to the irrational – among them dreams, metempsychosis, visions, drugs and somnambulism. All of these, it must be emphasized, were thought means to a higher rationality, not tools for a flight into the irrational as has been erroneously assumed by numerous post-Romantic critics.

In the protean concept "nature" many Romantics found an image for the realm to which they sought access. Besides providing a developmental pattern which dictated an organic unfolding of the coming together of antipathies within the individual, nature, they believed, was also man's complementary opposite. Since Rousseau, nature had been synonymous with the irrational dimension; perhaps most immediately in the wake of Shaftesbury, but just as surely as legatees of the Hermetic strain which had earlier contributed so substantially to Renaissance nature philosophy, the early Romantics interpreted the split between man and nature to have left nature in sole possession of the spiritual dimension. Indeed, such a conviction was the propellant for the various Romantic attempts at a philosophy of nature, the goal of which was thus to resurrect the correspondence between the two. Nature's additional role as the antipode to human existence was also assigned by Schelling, who maintained nature's traditional alignment, at least when in its original state, with the non-rational.[22] Seemingly paradoxical, this conception of nature as the structural model for human progress as well as man's complementary opposite was, as will be seen, important for the Romantic adaptation of the androgyne.

Religion was another, more conventional channel which offered a reunion with the spiritual world; however, religion for the Romantic seekers bore the stamp of Spinoza so that organic nature rather than a heavenly deity was the object of their reverence. Schleiermacher, whose theology was infused into early Romantic literature and philosophy, advocated religion because it alone offered participation

---

22 Friedrich Schelling, "System der gesammten Philosophie und der Naturphilosophie insbesondere," Abt. 1, vol. 6, 1860, pp. 406-418.

in the absolute, that is, with the infinite stirrings of the universe.[23] Not a religion of God and morality, his was rather a form of worship through which each human being could be permeated with a feeling of interdependence and oneness with spiritualized nature. Still another schema for wholeness is visible in the philosophy of Fichte and in the works of those whom he inspired, in which the roles not only of God but also of nature were minimized. Assuming the philosophical impossibility of reuniting spirit and matter, Fichte increasingly and consistently emphasized the role of the individual isolated from both a transcendent deity and the world. Eternity or the Golden Age of the future was thus to be attained only by a synthesis within the individual between his body and the spiritual infinitude of his own soul.

Whether they posited the spiritual element in nature, in religion, or within themselves, reunion with this allegedly opposing sphere remained a priority for the men associated with the Romantic movement. They expressed the dichotomies to be combined through various formulae: as antipodes of rational and non-rational thinking, of outer and inner worlds, of real and ideal spheres, and also of man and nature. Affirming this latter enunciation of wholeness, Schelling once defined philosophy as recalling the state of oneness with nature; as he expressed it elsewhere, a conscious reconciliation with nature would lead to salvation.[24] The considerable possibilities of this definition, as well as its applicability to androgyny, become apparent when one recognizes that Romantic ideology associated women with nature, with the forces of the non-rational, organic, that is, spiritual, world.

Prompted by the Enlightenment spirit of inquiry, many late eighteenth century thinkers attempted to investigate and comprehend sexual differences. Schiller had partially clarified his category of the "naive" by reference to women who, as those categorized by the

---

23 See for example his "Über die Religion," in *Werke*, ed. Otto Braun et al., vol. 4 (Leipzig: Meiner, 1911).
24 Friedrich Schelling, "Allgemeine Deduktion des dynamischen Processes," p. 77; and "Vorlesungen über die Methode des akademischen Studiums," Abt. 1, vol. 5, 1859, p. 290.

epithet, supposedly existed according to their own laws and possessed an inner necessity and harmony.[25] Novalis was incessantly philosophizing on the complementary differences between the sexes and was quite specific in his categorization. According to certain of his aphorisms, women live "in a truly natural condition;" their sphere is "the kitchen - the garden."[26] Friedrich Schlegel delivered himself of such definitions as "the *feminine figure* is completely flower and fruit."[27] As attested to by these examples, however, such efforts remained mired in age-old "wisdom."

Based on their understanding of the sexes as imbued with complementary powers, and spurred by a desire for their own wholeness, the Romantics posited restorative powers in the union between male and female as a concretely possible means of obtaining a merger between man and the non-rational. Perhaps love often serves as a unifying archetype when an age has analyzed its need for wholeness; to be sure, the Romantics venerated many kinds of love. Heterosexual and indeed often erotic love, however, was the unitive act through which they felt they could realize their philosophy. Whether the Romantic interest in love rendered its thinkers amenable to the image of the androgyne, or whether the latter instead inspired their high estimation of love is not clear. But it is certain that in their lives and in their writings, love based on an androgynous ideal became their inspiration. The attribution to love of redemptive powers evidences once again a proclivity to secularize Christian patterns.

---

25 In "Anmut und Würde," too, the qualities named in the title were defined in part by reference to sexual oppositions.

26 Novalis, *Schriften*, ed. Richard Samuel, vol. 3, 2nd ed. (Stuttgart: Kohlhammer, 1968), p. 568, # 92; and p. 556, # 6. Novalis' works are collected in four volumes (1960-1975) edited by Samuel, Paul Kluckhohn et al. Future references will be cited in the text according to the volume, page and, when necessary, fragment number.

27 Friedrich Schlegel, *Kritische Ausgabe*, ed. Ernst Behler, vol. 3 (München, Paderborn and Wien: Schöningh, 1963), p. 144, # 257. The critical edition of Schlegel's work, edited by Behler, Hans Eichner et al., is incomplete; where appropriate, references will be cited in the text according to the volume, page and, when necessary, fragment number and will be preceded by KA.

As certain Pietists had gone beyond Böhme in sanctioning earthly marriage -- although retaining its mission as a substitute for the divine union it would effect -- so, too, did the Romantics supersede their precursors. Their own contribution was a legitimizing of the physical pairing itself as proof of a divine union on earth. Various figures associated with *Empfindsamkeit* had already secularized the Pietist tendency toward equating heterosexual union with the assurance of heavenly salvation and made marriage instead an end in itself.[28] Voss, for example, offered literary expression of this eighteenth century accretion in *Luise, ein ländliches Gedicht*. Many Romantics likewise thought the combination of sexual opposites synonymous with marriage and thus glorified the marital state. Schleiermacher considered marriage a bond of such inviolacy that a divorce simply indicated that no true marriage had in fact existed.[29] Others, less influenced by Christian definitions, were not so concerned with labeling the combination. Transcending the versions of love transmitted to them in both the religious and secular legacies associated with Pietism, the early Romantics apotheosized the physical union of the sexes as the means for overcoming the dualism accepted by so many of their precursors and for establishing a heaven on earth. Because of their equation of the sexes as halves or antitheses -- equations the validity of which is still being investigated today -- that love is drawn into the sphere of androgyny.

It should not be inferred that the Romantic generation contributed to a definition of the essence of maleness or femaleness; in fact, the majority of their systems worked precisely because they did not doubt the validity of the stereotypes upon which those systems were premised. Their understanding of human nature reflects Christian patterns as surely as does their view of historical progress, for they were defining humanity according to theology. Although Böhme was not the initiator of the pattern declaring the sexes to be complementary opposites, his was a persuasive voice in its perpetuation. Woman in his theosophy was clearly associated with the fallen world. Thus

---

28 See discussion of *Empfindsamkeit* in Kluckhohn's *Die Auffassung der Liebe*, pp. 176-198.
29 Friedrich Schleiermacher, "Über die Ehe," *Werke*, vol. 3, [1911], pp. 227-265.

the most with which the Jena Romantics can be credited is the acceptance of both sexes as necessary to their ultimate goal, but even that equality was more an ideal than a reality. Flavoring their idealized portrait of woman as representative of organic nature and an embodiment of wholeness was a subtly negative value judgment which betrayed hierarchical thinking. As articulated in Schelling's philosophy, the Romantic thinkers reserved their primary appreciation for the mind, unquestionably the realm arrogated to the male; women and nature were thus deemed inferior. Kleist gives this idea typical expression in one of his epistles to Wilhelmine; in summary this effort declared his conviction that women were necessarily secondary because they were not associated with conscious mind. According to his classification of complementary powers, women compensated for their original inferiority by remaining the vessels of attributes so vital to men.[30] Women were, however, usually conceded a capacity for progress: after a long tradition of sole equation with the irrational, nature and thus the female as well were imbued in Schelling's system with a preoccupation to be translated into conscious mind, the highest value.[31]

Individual perfection was, of course, only a part of the Romantic dream. To realize their more expansive goal of cosmic harmony, the Romantics turned to literature, where symbols could give form to that ethereal world of perfection and indivisibility from which they felt alienated. Given the utopian quality in their perception of wholeness, by definition a product of their creative imagination, it is to be expected that the images and ideals adapted for its description were of a similarly imaginative origin. The Romantic turn to symbolic literature can be partially explained by reference to Rollo May's introduction to *Symbolism in Religion and Literature*. Although his concern with symbols is primarily a function of his interest in the symbolization process as it concerns his own discipline, psychology, he is also persuaded of their significance in literature. In fact, he advises prospective psychoanalysts to study literature

---

30 Heinrich v. Kleist, "Briefe," in *Sämtliche Werke und Briefe*, ed. Helmut Sembdner, vol. 5 (München: Hanser, 1970), pp. 506-508.
31 See for example "Von der Weltseele" and "Allgemeine Deduktion des dynamischen Processes," pp. 75-78.

because its symbols are uniquely capable of bridging various realities. Although the realities which May goes on to explore are defined differently, we recognize in them the same spheres for which the Romantics attempted a synthesis. May's definition, then, of a symbol as an expression of "the possible" and his basic assumption of its healing powers,[32] although formulated within the framework of psychological well-being, contribute to an understanding of the Romantics' tremendous faith in the powers of poetry.

Because the Romantics wanted symbols capable of bridging the spiritual world of wholeness and their own existential reality, some of their more forceful symbols were those which translated physical reality into its highest potential; conversely stated, they sought symbols which could be meaningfully approximated in their own lives. They were not engaged in a search for private or abstract symbols to express an individual truth, but were straining to express the harmony they believed the essence of the human experience. At home in a perfect world, but capable of concrete representation in heterosexual love, the androgyne, the *Urbild* of totality, gradually revealed its practical and symbolic potential.

The early Romantic appreciation for the androgynous ideal was, as has been discussed, dictated by philosophical, religious and literary aspirations. These, in turn, were outgrowths of a desire to somehow embrace a world of opposing forces in its entirety. This desideratum, which to a large measure defined Romantic ideology, was, if one is to accept Eliade's argument in *Mephistopheles and the Androgyne*, itself generated by the commitment to a broad concept of androgyny. According to Eliade, and as corroborated by numerous other critics, Goethe presented Mephistopheles in such a way that Faust's antagonist could not be simplistically despised. Eliade does not concern himself with the technique through which Goethe has accomplished this affirmation of evil -- it is surely related to the humor with which Mephisto relativizes all positions -- but rather with the philosophical implications. He concludes that Goethe recognized a deep stratum of

---

32 Rollo May, "The Significance of Symbols," in *Symbolism in Religion and Literature* (New York: Braziller, 1960), p. 33.

polarities in the world, and because of his own particular genius did not disavow or attempt to eradicate them, but instead incorporated them into a system of wholes. To Goethe, following Eliade's analysis, evil therefore was not only a counterpart but the necessary antipode, a promoter and perhaps even the needed impetus, to good. Consequently, evil and its representative Mephistopheles had to be imbued with at least some positive merit; the force he represented was no longer a categorical evil.[33] Mephisto was, it will be remembered, characterized by his progenitor as a part of that spirit which "always wants the evil, and always effects the good."[34]

A similar complex of ideas also supports the dialectical thinking so prevalent throughout German Idealism. The roots of that method have been identified in Böhme's conception of the *Ungrund*, the undifferentiated first principle.[35] Within the various thought systems developed between the time of Kant and Hegel, tensions between opposing forces were often assumed the propellants for progress. To Eliade, who works from a perspective avowing myth and archetype, these patterns would thus be examples of an androgynous ideal at its most subsuming. Indeed, once the world has been divided into dichotomies of good and evil or of nature and spirit, for instance, to apply to the oppositions sexual references is a simple extension; they are surely among the most pervasive and obvious images available to describe the *coincidentia oppositorum*. Parallels can, in fact, be noted between the structure Böhme outlined for salvation and the best known of these dialectic systems, Hegel's pattern for historical development: thesis, antithesis and synthesis. The synthesis which in turn becomes a new thesis bears comparison to a child, the result of

---

33 Eliade, *Mephistopheles and the Androgyne*, pp. 78-81. Thomas McFarland, in "A Complex Dialogue: Coleridge's Doctrine of Polarity and Its European Contexts," in *Reading Coleridge: Approaches and Applications*, ed. Walter B. Crawford (London: Cornell University Press, 1979), pp. 56-115, demonstrates the overwhelming importance of polarities to Romantic thinking in general.
34 Johann Wolfgang v. Goethe, "Faust," in *Berliner Ausgabe,* vol. 8 (Berlin: Aufbau, 1965), p. 190.
35 Robert F. Brown, p. 64; Brown provides a lucid discussion of Böhme's view of God, pp. 53-64.

love between a pair of sexual opposites and itself, in time, a new sexual being seeking its counterpart. In an essay on love written in the late 1790's, Hegel himself expounds upon the biological combination and shifts the focus to the child, who was later to become a preoccupation with the Romantics. In the child was to be seen proof of the union of polarities.[36] The rudiments of this pattern, showing an adherence to an androgynous ideal as a self-renewing principle, are present in Hegel's mature dialectic. As Abrams has observed, Hegel's "dynamic principle . . . seems, in the final analysis, to have acquired its attributes by analogy with bisexual reproduction."[37]

Goethe was apparently able to accept the tensions of the unresolved polarities. The task of consciously restructuring wholes thus remained for the early Romantics. As Novalis declared, "Polarity is an imperfection . . . in the future there shall be no polarity" (III, 324, # 479). Friedrich Schlegel's concept of *Universalpoesie* and, for example, his assessment of the proper life style as "the most fervent, completely indefatigable, almost voracious partaking of all life" (KA VIII, 49), were also motivated by his desire for wholeness. The predilection for harmony has been a part of most discussions on Romantic ideology; Eliade's intuitions offer a further, if archetypal, articulation of the yearnings which fueled these efforts. Of course, it is debatable whether this inclusive concept should even be termed androgyny; in any case it is the more specific application of the term, one true to its etymology, with which the present discussion is concerned. However, this more limited interpretation of androgyny should be recognized as a logical and consistent outgrowth of the early Romantics' overwhelming desire to understand, to label and to affirm those elements which they believed to form the basic polarities of their existence.

Ritter and Schubert, both loosely connected with the Jena circle, were among those during their age who perceived the value in an ideal of heterosexual recombination. The works of these two -- the

---

[36] Georg Wilhelm Friedrich Hegel, "Love," in *Early Theological Writings*, trans. and ed. T.M. Knox and Richard Kroner (Chicago: University of Chicago Press, 1948), pp. 302-308.

[37] Abrams, p. 176.

former a physicist, the latter a scientist preferring philosophical treatises – indicate the wide range of disciplines within which the ideal occurred. One of the underlying precepts in Schubert's *Die Geschichte der Seele* is the power of love to effect a unity out of a duality in emulation of the divine.[38] Ritter, who has been credited with the "unique creation of a genuinely 'Romantic' science,"[39] dedicated himself to reestablishing the link between man and the natural world. Many of his ideas in *Fragmente aus dem Nachlaß eines jungen Physikers* are described in alchemical language and are premised on a system of polarities which were assigned sexual designations. He, too, saw man's ultimate perfection as a reinstatement of his androgynous essence.[40] Even Wilhelm von Humboldt, allied more with the Rationalists than the Romantics, recognized the androgyne; in an essay "Über die männliche und weibliche Form" written in 1795 and published in Schiller's *Horen*, he projected his vision of a perfect human as an asexual entity combining the extremes within itself.[41]

There was also one philosopher who used Böhme's transformation of the androgynous ideal specifically and consciously as the matrix for his own philosophical system. Gray has called him Böhme's Romantic interpreter.[42] To August Wilhelm Schlegel he was "Boehmius redivivus."[43] He was Franz von Baader, a colleague of Schelling and Ritter at Munich, and a self-styled "Professor of love."[44] Little scholarly work has been done on Baader, a fact

---

38 Gotthilf Heinrich Schubert, "Von der Liebe der Geschlechter und der Zeugung," in *Die Geschichte der Seele*, vol. 1 (1877; rpt. Hildesheim: Olms, 1961), pp. 254-285.
39 Walter D. Wetzels, "Aspects of Natural Science in German Romanticism," *Studies in Romanticism*, 10 (1971), 1, p. 45.
40 Johann Wilhelm Ritter, *Fragmente aus dem Nachlaß eines jungen Physikers* (1810; rpt. Heidelberg: Schneider, 1969).
41 Wilhelm v. Humboldt, "Über die männliche und weibliche Form," in *Gesammelte Schriften*, ed. Albert Leitzmann, vol. 1 (Berlin: Behr, 1903), pp. 335-369.
42 Gray, p. 38.
43 Quoted in David Baumgardt's *Franz von Baader und die philosophische Romantik* (Halle: Niemeyer, 1927), pp. 37-38.
44 Franz v. Baader, *Sämmtliche Werke*, vol. 15 (Leipzig: Bethmann, 1856),

attested to and lamented by David Baumgardt, whose 1927 study has been the only attempt at a comprehensive presentation of Baader's philosophy to date.[45] Infused with a religious mysticism and tending toward brilliant and paradoxical aphorism in the manner of Friedrich Schlegel, Baader was never moved to organize his extensive writings into a system, though when finally collected in 1850 they filled sixteen volumes. Attempts at interpretation have been hampered by Baader's frequent inconsistencies; as Goethe once said about him, "I feel that there is something significant about the man, but I do not understand him."[46]

In Baader's own words, the desire for androgynous perfection (*Androgynenlust*) was the "secret, impenetrable, magic workshop of all life" (I, 46). A mystical exegesis of the Genesis account, he declared with prophetic certainty, would clarify humanity's role within creation. Böhme had described the mystery of heterosexual union in an essentially spiritual and non-physical context. But rejecting Böhme's condemnation of human sexual relations because, he insisted, androgynous perfection would then denote only "impotence" or "asexuality" or even "hermaphrodism," Baader hailed erotic union itself as the means to immortality. His works, written only after he had devoted ten years to the study of the Kabbala and Böhme's theosophy, pointed once again to an androgynous Almighty who created bisexual Adam and intended Adam to procreate "like Mary without man" (IX, 211). Without the same philosophical commitment to a dialectic, however, Baader declared quite simply that the division of sexes, as well as the fall, could be attributed to Adam's sexual desire for the woman within him. And only sexual union could restore the image of the divine on earth. In what was intended as part of a comprehensive doctrine, Baader saw the arms as extensions of the ribs; therefore, when a man embraced a woman he was drawing her once more into the enclosure of the ribs from which she had earlier been expulsed (VII, 236).

---

    p. 627. Baader's works are collected in 16 volumes (1851-1857) and will be cited in the text according to volume and page number.
45 See especially the introduction, pp. 1-13.
46 Johann Wolfgang v. Goethe, *Goethes Gespräche*, ed. Wolfgang Herwig, vol. 2 (Zürich: Artemis, 1969), p. 1006.

Although the influence of Böhme is clear, even more so when one analyzes Baader's language which contains much alchemical terminology, it is equally apparent that Baader was attempting to secularize Böhme. As a true Romantic, he was striving to synthesize all polarities to create a divine state on earth. He was also more concerned than his predecessor with the effect of love on the individual partners. While he clearly emphasized that the purpose of sexual love was the restoration of the creator's image in both lovers, the process he advocated reflects a conception of psychological wholeness. Sexual love was to help each individual develop his or her inner being from "halfness" into the "image of completed humanity" (X, 305).

It can be speculated that the reasons for Baader's obscurity lie at least partially in his exuberant calls for erotic union. The later, more genteel Biedermeier spirits living in the conservative Metternich years could probably not cope with his intensity, obvious even in the titles he gave to his works, for example, "Sätze aus der erotischen Philosophie" (IV, 163). The concept of androgyny has frequently been viewed with suspicion and those who value it have run the risk of contamination by association. Certainly reactions to Baader were vehement. He was, according to Schopenhauer, "the most disgusting scribbler next to Hegel."[47] As the Victorian age approached, accompanied by an entrenchment of misogynism, any ideal described in sexual terms was vociferously rejected. Baader was perhaps dismissed because his philosophic system -- if it can be called that – can not be discussed without mentioning his adaptation of the androgynous ideal. Even today, however, the few contemporary encyclopedias which include articles on his work are reticent on the subject.[48]

The androgynous ideal is also important in much of the literature of the Romantic age, although there is some divergence in the various applications. Certainly not all who recognized the power of bisexual totality saw it as a positive ideal. Tieck, for example, clearly viewed the sexes as opposing forces, but rarely did he invest the same hope

---

47 This judgment, contained in a letter written in 1856, is quoted in Baumgardt, p. 10.
48 Even the article on Baader in the *Encyclopedia of Philosophy*, vol. 1 (New York: Macmillan, 1967), does not mention the word.

in their reunion as did his Jena contemporaries. To be sure, in *Herzensergiessungen eines kunstliebenden Klosterbruders* which he completed with Wackenroder, Amalia in one letter is tributed as the redeemer, the madonna who through love awakens Antonio to art and the love of nature.[49] Likewise, in Tieck's own *Franz Sternbalds Wanderungen*, the hero of the title discovers near the end of the novel that his love for Marie is the beginning of religion; through love he could become whole. But these versions of love were not dominant in the works; more often Tieck linked women with the demonic. His *Der blonde Eckbert*, to take just one example, can be interpreted as a variation of the androgynous model, incest. Not a cause for salvation, the union of Eckbert and his sister Bertha instead leads to tragedy. Again linked with nature, woman is not only mysterious, but evil, man's counterpart and the vessel for his destruction. In *Die Wahlverwandschaften*, Goethe also dismissed the need for an ideal merging of sexual polarities in love; the attraction of opposites instead is the cause for great suffering.

There has also been variety in what little critical reaction the motif has generated. While Richard Exner has recently connected the Romantics' interest in the androgyne with their efforts to create a new and better world,[50] A.J.L. Busst has declared the symbol of bisexual totality in Romanticism to be "predominantly, but not exclusively, decadent." Following the argument Mario Praz advanced in *The Romantic Agony*, that the Romantics used symbols in which they no longer believed, Busst claims the German Romantics found satisfaction only in cerebrality. Ignoring their belief in the efficacy of a symbol, he states that reality was for them so horrible that it "occasioned withdrawal from reality into the mind, which became invaded by diseased imaginings."[51] If this does characterize the

---

49 Ludwig Tieck and Wilhelm Wackenroder, "Herzensergiessungen eines kunstliebenden Klosterbruders," in Wackenroder's *Werke und Briefe* (Heidelberg: Schneider, 1967), pp. 30-32.
50 Although specifically about Kleist, Exner's work includes discussions on many of the Romantics.
51 Busst, pp. 11, 40. See also Mario Praz' *The Romantic Agony*, trans. Angus Davidson (London: Oxford University Press, 1970).

androgyne in France after 1850 — and this is the focus of Busst's discussion — it does not apply to the early German Romantics who truly believed in the power of their art. August Wilhelm Schlegel's words in 1827 as he looked back to the days of the Jena group can not be dismissed as a lapse into sentimentality. Although he had been a part of many spirited circles and had met many notables, he wrote, he would always remember "the productive communion of spirits at an age when we were drunk with hope."[52]

As the quintessential ideal of perfection, the androgyne is as prominent thematically in the works of Hölderlin and Kleist as in works associated more definitively with the early Romantic movement; both Hölderlin's Diotima and Kleist's Natalie, for example, were ideal representatives of the unconscious, harmonious existence their male counterparts lacked. And as Hyperion longs, in Kluckhohn's words, for union with "his half,"[53] so Prince Friedrich is remarkably granted substance by his contact with Natalie. But the androgynous ideal finds its most comprehensive adaptations in the *oeuvre* of Novalis, where sexual convergence consistently serves as harbinger of universal harmony and individual salvation, and in the works of Friedrich Schlegel until 1800. Although a less metaphysical variant of the ideal is at first visible in Schlegel's writings, when he became part of the Romantic movement his conception of the ideal yielded to an adaptation similar to that of Novalis. The pattern which he subsequently espoused — love for a sexual opposite as the key to individual and cosmic wholeness — can be identified as the major Romantic appropriation of the androgyne. For this reason, the major works of Novalis and Friedrich Schlegel will be discussed in detail, as representatives of patterns which are frequently applicable in some measure to other texts of the period.

---

52 August Wilhelm Schlegel, *Sämmtliche Werke*, ed. Eduard Böcking, vol. 11 (Leipzig: Weidmann, 1847), p. 145.
53 Kluckhohn, *Die Auffassung der Liebe*, p. 340.

Chapter Three

NOVALIS' UNFINISHED NOVELS: ANDROGYNOUS WHOLENESS FOR THE GOLDEN AGE

Novalis was the most gifted poet among the group of Romantic poets and philosophers gathered in Jena. What has been said in the previous chapters about the early Romantic attempt to symbolize the perfection of the "other" realm and thus to capture in even so evanescent a way an impression of the "inexpressible" finds its ultimate articulation in Novalis' works and theory. His primary sensibility, he recorded, was of a world containing "two systems of senses" which, despite their differences, were nevertheless "interwoven in the most intimate fashion." Designated in a fragment as "body" and "soul," the binary frame is not unique; many of his precursors had premised their redemptive aspirations on similar conceptions. But in contrast to the dualism inherent in Christianity and in opposition to the Fichtean strain of Romantic ideology which had also affirmed the ultimate permanence of the separation, Novalis not only perceived these two spheres, but believed that each derived much of its potency from a thus very desirable exchange with the other. The completion of the above quoted fragment makes this point quite explicitly: both systems, he continued, "should relate to each other in a completely reciprocal fashion" (II, 546, # 111). Thus his poetic credo:

> The world must be romanticized. In this way one finds again the original meaning. To romanticize is nothing but a qualitative raising to a higher power. In this operation the lower self is identified with a better self. . . . When I give to the common an elevated meaning, to the usual a mysterious appearance, to the known the dignity of the unknown, to the finite an infinite lustre, I am romanticizing it.

So much is usually quoted to explicate Novalis' aesthetic theory. But just as imperative in order to avoid a limited interpretation is the remainder of the fragment: "The operation for the higher, the unknown, the mystic, the infinite, is reversed . . . it is given a familiar expression." The process is one of "alternating elevation and lowering [*Wechselerhöhung und Erniedrigung*]" (II, 545, # 105). It is consequently a reciprocal process infused with the Hermetic spirit which Novalis decrees. Empirical reality must be raised to its highest potential, expanded to its inherent perfection; or differently articulated, it must be expressed as its infinite model, its *Urbild*. No less important is the impulse from the obverse direction; the divine must be given finite form.

Given such an inscrutable doctrine, the aesthetic problem as it presented itself to Novalis was one of discovering an adequate vehicle for "romanticizing" or raising the world to the perfection of which it was capable, and conversely of crystallizing its infinite model. It was a desideratum, he soon realized, singularly achievable through the process of symbolization; only a symbol could effect the requisite "alternating elevation and lowering." Only a symbol could express the ineffable world of the spirit yet be meaningfully translated into empirical reality.

When Novalis declared his mission as a "shaping [*Bildung*] of the earth" (II, 427, # 32), he was issuing a mandate for the merger of the spiritual and physical realms through the efficacy of symbolic art. Although many of his contemporaries shared his concerns and even his method of assigning to art a mediating function, the degree to which Novalis believed an interchange between the two spheres possible, as well as the immediacy of his expectations, were unprecedented. Not content with a gradual evolution to perfection, Novalis awaited through the beneficence of the poetic medium an imminent earthly paradise. His trust in poetry can partially be explained by his faith in what he called the "magic wand of analogy" (III, 518). Unusual only because of its timing, his thinking was very much in the train of pagan and Renaissance nature philosophy. As Marjorie Nicolson has reminded us, an acceptance of the analogic relationship between the micro- and macrocosms was common to many thinkers after the Renaissance and before seventeenth century science offered a new way of looking at the world.[1]

---

1 Marjorie Hope Nicolson, *The Breaking of the Circle*, 2nd ed. (New York:

More than others in Germany, Novalis can thus be seen as an example of Abrams' argument that the early Christian faith in an apocalypse by revelation, replaced after the events in France by faith in an apocalypse by revolution, was transformed during the age of Romanticism to a faith in an apocalypse by imagination or cognition.[2] Certainly Böhme's crediting the imagination with creative powers influenced Novalis' thinking; that theosophist's *Ungrund*, which had been able to manifest itself in the world only after imagining it, proved as irresistible to Novalis as it did to many others. The age old belief in magic also helps explain to twentieth century sceptics Novalis' confidence in symbolic literature. A perceptive study by Anya Taylor, *Magic and English Romanticism*, although focused on Romanticism in England, is instructive for its German variant as well. Reminding us that creation even in Christianity was associated with magic words – God's "Let there be light," for instance – Taylor asserts that by the end of the 1700's magic was revitalized in spite of scientific argument and had reemerged as a way of thinking about art and creativity.[3] To be sure, Novalis' magic idealism to a considerable extent depended upon the incantatory power of words. Consequently, his works contain myriad "magic words" or symbols, one of the most rudimentary of which is that of the androgyne. Because it could mediate between earthly sexual love and the *Urbild* of perfect humanity, the symbol of the androgyne became Novalis' primary vehicle for realizing "the possible."

That Novalis gave the androgyne distinctly Romantic contours and that he allotted it such a prominent role in his works can ultimately be understood only by reference to Novalis as a dedicated

---

    Columbia University Press, 1962); Keith Thomas, in *Religion and the Decline of Magic* (London: Weidenfeld and Nicolson, 1971), attributes the decline in the belief in magic after the end of the seventeenth century to the new preoccupation with mechanical science and philosophy, p. 643.

2 Abrams, p. 334.
3 Anya Taylor, *Magic and English Romanticism* (Athens: University of Georgia Press, 1979), p. 13. See also Steven C. Schaber's "Novalis' Theory of the Work of Art as Hieroglyph," *Germanic Review*, 48 (1973), pp. 35-43.

artist with a unique vision. That the principle of bisexual totality was so consistently a part of that vision is less difficult to explain. It was, in fact, an ideal that he had encountered in various shapes since childhood. He was raised in an environment permeated by the beliefs of the Herrnhuters, that branch of Pietism founded by Count Zinzendorf and one fortunately more appreciative of art than most. Thus the saving function of marital love was a part of his religious heritage, a perhaps unquestioned truth for him as well as for others of his generation. In addition, his notebooks confirm a persistent and far more extensive interest in the natural sciences than is evidenced in the writings of many of his contemporaries. Not only did he know Schelling as well as Ritter and others who often applied sexual designations to the polarous forces they posited in nature, but he also studied their works. As much as any of his friends, Novalis believed that humanity could become whole, unfragmented, by understanding and accepting into itself the non-rational or spiritual world presumed to be residing within nature.

Mähl has demonstrated in an article entitled "Novalis und Plotin" that Novalis' often quoted phrase "my dear Plotinus" indeed encompassed a much wider frame than merely the specific works of Plotinus and was the rubric for a variety of esoteric arts such as theosophy, alchemy and Kabbalism, as well as the works of other thinkers, all of which Novalis studied and judged to be transmitters of Neoplatonic thought.[4] Straining to comprehend the physical world, Novalis embraced not only theoretical but also practical manifestations of an organic, living nature such as metallurgy, magnetism and electricity. He indulged as well a strong affinity for metempsychosis, mesmerism, magical numbers and galvanism. The appeal of these practices or "sciences" was presumably their challenge to the prevailing Enlightenment view of a mechanistic, clock-like universe. Rooted in Hermetic philosophy, they promised an intuition of the very soul of the universe. Several, electricity and mesmerism among them, were explained in the late eighteenth century in terms of sexual oppositions and attractions, and were thought means for bridging the

---

4   Mähl, "Novalis und Plotin," pp. 361-375.

polarities believed present throughout the natural world. In a recent study, *Spellbound: Studies on Mesmerism and Literature*, Maria Tatar has shown that mesmerism in its beginnings was credited as an aid in the recovery of the harmonious relationship which had once existed between man and nature; after the French Revolution, however, it was linked with a promise to expand consciousness by including the spiritual world. It can thus be understood as a nineteenth century attempt at psychology.[5] All of these practices helped to shape Novalis' world view. In fact, Novalis' intellectual avarice was such that it has been referred to as a "philosophy of spiritual gluttony."[6] Although his appreciation for an androgynous union can be traced to ideas conveyed through Pietism, it is quite certain these would not have accrued such force had it not been for his eclectic interests and the subsequent variety of thought which he so eagerly, some would say indiscriminately, absorbed.

In addition to the religious and intellectual currents which undoubtedly helped to shape Novalis' thinking, further insight into his dependence on androgynous culmination can be garnered from reference to easily accessible biographical data. Much has been written on the poet's relationship with Sophie, the twelve year old girl whom he met and loved until her death three years later in March, 1797. References in his notebooks and diaries at times idealize her and at other times indicate an aloof if serene awareness of her very real limitations. About her he could say: "She does not want to be anything. She is something," while almost simultaneously admitting her immaturity by questioning whether her "temperament" had ever been truly awakened (IV, 24). That the totality of her personage, however, became the model for his abstraction of woman is indicated by a phrase he once wrote in a notebook as a potential title for a future essay: "Sofie, or of women" (II, 598, # 336). Seen as a representative of non-rational, unthinking, organic nature, she provided the primary model for the female figures throughout Novalis' literary

---

5   Maria M. Tatar, *Spellbound: Studies on Mesmerism and Literature* (Princeton: Princeton University Press, 1978). See especially pp. 3-44.
6   Fanny Imle, *Novalis: Seine philosophische Weltanschauung* (Paderborn: Schöningh, 1928), p. 3.

production, each of whom exists in contrast to an incomplete or fragmented male.[7]

On May 3, 1797, Novalis by his own account experienced at Sophie's grave a mystic union with what he perceived to be Sophie and the infinite world of the spirit. A coincidence with Böhme's theosophy and with certain forms of Jewish mysticism no doubt intensified his interest, for the reunion they awaited between earthly man and the Heavenly Virgin Sophia bore comparison to his own mystic reconciliation. Whether or not Novalis actually would have become a poet had he not met and loved Sophie, and had he thus been denied the occurence at her grave, is debatable. That he himself credited this event as the impetus for his poetic mission is clear. About her death he asked, rhetorically one suspects, "Should I not thank God. . . . Is it not a calling to apostolic office?" (IV, 211). Mähl, however, is no doubt correct when he assesses this experience as the primary impulse for Novalis' development from empirical thinker who would only approximate the Golden Age to visionary who believed in the actualization of his dreams.[8] One can also conjecture that this happening triggered Novalis' later tribute to androgynous perfection. Certain it is that in 1798 he rather abruptly chose art as the medium through which to establish the Golden Age and devoted himself to a literature in which, as Abrams has remarked, the "persistent paradigm is sexual love."[9] Although particulars vary in his works, a resolution within a triadic pattern is inevitably the structural means of attaining

---

[7] Zinzendorf's influence can perhaps be noted here; in a letter to Friedrich Schlegel in 1796, Novalis speaks positively about Zinzendorf's conception of love and then turns the subject to Sophie (IV, 188). Heinz Ritter, in *Der unbekannte Novalis: Friedrich von Hardenberg im Spiegel seiner Dichtung* (Göttingen: Sachse and Pohl, 1967), argues against the opinion of the majority by naming Julie, Novalis' fiancée, as the main influence for Mathilde because it was she whom Novalis thought of as a bride, pp. 212-219. That Julie was for Novalis a far less ethereal creature than was Sophie is true. But his female creations are abstractions rather than real figures; Mathilde, as well as the others, is more an idealized virgin than a true-to-life bride.

[8] Mähl, *Die Idee des goldenen Zeitalters*, p. 286.

[9] Abrams, p. 298. Love was also a theme of Novalis' early poetry; "Vergiß mein nicht!" of 1794 is a case in point.

this paradise, and a union of sexual opposites is repeatedly the symbol for its inception.

Only after an extensive study of science and philosophy did Novalis dedicate himself to literature; although his career as a writer spanned but a few years, there is nevertheless a development to be noted in his literary production. His treatment of the androgyne is one measure of his artistic growth; only by the time of *Heinrich von Ofterdingen* had he become a consummate aesthetician, dependent on symbols to change reality. Despite his two unfinished novels' being unequal from an aesthetic perspective – *Heinrich von Ofterdingen* is without doubt a more mature work than is *Die Lehrlinge zu Sais* – the two will be discussed together. For although Novalis' treatment of an androgynous ideal in some ways parallels the qualitative difference between the larger works, there are basic similarities in its adaptation.

In the fairy tale of Hyazinth and Rosenblüte incorporated into *Die Lehrlinge zu Sais*, the first of his two novels fragments, can be detected the inherent three part structure as well as many of the themes and symbols of Novalis' work.[10] Related by one of the young apprentices of the title, the tale is an expression of that perfection and fulfillment for which all the novitiates are seeking. Hyazinth and Rosenblüte, the young man recounts, at one time lived in harmony with nature; they communicated with animals and plants and were secure in their union with one another. Only when a stranger presented to Hyazinth an illegible book, a symbol for knowledge, was their tranquility shattered. Thirsting now for consciousness, Hyazinth must leave; as he confesses to Rosenblüte: "I would like to tell you where I am going, I do not know myself; I am going there where the Mother of All Things lives, the veiled Virgin" (I, 93). After a search of indeterminable duration, he arrives in the realm of everlasting seasons where the flowers and streams greet him with familiar words. There in a dream state he confronts the Goddess of Sais and raises her veil to reveal none other than Rosenblüte, who falls into his arms.

---

10 Fairy tales played an inordinate role in Novalis' theory of art, for only in this genre could the boundaries of time and space be suspended. See for example III, 280, #234.

We are to understand that Hyazinth has regained the harmony with the spiritualized world of nature which was originally his and thus has attained the immortality of existence associated with the resurgent Golden Age.

Although the fairy tale ends joyfully where it had begun, Hyazinth's journey has not been circuitous, but rather could be described as a spiral. It has incorporated experiences and an expanding awareness, both of which have combined to make his final attainment one on a higher level. This personal growth, however, is not sufficient to usher in the Golden Age. The final stage of the triad, which the poet enunciates here as a revivification of the unity between man and nature, is ultimately possible only through Hyazinth's reunion with the woman behind the veil. Only then can he fuse his newly found consciousness with the unconscious joy of the natural world to which she belongs. In distilled form, the story is paradigmatic for the larger novel in which it appears as well as for the later *Heinrich von Ofterdingen*.

In the main body of *Die Lehrlinge* a coterie of young apprentices intuit and attempt to comprehend the harmony between man and nature which they feel had been integral to earlier periods but lamentably lost to theirs. It was a time when, as a personified nature says of man, "he understood us as we understood him." Paralleling the fairy tale, Novalis imputes the fatal split between man and nature to man's desire for knowledge. The same anthropomorphized nature pronounces judgment on man: "His desire to become God separated him from us" (I, 95). The result for man himself could only be fragmentation; according to the apprentice of the first chapter, his "inner being" had been gradually "split into such manifold powers" (I, 82). It becomes apparent that harmony and the Golden Age, the goal of all the apprentices, will be reinstated only when man and nature are again one. From the opening lines the importance of the apprentices in this attainment had been stressed; each was to trace the "figures" which are everywhere visible in nature, for these natural patterns would yield "the key" (I, 79). In a wistful tone one of the novices envisions the supportive role of nature in a future time when she will resume the role she played during the "old golden time" during which she was "friend, consoler, priestess and worker of miracles" to all human beings, when she lived among them and "intimacy with the divine made humanity immortal" (I, 86).

The concept of a past age in which man and nature were one is also essential to *Heinrich von Ofterdingen*, although Novalis has altered his basic conception of nature. That he no longer anthropomorphizes nature has a bearing on his treatment of the androgynous symbol. Despite numerous references to the fall of man from his blissful existence in paradise, the lost age in this second novel is less lamented; rather the focus has shifted to a future which accomodates the possibility, even certainty, for recapturing the primeval paradise. But even very early in the novel a stranger's remarks about a blue flower stir vague recollections in Heinrich. He musingly compares the stories to others he has heard about an incomparable time in the past when "beasts and trees and mountains had spoken with humanity." The images evoke a further response, one conditioned not by melancholy but by hope: "It seems to me as if they wanted to begin at any moment, and as if I could tell by looking at them, what they wanted to say to me" (I, 195).

The triadic structure schematizing a lost state of felicity and its final resurgence finds its most eloquent expression in the interpolated fairy tales of *Ofterdingen*. The extremely complicated fairy tale told by Klingsohr – written by him, he avers, before he became so rationalistic – provides a good example. When love and poetry are rejoined, the scribe, embodiment of intellect and therefore of division, simply disappears; nature is reunited with man and suddenly "everything" seems to have a soul. "The beasts approached the awakened human beings with friendly greetings. The plants entertained them with fruits and fragrances, and decorated them most elegantly" (I, 312-313). In the tale of Atlantis a similar pattern emerges, expressed so enchantingly by a young man whose song the narrator relates:

> [His song] dealt with the origin of the world, with the origin of the stars, of the plants, beasts and humanity, with the all-powerful affinities within nature, with the ancient Golden Age and its rulers, love and poetry, with the appearance of hatred and of barbarism and their struggles with those beneficent goddesses, and finally with the future triumph of the latter... the rejuvenation of nature and the return of an eternal Golden Age (I, 225).

Even such fleeting reference to these fairy tales reveals their basic similitude: along with the story of Hyazinth and Rosenblüte they are variations upon a common theme. Each depicts a progression of events which culminates inevitably in a joyous oneness between man and nature, in other words, in a resurgent Golden Age.[11] The novels, too, following this prescription, represent attempts to induce aesthetically the union of these two antithetical forces through the peregrinations of the title characters, attempts which, had the novels been completed, would presumably have come to fruition. *Ofterdingen* is unfinished, but notes left by Novalis indicate an ending as presaged by the fairy tales; for example: "It is the primeval world, the golden time at the end" (I, 345), or: "The entire human race at the end becomes poetic. New golden time." And in that time "humanity, beasts, plants, stones and stars, flames, sounds, colors must . . . act and speak as One Species" (I, 347). The same structure is latent in *Die Lehrlinge*, a conclusion attested to by Bruce Haywood who, after a study of Novalis' imagery, concluded that the structure of the Hyazinth and Rosenblüte tale, including the final recombination of man and nature, could be extended to the novel as a whole.[12] Fragments also indicate this to have been Novalis' intent.[13]

The specific contours of Novalis' paradise are traceable in both novel fragments to his apprehension of a broadly conceived nature as man's complementary opposite. Peckham has concluded that during the Romantic era man saw himself as nature's redeemer.[14] Certainly this captures the essence of Fichte's excessive individualism which granted value to nature only as a subjective postulation of the "I." Such an analysis, however, completely ignores the counter strain which granted approbation to a spiritualized nature which could save humanity. Novalis' definition of man as the "Messiah of nature" (I, 110, #4) would seem to place him in the Fichtean train; however,

---

11 The reunion of man and nature was basic to the idyll, which Mähl found so important for Romantic dreams of a paradisiacal future. See Mähl's *Die Idee des goldenen Zeitalters*, pp. 103-186.

12 Bruce Haywood, *Novalis: The Veil of Imagery*, Harvard Germanic Studies I ('s-Gravenhage: Mouton, 1959), pp. 40-43.

13 Phrases such as "new Jerusalem" and "consecration into the secrets" (I, 111, #7) in the paralipomena to the novel presage a final Golden Age.

14 Peckham, pp. 32-33.

this construction, just as many of Novalis' fragments, is not definitive; it represents a flash of illumination, not a complete, developed system, although many critics have tended to read it as such.[15] For the saving of nature, which Novalis surely did avow, was within the framework of reciprocal beneficence in which the obverse was just as true. In *Die Lehrlinge* it is only union with nature which can save man. After Novalis had set this first novel aside and had completed half of *Ofterdingen*, he wrote to Tieck about his recent study of Böhme's works. After finally understanding that theosophist "as he must be understood," he had, he confided to his friend, decided to change the focus of *Die Lehrlinge* so that it would be "a genuinely symbolic novel of nature" (IV, 322-323). Although he presumably intended to make of nature an even more important component, it is doubtful whether such alteration would have affected the balance between man and nature; for Böhme, despite his mystical approach to nature, was interested in the natural world only as tangential to man's salvation. In any case, the change Novalis predicted was never initiated, and in the form left to us, nature in that first novel is merely an agent; it has been appropriated value almost solely within the context of man's redemption.[16] Although its puissance has diminished in the later *Ofterdingen*, nature remains the counterpart to man, the partner who can assure the cosmic wholeness demanded by Romantic philosophy.

Nowhere in Novalis' works is there an appreciation of physical nature for itself. Instead the importance he ascribes to nature in his fiction results from an attempt at making palpable the more abstract ideals with which he associated the natural world, the very qualities of which the Romantic male felt such a paucity in his own life -- emotion, spirituality, the non-rational. The transference of these attributes to woman as partner represents a further effort to make this sphere accessible. Rather than questioning the presumed similitude

---

15 See for example the critical edition of Novalis' literary works in which Kluckhohn and Samuel refer to the concept as one of the poet's "favorite conceptions" (I, 73).
16 Paschek's study, the most recent assessment of Böhme's influence on Novalis, confirms that the influence in *Die Lehrlinge* is very slight, pp. 72-81.

between women and nature, Novalis saw in the prevailing late eighteenth century attitudes a confirmation for his conviction of "women's similarity to plants" (I, 434, # 15). The correspondence was deemed so sound that even a reverse arrogation was thought justified: "All of nature," he wrote in another fragment, "ought really to be feminine, Virgin and Mother simultaneously" (II, 618, # 429).

So basic to *Die Lehrlinge* is the identification between nature and the feminine that the elusive union with the natural world is crystallized in union with a woman. An apprentice provides an oblique reference to the configuration of the merging when he realizes that cerebrality will not be the means for reintegration; the times for which he yearns, he is told, will only be restored "through feeling," linked here with an inner light (I, 96). The specifics become clearer when the apprentice of the first chapter, confused about his path and only vaguely aware that his mission is to reunite man and nature, intuits the association between his goal and the Virgin. Gazing at the various objects in the temple of the Goddess of Sais, he muses that perhaps they were there to guide him to the place "where the Virgin is in a deep sleep, the Virgin for whom my spirit yearns" (I, 81). The same novitiate, attempting to logically comprehend his unifying mission, is admonished by another about the limits of introspection and told that the new world will become a reality only "with the first kiss" (I, 91). Precisely at this juncture Novalis inserted the fairy tale of Hyazinth and Rosenblüte, underscoring the catalytic powers of union with the feminine.

Hyazinth, who perceived his path to be directed toward the "Mother of All Things" or the "veiled Virgin," had gone to the temple of the goddess and by lifting her veil had established the equilibrium so important throughout the novel. Removing the veil of the goddess is also the articulated goal of the novices, each of whom, it is emphasized, will have to find his own path by "tracing" nature's patterns.[17] The act of raising the veil eliminates the barrier between the various sets of antipathies, most obviously those between man and woman and between mortal and divine; thus it initiates the

---

17 The original title, *Der Lehrling zu Sais*, was changed to the plural presumably to stress the necessity for each to find his own way.

Romantic corollary, the Golden Age.[18] Haywood's study confirms the importance of this image as the symbolic barrier between man and nature as well.[19] Only because of the association in Novalis' mind between nature and the feminine is the raising of the veil of Isis so potent an act. Critics have not overlooked the substitution; early in this century Edgar Ederheimer recognized that the natural world, especially in *Die Lehrlinge*, took substance in the woman behind the veil.[20] More recently Mähl has defined marriage for Novalis as the symbolic image of the "longed for communion between humanity and nature."[21] But it has not been generally recognized that the pattern has roots in a concept of androgynous perfection.

Clearly Novalis attributes to heterosexual reunion a redemptive function. Less so than in the *Hymnen an die Nacht*, to be discussed later, but also in this first novel fragment, he portrays the all-important union with nature through erotic images; the prevalence of these descriptions lends support to the foregoing analysis. Envisioning a future oneness with nature, a youth intones near the end of the fragment:

> Whose heart does not stir with leaping desire when nature's innermost life in all its fullness becomes a part of him, when that powerful emotion for which language has no name but love and voluptuousness[22] spreads through his being like a mighty, all-dissolving vapor and he sinks, quivering with sweet anguish, into the dark seductive womb of nature, the poor self is consumed in the spreading waves of desire, and nothing remains but a center of immeasurable procreative power, an engulfing whirlpool in the great ocean (I, 104).

---

18 The goddess Isis, above whose statue according to legend were the words "I am present, future and past" (Mähl, *Die Idee des goldenen Zeitalters*, p. 361), held a great fascination for many late eighteenth and early nineteenth century figures, among them Mozart (*Die Zauberflöte*), Schiller ("Das verschleierte Bild zu Sais"), and Friedrich Schlegel ("Hymnen"). In contrast to Novalis, Schiller, for example, believed the truth behind the veil too powerful to be known by mortals.
19 Haywood, pp. 42, 43 n. 11; Haywood states this most clearly when refuting the views of earlier critics.
20 Ederheimer, p. 73.
21 Mähl, *Die Idee des goldenen Zeitalters*, p. 331.
22 Haywood translates *"Wollust"* as voluptuousness and explains his reasons, p. 47 n. 14; I use his translation.

Sexual allusions continue throughout this speech of the novitiate which concludes with his fantasizing about the eventual reconjunction of man and nature; embracing her, man would then feel "as at the bosom of his chaste bride" and in "sweet intimate hours" (I, 106) he could confide to her his innermost thoughts. Haywood has labeled this "hymn to love" the "dominant chord of the chapter" because, he explains, it is "erotic love that is the . . . key to man's mystic union with nature."[23]

Certainly the portentous results of man's marriage to nature -- whether couched in concretely erotic or more symbolic phrases -- were not attributed by Novalis alone. Hölderlin's Hyperion also describes a future, historical perfection in terms analogous to his own awaited union with Diotima; in the Golden Age, he avows, there will be "only One Beauty . . . and humanity and nature will unite in One all-inclusive Divinity."[24] Given the Romantic longing for the spiritual world of nature and the equation of woman with this supposed antipode to the male being, the efficacy of the pattern in many works of the age was all but assured. Abrams was one of the first to recognize the prevalence of the union between man and nature in literature and philosophy around 1800; he has explored it in English Romanticism and identified it in the works of the German movement as well. Further, he has suggested that the direct prototype for this period-metaphor is to be found in the Biblical apocalyptic marriage from which ensued the millennium, the New Jerusalem.[25] A note to *Die Lehrlinge* indicates that Novalis to some extent connected his vision with such a model: "*New* Testament -- and new nature -- as *new Jerusalem*" (I, 111). In that first novel fragment, he had indeed focused on the exigencies of recovering a paradise for the collective. While maintaining faith in the androgyne as the paradigm for reinstating paradise, other works of German Romanticism approached the model in ways other than by arranging man's reunion with a simplistically designated nature; although remaining in the service of

---

23 Haywood, p. 47.
24 Friedrich Hölderlin, "Hyperion," in *Sämtliche Werke*, ed. Friedrich Beissner, vol. 3 (Stuttgart: Kohlhammer, 1957), p. 90.
25 Abrams, pp. 37-46.

cosmic accord, heterosexual union also gained prominence as a literary symbol capable of the all-important mediation between the individual psyche and the divine. Latent within *Die Lehrlinge*, this pattern is more openly acknowledged in *Ofterdingen*, although still encompassed within religious and aesthetic frames.

Although this intensified appreciation for the sexual pairing in Novalis' second fiction represents a perceptible shift, it does not signal a major adjustment in his thinking; sexual coalescence is still the cue for the merger of the larger rational and non-rational worlds. The more noticeable development in *Ofterdingen* is the glorification of poetry. Even in the earlier novel, Novalis had allowed the apprentices to rhapsodize on the exclusive capacity of the poet to comprehend nature (I, 99). In *Ofterdingen*, however, the connection becomes unambiguously causal: only poetry can bring about the Golden Age. Its unifying symbols alone can restore spirituality to the physical world. Thus Novalis confided to Tieck that he intended *Ofterdingen* as an "apotheosis of poetry" and a novel in two parts, the first delineating Heinrich's maturation to poet and the second showing him as a poet "transfigured" (I, 356). But beyond this new configuration, we discover familiar territory. The precondition for Heinrich's becoming a poet is his wholeness, and that is effectuated only through a heterosexual union with his complementary opposite, this time in a fusion credited explicitly as love. Although the stages in the transition to a cosmic paradise have altered and although sexual union is not the preponderant goal, recombination with the feminine polarity is again pivotal.

As Heinrich embarks upon his journey to Augsburg, he not only hears many stories extolling poetry, but, in the tradition of the *Bildungsroman*, he experiences the physical world. However, even after his arrival in that city, the narrator reports, his inner core remains untouched. Paralleling what the apprentice has been told about the impact of the first kiss, Heinrich's most crucial experience is his meeting with and almost immediate love for Mathilde. The Mathilde who plays such a crucial role in *Ofterdingen* is never simplistically equated with nature as had been the feminine in the earlier novel. The results with which Novalis credits her, however, remain consonant: reunion with her bestows equilibrium and thus completion upon

Heinrich. Mathilde is thus meritorious within the framework of Heinrich's development to poet. In this all-important context she functions as complement to Klingsohr who, although by no means completely one-sided, is nevertheless the strongest voice advocating logic, clarity and order in poetry. "Poetry wishes," Klingsohr proclaims, "to be undertaken as a disciplined art" (I, 282). "Enthusiasm without understanding," he insists, is "useless and dangerous" (I, 281). Although these are qualities which Novalis did not disdain, it is nevertheless this same Klingsohr whom critics have identified with Goethe. Since the impetus for the writing of *Ofterdingen* was Novalis' expressed dissatisfaction with Goethe's *Wilhelm Meister* -- which Novalis on second appraisal and only after studying Böhme judged too orderly and lacking in a sense for the infinite (II, 640-642; III, 646, # 536) – Klingsohr must be seen as a figure embodying a limited scope.

Thus the lessons of Klingsohr, while necessary, are only penultimate and need to be fired by those of Mathilde, the benefit of whom Goethe lacked. In her presence and through love for her Heinrich learns to value the non-rational and instinctive and finally gains an intuition of the infinite; in the typical Romantic euphemism, his inner soul is awakened, the credit for which belongs quite certainly to Mathilde. To Mathilde's "I think . . . I have known you since time immemorial," Heinrich avows: "My Mathilde, only now I feel what it means to be immortal." Even more to the point of causality, Heinrich continues: "Yes, Mathilde, we are eternal because we love one another." But such personal immortality, which was credited as the sole instigation for the Golden Age in the world of the apprentices, is no longer potent enough to induce a cosmic paradise. In *Ofterdingen*, the Golden Age can only become a reality through the mediation of poetry. That the union with Mathilde has been productive even to this end, that is, in helping Heinrich to become what he has been meant to become, a poet, is clearly acknowledged as Heinrich avers to Mathilde: "It seems to me as if I only now am beginning to live. . . . I am only through you what I am" (I, 287-288).

Although Novalis eulogizes heterosexual love as the quintessential unifying power, there is curiously little advocacy of erotic love. In fact, Mathilde preserves her virginity apparently to the point of conceiving Astralis through one embrace (I, 341-342). Erotic overtones are detectable mainly in the fairy tale of Klingsohr. This very difficult tale, containing as it does images from innumerable traditions, has already been mentioned in another context. Although there is no consensus as to an overall interpretation, critics generally agree that the ending of unalloyed rejoicing is an overcoming of some form of dualism, seemingly through sexual love. With the realization of the Golden Age, as the narrator proclaims, the throne was transformed into a magnificent marriage bed and, following the example of the king, the populace embraced. And in this realm of eternal love, as Sophie the "eternal priestess of the hearts" intones, "the Mother is among us, her presence will make us eternally happy" (I, 315).

Although the ostensible terminus in both narratives is the rejuvenated Golden Age, the reclamation of that historical condition is, as has been seen, contingent upon the heroes' personal development. The idea of predestination implicit in Novalis' view of historical progress becomes explicit when he applies the triadic model to individual progress. Novalis construes wholeness as a birthright from which his heroes have become alienated. In *Die Lehrlinge*, before he knows the object of his search, the spokesman for the apprentices realizes: "Everything leads me back into myself." After the teacher has given them a premonition of the absolute, the same novitiate declares the experience memorable because it had given them an intuition, if fleeting, of "this wonderful world within our souls." He wishes he could have prolonged a particularly fortuitous meeting with a child because "everything seemed in its presence to become inwardly brighter. If it had remained longer, I would surely have discovered more within myself" (I, 81-82). The inner world, which Novalis gradually reveals to be the locus for the actualization of the apprentices' dream, is also expressed as a homeland. Their teacher, one novice explains, grants them great freedom in their search, for he knows that regardless of their path, they will be led ultimately "to these dwellings, to this holy home [*Heimat*]" (I, 82).

Similar sentiments are expressed in the later novel when Heinrich intuits that the search which leads him away from his home will, despite his divagation, ultimately ensure his return. The narrator reports Heinrich's musings at the moment of his departure: "The wonderful flower was before him and he looked toward Thuringia, which he was now leaving behind, with the strange premonition that he would return to his fatherland after long peregrinations throughout the world and as if he were actually traveling toward that destination" (I, 205). Indeed, most of his adventures on his journey to Augsburg, from those with the merchants and miners to those with various female figures, arouse within Heinrich vague perceptions of familiarity. These experiences can be attributed to Novalis' belief in the unity of all things or to his fascination with metempsychosis as Haywood suggests;[26] however, it seems that Novalis also intended them as external manifestations of patterns which, by awakening corresponding internal or archetypal models within Heinrich, could accomplish that decisive awakening of the inner world. Such an intent is also apparent in Heinrich's meeting with Mathilde, for in seeing her he recognizes the face he had once glimpsed in the corolla of the blue flower while dreaming. Later in the novel the recurrent question "Where are we going?" receives the answer: "We are going home, always" (I, 325). Numerous allusions to Heinrich as a born poet who needs only to become aware of that which he possesses within himself – Heinrich was, we are told, "born to be a poet" (I, 277) – emphasize the homeward and inward direction of his pilgrimage. Thus the notion of a predetermined fate is as fixed in this novel as in the previous; a benevolent and omnipotent guide has charted Heinrich's immutable path.

The proclivity to euphemize the goal of a spiritual quest has been present in literature at least since the time of St. Augustine. In his *Confessions*, long regarded as the model for a literary quest, he referred to spiritual fulfillment as reaching "home," or as finding a "bridegroom" or "spouse." That the human regimen for fulfillment involves an inwardly directed search or the reaching of "home" has been a factor in German literature since *Parzival*. Wolfram's hero, it will be remembered, was also predestined to reclaim through his wanderings that which from the beginning had been latent within him. Such illuminations are not only the prescript of the mystics;

---

26 Haywood, p. 93.

they are fundamental to many forms of transcendental philosophy, and even to the occult sciences, all of which, according to A.E. Waite, have often been regarded as attempts at magic. Associated with the Hermetic tradition, they are premised on the assumption of a world beyond the senses which could somehow be attained by awakening, in Waite's words, the "latent potentialities which constitute, by the fact of their latency, what is termed the interior man."[27] He alone, the "interior man," was divine. The earliest secret gnosis, Pagels claims in her study of the early Christian Gnostics, was the recognition that to know oneself meant to know God.[28] Böhme's conception of man as *microtheos* also impelled a search for the self or for the inner light which would proffer eternal reward. A similar interpretation of salvation formed the underpinnings of Pietism; along with other euphemisms, Pietists frequently defined the endpoint as a discovery of the center. This attempt at discovering the whole person was, in fact, a part of many esoteric anti-Enlightenment practices; religion for these seekers had thus become an exploration of the psyche.[29]

For many reasons the emphasis on the inner world and its divine center became an important tenet of early German Romanticism. Novalis' logical defense of this persuasion, "How can a human being have a sense for something, if he does not have its seed within?" (II, 419, # 18), as well as his rather dogmatic assertion, "One born blind never learns to see" (I, 105), were echoed by numerous contemporaries. Deeply influenced by Böhme, Schelling confidently declared that a knowledge of self equaled knowledge of the divine and that the eternity for which they all yearned was to be found within:

---

27 Waite, p. 1. Waite includes mesmerism, spiritualism, theosophy, Kabbalism, mysticism, the Rosicrucian Order, Freemasonry and alchemy in his discussion of the occult or Hermetic tradition, viewing them all as manifestations of the same human need for harmony.

28 Pagels, pp. 119-141; the chapter is titled "Gnosis: Self-Knowledge as Knowledge of God."

29 Pietism should be associated as much with these practices, Hermetic in origin, as with Protestantism. See Tatar's *Spellbound* for other late eighteenth and early nineteenth century practices aimed at the discovery of what Mesmer called the sixth sense.

> The sudden realization ... that one has eternity within oneself is similar to a sudden clarification and illumination of the consciousness which one could explain only by reference to the eternal, that is, to God. ... The Golden Age would come on its own accord if each human being would display it within ... not through endless and restless progress and activity toward the external, but rather by a return to the point from which each has set out, to the inner identity with the absolute.[30]

Similarly, to Schleiermacher religion came into existence only when man found infinity within himself. In one of his *Monologen* he stated: "Whenever I turn my gaze into my inner self, I am at the same time in the province of the eternal; I gaze at the activities of the spirit which no world can change and no time can destroy." With confidence he therefore concluded: "At each moment, a human being can live outside of time, simultaneously in the higher world."[31]

Not only in his novels did Novalis align himself with such insights, but in many fragments he also offered espousals of a similarly directed search for the absolute. Quite categorically he once stipulated: "The mysterious way goes inward. Eternity is in us, or nowhere" (II, 419, # 16). Even philosophy, for Novalis along with art the quintessential manifestation of human striving for truth, he defined as the "longing for home [*Heimweh*]" and the "drive to be at home everywhere" (III, 434, # 857). His various descriptions of the inner world are laced with adjectives derived from a similar phraseology; that region is "so homelike...so like the fatherland" (III, 376, # 617). Such expressions can be subsumed under the frequently discussed rubric *Heimweh* and have been linked by critics, Alexander Gode-Von Aesch among them, to the desire to find the real self.[32] To be sure this was in part Novalis' goal. In *Die Lehrlinge*, however, he was not yet prepared to acknowledge this level of androgynous completion. Hyazinth's reconciliation with Rosenblüte is an almost magical act, important because it unifies the disparate forces of the universe. The

---

30 Friedrich Schelling, "System der gesammten Philosophie und der Naturphilosophie insbesondere," pp. 562-563.
31 Friedrich Schleiermacher, "Monologen," in *Werke*, vol. 4, p. 413.
32 Alexander Gode-Von Aesch, *Natural Science in German Romanticism*, Columbia University Germanic Studies 11 (Morningside Heights, N.Y.: Columbia University Press, 1941), p. 112 n. 74.

novices' own goal, although identified as the inner world, remains too incomplete to furnish the basis for any further conclusion. A much debated alternative ending to Hyazinth's search does, however, indicate the poet's awareness of the androgyne's potential for psychological wholeness: "One succeeded — he raised the veil of the Goddess at Sais — / But what did he see? He saw — wonder of wonders — Himself" (I, 110, # 2). To be sure Novalis rejected this ending, and the priority remains with cosmic harmony, but the rejection does not signal a disdain for individual wholeness. Instead it indicates that Novalis had not yet become convinced of the symbolic capabilities with which he attributed the androgyne in *Ofterdingen*.

The pattern for wholeness in Novalis' novels, be it individual or cosmic, involved heterosexual combination; however, since Novalis believed the sexes to possess complementary powers which in his scheme were not free of stereotyping, he assigned to the male the role of conscious seeker. There are numerous historical precedents for what followed: the idealization of the passive, waiting female. The "feminine" for Novalis, in fact, took on mythic dimensions. The story of Hyazinth and Rosenblüte again provides a model; although specifically with Rosenblüte, Hyazinth's recombination is also with an enigmatic goddess Isis presumed behind the veil. And even within the scope of the short fairy tale, the associations are extended to the Virgin and to the Mother of All Things, all of whom merge into an incorporeal feminine principle thought to offer salvation. Not an individual female, but a broadly conceived feminine partner would presumably be the basis for coalescence in *Die Lehrlinge* as well. A fragment included in the paralipomena to *Ofterdingen* reads: "Longing for the Virgin. . . . Jesus in Sais" (I, 340); although unnecessary for and probably illegitimate as a tool for interpreting *Die Lehrlinge*, it is nevertheless indicative of a continuing symbology. The importance, to be sure, is not in the Christian reference for itself, but rather in the allusion to the feminine redeemer behind the veil. As Hyazinth experiences the catalytic powers of the feminine, so can we assume that, had the novel been completed, "the shaping [*bildende*] eros"[33] would have been the major factor in the education of the apprentices.

---

33 The phrase is Giese's adroit definition of Romantic love, p. 222.

For Heinrich, Mathilde functions as did the Virgin-Rosenblüte-Isis complex of the earlier novel. She offers participation in the spiritual realm, and as such is the medium through which he establishes his own personal completion. The context within which she makes her offering, however, has altered. It becomes apparent that the pagan and to a degree the Renaissance arrogation of spirit to the natural world is no longer such an important factor. Instead it is a god whose perfection infuses the intangible world of the spirit. As a religious tone decidedly more Christian than that in the earlier novel asserts itself, the pagan goddess is completely repulsed from the pantheon of feminine redeemers. Novalis tacitly signals the association with Christian references when the Mother of God smiles benignly upon Mathilde; religious overtones prevail as Heinrich responds with a paeon to Mathilde's mediating function: "O beloved, heaven has given you to me to venerate. . . . You are the holy one who brings my wishes to God, through whom he reveals himself to me" (I, 288). The transference of the spiritual force from nature to God is an important clue for comprehending Novalis' reverence toward the female figures of his works. That he could associate Mathilde with religion rather than nature demonstrates that the "feminine" existed not for itself, but as an agent offering initiation to the spiritual realm; he believed it a means which could be categorized according to necessity.

Such a perspective also explains why, despite the overwhelming importance of the feminine figures in Novalis' various reveries, the females themselves remain abstract ideals. Mathilde, for example, represents for Heinrich only the archetype of the feminine as Novalis experienced it. It is these archetypal components rather than her personality or individuality -- one could indeed ask if there was any -- that are significant. As all the qualities which Heinrich valued or needed in Mathilde are reflections of Novalis' assessment of woman, they could be and are reflected infinitely upon others. Even though in the course of the narrative Novalis found it necessary that she die, presumably because Heinrich had already absorbed the benefits she could bestow, and because his existence as poet required her sacrifice, the "feminine" principle remains in the persons of Cyane, Edda and the other women who resemble Mathilde.[34]

---

[34] Such role merging is prefigured in the "Zueignung" (I, 193) and is also

In *Ofterdingen*, Novalis terms the momentous coming together of male and female polarities love. More receptive to Christianity than he had been earlier, he had discovered the value of love as a force which could regenerate both the individual and his world. He had also come to regard heterosexual love as the highest form of religion. "Absolute love independent of the heart, grounded in faith, is religion" (II, 395, # 56), he stated in a fragment. The correspondence is basic to *Ofterdingen*. "What is religion," Heinrich inquires, "but an infinite understanding, an eternal union of loving hearts?" The poet provides the rationale for construing androgynous union as a religious act when Heinrich explains to Mathilde that through her he has contact with her eternal essence. He further intones: "Your earthly shape is only a shadow of this image. . . . the image is an eternal prototype, a part of the unknown holy world" (I, 288-289).

The literature and philosophy of German Idealism was saturated with a premonition of the *Urphenomen*.[35] It is well known that Goethe, for example, sought the *Urpflanze* and that Schleiermacher very specifically credited a concept of original forms. Before his turn to poetry, Novalis had even contemplated the colation of an encyclopedia attesting to the unity of all things, to an *Urprinzip*.[36] Indeed, the Romantics' assurance of and faith in original models — whether referred to as *Urbilder* or conceived within the Neoplatonic frame of a spirit world — was a prime impulse for their intensive preoccupation with the symbolization process. There are numerous reasons for such fealty to a concept of original forms; certainly it testifies to

---

    instrumental in the Pilgrim's Song of the second part of the novel (I, 323-324), especially in the sixth verse. Role merging was a part of the alchemical tradition in which the saving stone was variously referred to as bride, sister and mother (Gray, pp. 221-223). The same tradition can be noted in Pietism; Arnold, for example, referred to the Virgin who would descend to earth as virgin, bridegroom, and even mother (Arnold, *Das Geheimnis der göttlichen Sophia*, part 1, pp. 42-43).

35 Arthur O. Lovejoy, in *The Great Chain of Being* (Cambridge: Harvard University Press, 1961), pp. 269-280, discusses the origins of this idea and its acceptance in Germany with Herder and Goethe. See also Gode-Von Aesch's *Natural Science in German Romanticism*.

36 Mähl discusses this plan in *Die Idee des goldenen Zeitalters*, pp. 349-353.

the conservative nature of the thinkers involved, for what they were attempting was a preservation of the "truths" which the new science had rejected. In *Ofterdingen* it is Heinrich's need to restore within his own person the *Urbild* of androgynous perfection which motivates his worship of Mathilde. Their reunion offers him what man lost after the fall from grace: the essence of the feminine polarity.

Several critics have attempted a definition of Böhme's influence on Novalis.[37] In one of the most recent assessments, Carl Paschek credits Böhme's thinking as the primary incentive for Novalis' apotheosis of poetry and for his conception of that endeavor as divinely inspired. According to Paschek, Böhme's influence is also responsible for Novalis' equation of poet and God. Although he alludes to it only briefly, Paschek does acknowledge Böhme's theory of androgyny; he recognizes Böhme's *Urmensch* as bisexual, and that theosophist's system as according salvation to a "reborn primal man." He also mentions the androgynous Adam in Pietist thinking, most specifically in Oetinger's theosophy.[38] Although he does recognize Böhme's impact on Novalis' appraisal of the power of love, he does not explore the underlying pattern.[39] Kluckhohn noted the same connection in *Ofterdingen*, where Böhme's conception of love as capable of restoring the image of God to humanity through "an inner rebirth," he admits, "plays a role."[40] But neither critic offers further analysis.

The present study is not an examination of Böhme's influence and will not develop the main points of comparison between his and Novalis' works. For purposes of this discussion it is also inessential to determine whether Novalis derived his ideas from Böhme or whether his study of the theosophist's writings accorded with and reinforced his own assertions -- a far more likely prospect. It suffices

---

[37] In addition to Ederheimer's study, see also Walther Feilchenfeld's *Der Einfluß Jacob Böhmes auf Novalis* (Berlin: Ebering, 1922).
[38] Paschek, pp. 28, 78, 240.
[39] Paschek, p. 344. Paschek also acknowledges Böhme's influence in Klingsohr's *Märchen* where the "cult of Sophie," as he phrases it, is most apparent and where a role is reserved for Sophie as mediator, pp. 269-290.
[40] Paul Kluckhohn, *Das Ideengut der deutschen Romantik*, 3rd ed. (Tübingen: Niemeyer, 1953), p. 70.

to recognize that Novalis admired Böhme's thought enough to document a concern with his theosophy, to study it, and to pay homage to its formulator in several poems (I, 411-413; 436, # 32). Although no detailed study on the link between Böhme's androgynous *Urbild* and Novalis' works has been done, it is clear that the poet's tribute to an androgynous ideal gathered momentum because of its paramount importance in Böhme's works.

Baader, who provided the Romantic metamorphosis of Böhme's theosophy, albeit with an increased focus on marital eroticism as the force for actualizing the divine *Urbild*, also provided corroboration for Novalis' thoughts. The influence of this flamboyant thinker on Novalis is even more difficult to document than was Böhme's, because Baader did not begin to systematize his theosophy until 1810, by which time Novalis had been dead for several years. Novalis, however, knew and admired Baader's precepts, although certainly that admiration was mutual, and it is just as likely that Novalis contributed a reciprocal influence to Baader's thinking.[41] Novalis, in fact, found Baader so significant that he declared him to comprise along with Fichte, Schelling, Hülsen and Schlegel "the philosophical directorate in Germany" (II, 529, # 25). Especially in the field of science was Novalis familiar with Baader's theories, which were also premised on the belief in the unity of all things. As early as 1798 Novalis expressed a desire for Baader's inclusion within the Romantic circle, and as an alternative recommended to Friedrich Schlegel that the latter study Baader's works. "His magic reunifies, / What the sword of imbecility has sundered" (IV, 263), he promised his friend.

In the tradition espoused by Böhme, Baader and many of the Pietists, heterosexual union has "saved" Heinrich but with a typically Romantic flavor. As the narrator formulates in a Romantic interpretation of Matthew 18:20: "Where two are gathered together, he is also among them" (I, 288). Heinrich and Mathilde have actualized the *Urbild* of androgynous totality and in so doing have become divine, the proof of which is Astralis. As their creation, the child testifies to their indivisibility, to their partaking of spiritual powers

---

41   Baumgardt sees the possibility of a mutual influence, pp. 82-104.

on earth;[42] because of Astralis the poetic narrator in the second part of the novel can aver that Heinrich and Mathilde no longer exist as separate individuals, and that they have instead joined themselves into "One Image" (I, 318). Their own wholeness, and it is only Heinrich's which interested Novalis, was to lead to an analogous perfection of the world.

At this stage of his thinking, Novalis attributed such potency to the aesthetic reality and made so little differentiation between it and its empirical counterpart, that he deemed the paradise he would create capable of realizing itself in the physical world. In the widest sense possible, poetry was for Novalis the mediator between god and man. The second part of the novel, if completed, would have followed Heinrich's poetic mission culminating in his plucking of the blue flower. The physical and spiritual worlds would thus have fused in a state of undifferentiated harmony described as "One in all and all in One" (I, 318). Notes to the work also indicate the extent to which Novalis envisioned this coalescence. "Conversations among flowers. Beasts. Heinrich von Afterdingen becomes flower − animal − stone − star," he wrote. "According to Jakob Böhm at the end of the book" (I, 341 [sic]). The world into which the mysticism of Böhme was to have been infused is to be understood as the universal Golden Age.

Thus a unique series of correspondences was to have reinstated paradise in both *Die Lehrlinge* and *Ofterdingen*. Important because it was to have unified man and nature, and defined in part as a search for the inner world, the apprentices' reunion with nature was to have been concommitant with the transition to a cosmic heaven. Although Heinrich's own completion in *Ofterdingen* is achieved in the same manner, an aesthetic dimension has been added, which reference to fragments helps clarify. "*Representation* of the *soul* [*Gemüt*] – of

---

42 Creation of all kinds was a central concept to most Romantics, including the creation of children as the synthesis of opposing forces. Schubert's "Von der Liebe der Geschlechter und von der Zeugung" exemplifies their attitude. Various fragments attest to Novalis' high estimation of children: II, 457, # 97 for example. Mähl deals with this aspect of Novalis' thought in *Die Idee des goldenen Zeitalters*, pp. 362-371.

the *inner world"* (III, 650, # 553) was Novalis' definition for poetry. In a later fragment came the completion: "Not as it is, but as it could and must be" (III, 650, # 557). Granted access through love to the inner world, Heinrich was to poetically render this private sanctuary and thus bring about the long awaited paradise. But despite the dominance of poetry in *Ofterdingen*, the paradigm identified as essential to *Die Lehrlinge* remains: the Golden Age can be attained only by an individual's going "home" or to the "center," and the discovery of such a locus can be facilitated only through heterosexual love -- behind which is Novalis' homage to the ancient dream of androgynous perfection.

Not only in the basic structure of his novels with their androgynous resolutions, but also in many of the symbols and images within those works does Novalis show an affinity for the concept of androgynous wholeness. Isis, for example, in mythical accounts, because she bears without consort, possesses elements of bisexuality and is associated with rebirth. There is in Novalis' earlier novel thus a credible merging of the roles of Isis and the Virgin Mary, who in Western tradition does likewise.[43] In the same novel, nature, the formulaic expression for the "feminine" principle as Novalis chose to perceive it, is also awarded dual-sexed powers. A youth speaks with great enthusiasm of the joy granted to those living in harmony with this nature; such intimacy allows them to see her "in her duality, as a procreating and birth-giving power, and in her unity, as an infinite, everlasting marriage" (I, 106). Novalis' nature is thus a singular entity but androgynously complete in the ability to engender as well as to bear. Astralis, too, the herald of the age of love, is a strangely hermaphroditic creature, born of an embrace and truly conceived as a combination of Heinrich and Mathilde.[44] Novalis seems to envision this creature

---

43 Campbell, in *Occidental Mythology*, declares Mary to be the Christian form of Isis, the Mother of All Things, pp. 42-45.
44 Mähl, in *Die Idee des goldenen Zeitalters*, recognizes that the value of a child for Novalis lies in its essence as a true "Einswerden" of sexual polarities, pp. 365-366. Feilchenfeld connects Astralis to Böhme's conception of magic birth, p. 83. In the critical edition Kluckhohn and Samuel suggest the various influences which went into this strange creature and include Böhme's theories (I, 610).

as feminine, but critics usually refer to Astralis as male. Kluckhohn, for one, even apologized for having been susceptible to this tendency.[45] Bequeathed to his contemporaries as the quintessential Romantic symbol, Novalis' blue flower also has a long history of ambiguous definition. Jung, whose debt to the Romantic movement and to the Hermetic strain which fed it is beyond doubt, refers to the "sapphire blue flower of the hermaphrodite" in alchemical writings.[46] Novalis was perhaps aware of the reference, for on at least one occasion Heinrich calls Mathilde "a pure and precious sapphire" (I, 280). Inferences are not to be made that Mathilde was a hermaphrodite or that Heinrich's search was for such a strange being, but rather that a concept of merging was persistently present in Novalis' thought.

So basic to Novalis' thinking was the configuration of an androgynous whole that he even defined the subject of true philosophy as being the "marriage between nature and spirit" (III, 247, # 50). His vision of future harmony in *Glauben und Liebe* – as a time when all humanity will "fuse like a pair of lovers" (II, 488, # 16) – is further testimony to his belief in the power of sexual union. That a marriage between a king and queen in that work represents an ideal political system is partially attributable to what Novalis thought he saw in Berlin, but even that myopic view was conditioned by his immense faith in the merging of sexual opposites. The separation of the sexes was, in fact, for Novalis prototypical of all division; as Mähl has phrased it, the sexes were for Novalis the "prototype of all polarities."[47] By the time he wrote *Ofterdingen*, he was convinced that the harmony following the reunion of those oppositions was a condition which could be attained within the human psyche and then, through the symbolic power of art, be extended to the entire world.

---

45 Kluckhohn, *Die Auffassung der Liebe*, p. 478.
46 Jung, "Individual Dream Symbolism in Relation to Alchemy," in *Psychology and Alchemy*, p. 80.
47 Mähl, *Die Idee des goldenen Zeitalters*, p. 366.

Chapter Four

HYMNEN AN DIE NACHT:
THE SAVING GRACES OF "CHRIST AND SOPHIE"

The pattern which determined the structure and content of Novalis' unfinished novels is also operative in *Hymnen an die Nacht*. Once again a convergence of sexual opposites reestablishes man's harmony with the spiritual world. Oscillating between verses childlike and sincere in tone and other passages turbulent with emotion, the mood of the hymns, however, does not resemble that of the novels. *Die Lehrlinge* had been a vehicle for Novalis' philosophical musings; by the time he wrote *Ofterdingen* he had learned to further aestheticize his desires. Composed between these unfinished works and in contrast to both, the hymns present no masks; neither an apprentice nor a Heinrich stands between poet and reader. Narrated by a poetic "I," the *Hymnen* speak more directly to the reader than did either novel. The strident claims at actually overcoming the barrier between man and the divine have, therefore, an immediacy which the more romantic fictions lacked. Critics protest the excessive employment of biographical information as an interpretive tool for Novalis' writings; but when dealing with the hymns, the surfeit of correspondences between the poet's life and the fiction of the work makes the practice almost unavoidable. Most critics, in fact, equate the poetic speaker with the author. Even Haywood, who attempted to interpret the hymns, as he did all of Novalis' works, without recourse to the person of the poet and instead through the study of its imagery, admitted that the events surrounding Sophie's death were necessary for an understanding of the *Hymnen*. The mystic reunion with her and the spiritual world assumed for the poet, says Haywood, "universal reference" and "symbolic character."[1] That intensely personal experience at her grave -- what Kluckhohn refers to as the central

---

1 Haywood, pp. 3, 53.

91

experience of Novalis' life (I, 15) -- forms the axis of the hymns. The genre Novalis chose is consonant, for the lyric has always been a convenient vehicle for personal outpourings.

Novalis described his graveside experience as one which transcended time and space and which nullified the power of death. In his diary he wrote: "In the evenings I went to Sophie. I was indescribably joyful there − flashing moments of enthusiasm − I blew the grave away in front of me like dust − centuries were like moments − I could feel her nearness − I believed she would appear at any moment" (IV, 35-36). In words recalling this diary entry, the speaker in the third of the hymns to the Night remembers his own miserable loneliness at his beloved's grave. Suddenly, he declares, the grave was transformed into clouds of dust and through the clouds became visible "the transfigured features of the beloved." In her eyes he fathomed eternity and through her embrace he gained entrance to the world of spirit without time. "I grasped her hands and the tears became a sparkling, unbreakable band. Millennia receded into the distance" (I, 135). Co-editors of the critical edition of the *Hymnen*, Kluckhohn and Richard Samuel have confirmed that the vision Novalis described in his diary in May of 1797 was the nucleus of the third hymn, with correspondences to the poetry "which can not be merely coincidental" (I, 116). Understood as the distillation of Novalis' own experience, this third hymn is generally recognized not only as the first written, but also as the core of the entire work.[2] The other five hymns represent the poet's attempt to make possible for all humanity the same sudden oneness with the realm of the spirit he had enjoyed at Sophie's grave. Disagreements over the interpretation of the hymns are inevitable, for the chronology of events is

---

2   See Kluckhohn and Samuel for general information on the conception of the *Hymnen* (I, 115-120); the third was probably written in the fall of 1797. Two versions of the *Hymnen* are extant: the first in manuscript form and dating from 1797, the second the *Athenäum* version published in 1800. Novalis made the changes for the published version himself; although some feel it inferior -- Heinz Ritter, in *Novalis' Hymnen an die Nacht* (Heidelberg: Winter, 1974), exemplifies such a position -- the references in this study will be to the *Athenäum* version unless otherwise stated.

difficult to ascertain and much of the imagery seems abstruse. But as an exegetical perspective, the androgynous ideal has much to commend itself; indeed the myth of androgynous perfection provides once again the scaffold for inducing the universal harmony so fundamental to Novalis' thinking.

As did the narratives, the hymns assume a world of polarities in need of a propellant for moving the separated spheres toward reunion. Although the fusion of sexual opposites will again be this catalyst, Novalis alludes to such pairing only indirectly; a metaphoric union between Light and Night is instead the overt concern in the work. Lost primal harmony, the speaker claims, has resulted in a world of Light which has vanquished the supremacy of the realm of Night. Only the reunion of these antipodal forces can create a harmonious future. The particular attributes of the opposing principles, which are sustained throughout the work and gradually subsume the entire world, are associated from the beginning with sexual dichotomies. Further defining the metaphoric frame for his binary world in the first hymn (I, 131-133), the speaker refers to Light as the "King of Earthly Nature;" to him he imputes the power for revealing the "wondrous glories of the kingdom of the world." Night is the opposing "World Queen," the "revealer of holy worlds." She alone can open "the infinite eyes" which can fathom "the depths of a loving soul."[3]

As the speaker contrasts the two opposing realms, it becomes clear that the pattern of the novels is intact. For the world which draws the poetic narrator is not the empirical world of Light, but the nocturnal world with its promise of infinity. Only the realm of the Universal Queen, he claims, can foster a reunion with the sexual opposite who is now a part of that dark domain. The World Queen

---

3   From all-seeing eyes to magic birth to magic sleep, many motifs in Novalis' works recall similar images from Böhme's writings. Many of these images are found within the space of a few pages in *Mysterium Magnum*, vol. 5, pp. 94-100. The Light and Dark dichotomy, however, does not recall Böhme's work. Although in the same section of *Mysterium Magnum* which contains so many other references Böhme did declare a time when there would be no need for the sun, he otherwise associated Light with the feminine wisdom Sophia, within. The Inner Light Protestants in England, for example, were directly influenced by this conception.

is the "guardian of blissful love." Praising her to his beloved, the speaker stresses this causal relationship: "She sends you to me — tender beloved." Because he interprets the gift of Night as the means for transcending the finite world, the poet in the first hymn seems content to resign himself to his existence in that diurnal realm. Through contact with his beloved, and through her with the world of Night, he believes he has found a way to become whole. As he declares to his sexual counterpart: "You have revealed the Night to me as life — made me human."

The humanness the "I" has found, the totality he associates with perfection, results from his own reunion with his feminine counterpart. The conclusion to the first hymn underscores the erotic ingredient in this formula for salvation. Yearning for an end to the tyranny of the physical world of Light, the speaker demands of his beloved: "Consume my body with spiritual passion." Only in this way will he be able to "fuse more fervently" with her. The locus for an individual's comprehension of infinity is again, as it was in the novels, the inner self. Only love will restore the "inner" blending of the sexes necessary if the speaker is to regain his spiritual essence and thus his divinity. As he phrases it, such a merger would render possible his celebration of an eternal "wedding night." To be sure, the larger context for this hymn is still the reinstatement of a paradisiacal Golden Age, but that universal felicity is to be a consequence of individual fulfillment.

In the shorter, less intense second hymn (I, 133-135), the terms of harmony revert to the metaphor of Night and Light. In despair, the speaker laments the return of morning and looks forward to a time when earth's power will end. Such a time must come, for Light's realm in time is "measured." "Without time and space," on the contrary, are the powers of Night. The means for neutralizing the opposition, however, are still entirely personal. The erotic component is unmistakable as the speaker offers a paeon to sleep. Loftily he separates himself from those whom he deems incapable of recognizing Night and its partner, sleep, as the inspirations of erotic love. To this adulated sleep the poet intones: "They do not know that it is you who hovers over the tender maiden's breast and makes her womb a heaven — they do not fathom that out of tales of old you come to meet me, opening the heavens and carrying the key to the dwellings of the blessed." No mere physical sleep is this – for that the poet employs the word "shadow" – but instead a "holy sleep." It is a condition to be sustained "in the golden flood of the grapes – in the magic oil of the almond tree, and in the brown juice of the poppy." Along with erotic love, the speaker commends these offerings of "sleep" for granting access at least temporarily to another more veritable level of reality and thus making bearable the diurnal life. Although the specifics apply to the individual in his quest for communion with the spiritual world, the speaker attempts to subjugate the eternal "wedding night" to the position of agent, a feat he had only intimated in the first hymn. The foremost purpose of this less emotional hymn is to clarify the role of heterosexual love within the larger pattern of overcoming that split between forces which, according to the speaker, has separated heaven from earth.

Already identified as the aesthetic rendering of Novalis' own unique rejuvenescence, the experience of the third hymn (I, 135) is the foundation for the personal resolution the speaker has offered in the first two hymns. By recounting it in the past tense, Novalis provides linguistic distance from the preceding hymns and in so doing somewhat objectifies the events it relates. The reunion can therefore better serve as a model for the reality the speaker intends to repeat and eternalize. Here in this hymn is the speaker's proof that an individual can regain access to the spiritual world through heterosexual love. As he tells it, this first and only dream of reconciliation with his beloved has left him with an "eternal, immutable belief in the heaven of Night and ... the beloved." With his claim to having induced a synthesis of the disparate spheres by tearing loose "the bonds of Light" the hymn peaks; the speaker, we are to understand, has entrusted himself to Night with its promise of erotic love and timeless existence. At this point in the maturation of the apprentices, *Die Lehrlinge* presumably would have ended; at the same stage Heinrich in *Ofterdingen* would have become capable of poetry. Androgynous union would have served its purpose as the portent of a renewed age of perfection. The encounter of sexual polarities is no less powerful in the *Hymnen* than it was in the novels; it is still the prototypical union, but it lacks the symbolic thrust which Novalis had discovered by the time he wrote *Ofterdingen*. At the same time, Novalis is attempting to go beyond a mere dependence on the fairy tale magic which seems to have restored Hyazinth's world. In this intermediary work, sexual consummation unifies two contiguous worlds by its magical or symbolic potency, but does not then, having served its function, become unnecessary; it is rather an artistic representation of a reality which itself, because of its merging capabilities, must be sustained. In the final three hymns Novalis strives to extend this precarious and entirely personal resolution to a more universally accessible -- and not just coincidentally more traditional -- framework for salvation.

The speaker in the fourth hymn (I, 135-139) believes he has found a means for eternalizing his experience of oneness with the spiritual world. Following his confident declaration that he knows the time of the "last morning," he abruptly and with great effect proclaims that the "pilgrimage to the holy grave" became "long and wearying;" the "cross" weighed him down. Such imagery cannot but conjure immediate Christian symbols. But the use of the past tense in this important phrase, as well as the word "hill" which follows shortly, recalls the third hymn. Novalis had used the same word both in the diary description of Sophie's grave and in the poetic translation of that experience, the third hymn. He intends the "holy" grave in the fourth hymn to establish a link between the redemptive forces of heterosexual and Christian love. Retaining its connection with Christ, the image remains as well a reference to the grave of the beloved which had figured so dramatically in the previous hymn. Not until the end of the fourth hymn, however, does the speaker relate his vision once again to Christian salvation. Reasserting his conviction instead within the predominant metaphor of Light and Night, the speaker expresses again the superiority of the world of Night. "Can you show me," he questions Light, "an eternally faithful heart?" When he does reassert Christian references, he does so within the main metaphor. Consistent with the set of imagery he has already developed, he links Christianity with the world of Night, the conqueror capable of overcoming all adversaries. Convinced of the inevitable reclamation of the spiritual world, he pronounces universal harmony a certainty despite Light's recalcitrance. "Your anger and rage are in vain," he states to Light near the end of the hymn for, he continues, the "cross," the "triumphant banner of our race," is "indestructible." Besides reaffirming the link between Christianity and the realm of Night which will ultimately subsume its opposite, these intimations prepare for and make more credible the later overt role the poet allots to Christ as Savior.

The fervidly erotic ending to the fourth hymn reinforces the ambiguity between Christian and erotic forms of union: "Oh! drink beloved, / powerfully of me, / So that I can fall asleep / and love. / . . . / I live by day / full of belief and courage / And die by night / in holy passion [*O! sauge Geliebter, / Gewaltig mich an, / Dass ich entschlummern / und lieben kann. / . . . / Ich lebe bei Tage / Voll Glauben und Mut / Und sterbe die Nächte / In heiliger Glut*]." Most critics have treated this finale as an admittedly rather curious call to Christ; concerned with documenting Novalis' interests beyond the mere personal to a desire for universal salvation, they point here to Christ as the medium for such a premise. A more impartial analysis would not deny Christian implications, but would argue that they do not eclipse the more private yearning for a "beloved" which has surged forth in the previous hymns. The first three hymns have established quite definitively the importance of the sexual counterpart. Although the Christian allusions in this fourth hymn are forceful, they do not justify an eradication of the personal goal of union with that partner. Rather than the poet's ambiguity, one should speak here of a deliberate role merging. The association of Christ and a sexual partner may be ironic, for the orthodox faith has always opposed any expression of eroticism,[4] but it is not unique. Christianity has always been considered a religion of love and Novalis' emphasis on the erotic variant is merely a secularization of Christian patterns.

Novalis' identification of the two saviors is part of the long tradition indebted to Böhme, whose *Weg zu Christo* had even been subtitled *Christosophia*. Novalis, however, was not merely reviving Böhme's thinking in the *Hymnen*, but was bringing to the work his

---

[4] Other of Novalis' works maintain this association; see for example the seventh of the *Geistliche Lieder* in which Christian symbols of eating and drinking are identified with erotic love (I, 166-168).

own experience of mystic union and salvation. Shortly after Sophie's death, he had written in his diary the simple phrase, "Christ and *Sophie*" (IV, 48). Although Böhme's influence is unmistakable, salvation in the hymns also reflects the thinking of a more secular age. Böhme had venerated an androgynous Christ who offered a reunion with the Heavenly Virgin lost to man during the fall. The marriage partner he had viewed as the earthly substitute, and to be sure an inferior one, in the androgynous combination he associated with salvation. For Novalis the substitution proceeded from the obverse direction. It is personal heterosexual love which offers the primary experience of wholeness, but the universal application comes through the saving love of Christ, whose power emanates from the "feminine" world of Night. As Böhme before him, Novalis too in the *Hymnen* is attempting to combine the Hermetic claim that divinity was to be revealed by self-awareness with the Christian promise of paradise.

In the fifth and longest hymn (I, 141-153), Novalis imposes a historical framework upon the antagonistic forces of the Universal King and Queen. Intent upon eternalizing the fulfillment he had experienced in his dream, the poetic narrator associates Light and Night with the pagan and Christian worlds, respectively. Despite his acceptance of Christian redemption, Novalis' world view is his own. The somewhat anachronistic conception of historical progress he offers in this hymn shows basic similarities to passages in the novels. Once again the speaker refers to the original historical stage as a time of pristine harmony between man and nature; he depicts that world as the majestic domain of the early gods who existed when rivers, trees and flowers all exhibited "human sense," and when "an eternally bright festival of the children of heaven and the denizens of earth intoxicated life through the centuries like spring." In the description of the divinity as "a God in the grapes — a loving maternal Goddess rising forth in full golden garb," there is also a vague tribute to a conception of an early bisexual deity in this perfect time. But gradually, as the speaker tells it, the inescapable aura of death permeated this blissful existence and, as the ancient world succumbed to its fear, the gods disappeared. Nature, robbed of its soul, became lonely and lifeless. In a departure from *Die Lehrlinge*, however, spirituality did not remain the sacred trust of nature. Man's perception of infinity instead, we are told, found a sanctuary in the "higher realm of the soul." Despite the religious and historical overlays, the regaining of oneness with the spiritual realm remains a personal process. Following mystic and occult traditions, it leads one into the self.

As postulated in this fifth hymn, it is death and the fear of death which have ruptured primal harmony. In the world histories of the novels, Novalis had attributed this result to knowledge and consciousness. The modification in the hymns is not surprising, for Christian thinkers have traditionally faulted consciousness for bringing cognizance of death. Christian orthodoxy, however, has also made much of its power to neutralize death's potency, of its capacity to offer an eternal reward to replace a life in time. By linking his personal vision to Christianity, Novalis assumes the benefit of this promise; he hails religious salvation, already allied with Night and erotic love, as the path to immortality. "Night became the mighty womb of revelation -- into it the Gods returned" to come forth in the form of Christ, the "son of the first Virgin and Mother – the infinite fruit of mysterious embrace," who would by his love and death redeem the world.

Given Novalis' perception of the nocturnal realm, this alignment with Christianity is quite plausible. Historically, Christ is the prototypical example of a mediator. In the *Hymnen* redemption depends solely on the love and sacrifice of an intercessor. Although the concept of sacrifice did not figure in *Die Lehrlinge* – the "Jesus in Sais" notation, however, indicates that such a necessity was not far from Novalis' mind -- it was present in *Ofterdingen*, though not defined as such. Mathilde's death is from a certain perspective the requisite sacrifice for Heinrich's immortality as a poet. Recalling Novalis' reaction to Sophie's death – it was for him a "calling to apostolic office" -- helps as well to define her importance in the poet's life. And such is the pattern in the *Hymnen* where the beloved has so propitiously died. In the second hymn after lamenting the coming of day, the speaker had asked impatiently when the "mysterious sacrifice of love" would burn eternally (I, 133). The Fichtean influence so visible in the goal-oriented searches of the novels has thus been replaced in the hymns to the spiritual world of Night by Christian and especially Pietist prescripts; there is in the *Hymnen* a passive dependence on a mediator whose loving sacrifice will ameliorate the anguish of mortality. As developed in the artistic work, the mediator role represents a merging of the historical Christ with a female intercessor, a sexual opposite at home in the spiritual world. The final verse of this fifth hymn affirms once again the correspondence between the two. "One night of bliss" is equated with standing in the presence of the Almighty, humanity's sun. As the grave with its dual reference, so here the sun links personal and historical salvation, for it is not only a signal of religious fulfillment. Although the speaker terms the spiritual realm the world of Night, that all-inclusive nocturnal realm also has its sun; the "beloved," referred to as the "light of Night" (I, 135) and the "sun of Night" (I, 133), was its center.

Numerous critics have remarked that Novalis' religion, though ostensibly Christian, has nothing to do with sin and its consequences. In addition, it is clear that the utopia he envisions has little in common with a Christian heaven. Novalis' lack of orthodoxy is also apparent in his conception of Christ as a transfiguration, indeed a rebirth, of the old gods who "had gone to sleep in order to go forth over the changed world in new, wonderful shapes" (I, 145). More examples from the hymns to the Night could be cited; each would underscore the conviction that Novalis formulated his conception of Christianity and Christ to serve as a framework within which he could find fulfillment for his intense yearning for universal accord. By the time he wrote the hymns, he had studied history enough to think he had found the stability he associated with perfection in what he took to be the Christian Middle Ages; in *Die Christenheit oder Europa* he had adumbrated that view, positing in Christianity a spiritual power which could bring peace to the world. But there, as well as in the *Hymnen*, he pays his tribute to that religion not because of its dogma, but rather because of the harmony with which he thought it actualized itself. Despite his frequent praise of Christianity, Novalis was decidedly undogmatic. The phrase "Reconciliation of the Christian religion with the pagan" (I, 347) in the paralipomena to *Ofterdingen* can be seen as his general intent.

When in the fourth hymn the poet had restated his preference for the world of Night, he had named as one of its aspects, death. "Which voluptuousness, which enjoyment," he had rhetorically asked the realm of Light, "does your life offer which would outweigh the delights of death?" (I, 137). Important as part of the mediator's role, death is also a positive goal for each individual. For Novalis the "Virgin" dwells in the world of the spirit, "in the kingdom of love;" and that is also the site of the "temple of heavenly death" (I, 149). By the fifth hymn, the "beloved" has become a part of an idealized "feminine" principle; as was the case with the feminine redeemers in the novels, she is linked with the "Mother," with "the Heavenly Virgin," and with Maria. All are included in the realm of the Universal Queen, the world of Night and, according to Novalis, are a part of a historical Christianity. Reunion with the feminine will offer the experience of death necessary as the prelude to a new life. A renewed and zealous outpouring of that emotion expressed in its title, a "yearning" for death, permeates the sixth and last hymn (I, 153-157). Gradually it becomes apparent, however, that the death for which the speaker longs is to be understood as a spiritual rebirth; as such, the formulation evidences the influence of the mystical and Christian tradition of dying to be born again. We need only to think of St. Augustine or St. Paul or of the "sleep of death" which was the coinage for salvation in, for example, Psalms 13 to realize the strength of this euphemism. Historically, this tradition has been antipathetic to many because it has so often represented a narcissistic desire for personal salvation unfettered with ethical or social implications. Novalis cannot be so faulted, at least in his intentions, for in the final three hymns the speaker has tried to extend his own *unio mystica* to a permanent, cosmic condition. The final hymn attests to his success, for the "I" is now an expansive "we." "Death" made possible by a mediating "savior" will usher in the universal Golden Age.

The other refrains hailing spiritual rebirth through "death" recall similar passages throughout the novels. The apprentices and Heinrich had spoken of their ultimate destination as "home," and so, too, in the hymns is such a location the goal. Speaking for all humanity, the poetic narrator disclaims all desire for new experiences. "We want," he affirms instead, "to go home to the father." Repeating the association, he asserts that the finite world will never satisfy humanity's yearning for peace. "We must go to our home [*Heimat*]," he instructs, if we are to experience the "holy time." The death of the old self, we are to understand, will lead to a regeneration of the new; as he did in the novels, Novalis intends here a reemergence of an individual's androgynous center. As the speaker had stated earlier: "Death calls to the wedding."

The final hymn concludes with a merger of the two mediators which will make possible Novalis' synoptic vision. All vacillation between distinct references to Christ on the one hand and to a sexual partner on the other disappear in the poet's final euphoric proclamation of his goal: "Down to the sweet bride, / To Jesus, the beloved." Indeed now that the poet has found a way to link the supreme world of the Universal Queen with a historical Christianity and through that merger been able to affirm the possibility of "salvation," all antinomies are overcome. As the metaphoric veil once again encloses the work, the hymns to the Night conclude in the "twilight," a signal that the supremacy of Light has been superseded and must now yield to a merger with Night.

Novalis' novel fragments and the *Hymnen* are testimony to the poet's strong intuition of a divine world beyond the senses and to his surety that humanity, when restored to its original androgynous perfection, could exist in that resplendent world. Love is inevitably the key to the wholeness thought tantamount to salvation and immortality. Kluckhohn, in recognition of the importance of love to Novalis' vision, has suggested the poet's prophetic definition of love as the "ultimate goal of *world history*, the One and Only [*Unum*] of the universe" (III, 248, # 50) to be a suitable motto for the poet's entire *ouevre*.[5] Whereas most critics have recognized the importance of love in his work, few have placed it within the framework of androgyny.[6] Hermann Korff, for example, describes the Romantic vision in general as man's search for and redemption through a

---

5 Kluckhohn, *Die Auffassung der Liebe*, p. 484.
6 Those who have include, in addition to Huch and Giese, Benz, in *Adam*, p. 26; Raymond Furness, in "The Androgynous Ideal: Its Significance in German Literature," *Modern Language Review*, 60 (1965), pp. 60-61; Busst, pp. 58-67; and Exner, pp. 56-57.

woman.[7] Nowhere, however, does he avow its origin in the ancient dream of androgynous perfection. In *Das Ideengut der deutschen Romantik*, Kluckhohn also makes frequent mention of Böhme's concept of androgyny, but rejects its application to Novalis and Romanticism quite categorically. The notion of a primal androgyne, he insists, should "in no way be spoken of as the main ideal of the Romantics." His own definition of Romantic love, however, provides justification for that which he denies; such love, he analyzes, is a true union of sexual opposites: "The polarous opposition of the sexes ought . . . to find its fruitful synthesis in love and marriage."[8] Although Mähl recognizes Novalis' belief in the sexual polarities as the prototypes of all dichotomies to be synthesized, he does not see the larger context. Indeed, the word androgyny is not even mentioned in his study, although he does acknowledge the potency of an *Urbild* in Novalis' works and Böhme's influence in that conception. He summarizes that Novalis saw in marriage the "prototype of the Golden Age," because it incorporated the "secret of loving Oneness out of two beings."[9] Such an analysis can only reflect Novalis' affirmation of androgynous wholeness.

Pivotal as it was to his vision, love was not for Novalis a unifier of people, but rather an agent which could facilitate a merger between contiguous realms of physical and spiritual phenomena. Whether he was primarily concerned with that merger as an individual or cosmic attainment is another question. Although he repeatedly enunciated his goal as the cosmic Golden Age, his works indicate a preoccupation with individual fulfillment. Unsympathetic readers have thus criticized him for seeking to lose himself in an individual ecstasy of union with some absolute. Some of his fragmentary illuminations do court the danger of such a reading, but he was more concerned with his world than such objections would suggest. To be sure, his idealism precluded any grasp of social or political reality, but that in itself is

---

7 Hermann August Korff, *Geist der Goethezeit*, vol. 3 (Leipzig: Weber, 1940), pp. 86-87.
8 Kluckhohn, *Das Ideengut*, p. 68.
9 Mähl, *Die Idee des goldenen Zeitalters*, p. 270 n. 30; this unity from duality, claims Mähl, is the core of all his fairy tales.

not synonymous with a disregard for the welfare of the collective. Ultimately the importance of universal versus individual wholeness in Novalis' works can best be understood if one is willing to grant the necessity of the latter to the former. Such a notion was indeed Novalis' ostensible intent. "The world will change," he penned on the manuscript of the *Hymnen*, "with humanity" (I, 140).

Given that perception of the progression necessary to bring about eventual world peace, a chronology accepted by many thinkers before him, Novalis' concentration on the individual is understandable. A world of perfected individuals was to be the impetus for earthly peace. The *Hymnen*, for example, could end only after the poet has been able to shift the narrative point of view from an "I" to a "we." Even in *Glauben und Liebe* where his conservative, if not reactionary, thinking reigns at least on the surface and where his concept of political reality tends toward the mystical, his views are not without democratic implications. "All human beings ought to be capable of occupying a throne" (II, 489, # 18), he asserted there. In *Die Lehrlinge* he expressed the same idea with a metaphor of the sun. After the Golden Age would be reinstated, the sun would lay down "its stern scepter" and become "once again a star among stars" (I, 86).[10]

More than his contemporaries, Novalis gave to self-fulfillment a metaphysical dimension. But the focus on the solitary perfectible individual in his works brings with it a suggestion of narcissism. Indeed, the love Novalis recommends is not one which unifies human beings, but one which accrues benefits for the lover; it is primarily an exploitative union and one which benefits the male protagonist. When he rejected the alternative ending to the fairy tale of Hyazinth and Rosenblüte, he seems to have put aside a narcissistic fascination with the self. In the introduction to the critical edition of Novalis' literary works, Kluckhohn makes much of the fairy tale, seeing its

---

10 Richard Faber, in "Apokalyptische Mythologie: Zur Religionsdichtung des Novalis," in *Romantische Utopie. Utopische Romantik*, ed. Gisela Dischner and Richard Faber (Hildesheim: Gerstenberg, 1979), sees Novalis' collective aims more positively than do most critics; he argues, for example, that if the world is going to be changed, the new must be first imagined, p. 79.

glorification of the powers of love as proof that Novalis had overcome an earlier "solipsism nourished on Fichte" (I, 75). In the fairy tale, however, and in the novel framing it, and in *Ofterdingen* and the *Hymnen* as well, the love relationship is important solely because through it the male achieves wholeness. The female partner in these works is important only because she "saves" the male. From this perspective Novalis' works can be seen as variations of his preoccupation with, if not solely self-improvement, then male fulfillment.

Although his aesthetic works make the point only subtly, it was the erotic element in the love union which Novalis saw as efficacious. In fragments, however, he was more direct. "Body and soul," he once wrote, *"touch each other* in the act." Written between 1798 and 1799 when he was still contemplating a comprehensive encyclopedia, this statement is part of a larger fragment of the Brouillon collection and appears under the heading *"Physik."* In its entirety the fragment clarifies Novalis' obsession with the sexual synthesis. A part of the remainder reads:

> As the *woman* is the *highest visible* means of nourishment which accomplishes the *transition from body to soul* — So are the sexual parts the highest *external* organs which accomplish the transition from visible to invisible organs.
> The *glance* — (speech) — the *touching of hands* — *the kiss* — *the touching of breasts* — *the holding of the sexual parts* — the act of embracing — these are the rungs of the ladder — on which the soul descends — in contrast to this ladder there is one — on which the body ascends — up to the embrace (III, 264, #126).

Fortunately Novalis turned to literature where he could aestheticize and somewhat reshape these musings; however, the hope for female fulfillment which the fragment offers did not become a part of his literary concern. His works focus on male perfectibility, and it is not difficult to see the poet himself as the model for such totality. It seems thus that Novalis' synoptic dreams spring primarily from the narcissistic impulse to transform the world according to his own vision. Especially in the intensely personal hymns, the elaborate religious scheme seems to have been postulated in order to justify his own experience of union with an absolute or to give it more acceptable contours. Indeed, it seems as though he felt it necessary to couch his own personal desire in a universal, religious experience.[11] Throughout his work, in fact, it is difficult to separate the male protagonist completed through love from Novalis, himself, who believed his poetry could usher in the Golden Age.

Whether in the services of effecting a macrocosmic or a more individual fulfillment, the androgynous ideal is central to Novalis' vision. His thinking is, in fact, a good example of Benz' proposition that the myth of the androgyne has created a metaphysics of sex and has even been a formidable impetus to metaphysical speculation *per se*. It is the "hidden source of metaphysics" according to Benz, because humanity is fated to strive to realize the myth.[12] And to follow Benz' argument, given the impossibility of a concrete physical manifestation, human beings turn to literature, philosophy and metaphysics. Although Benz is not so specific, it is the symbolic potential in these disciplines which makes them so attractive. For Novalis the androgynous configuration was a symbolic expression of a psychically held and philosophically reinforced model for perfectibility, one which corresponded with his own external reality.

Especially after *Die Lehrlinge* there was in Novalis' thought and works a definite proclivity for seeing in the symbol of the androgyne a transcendent reality on the verge of manifesting itself in the cognitive world. He articulated the role of art in this process when he applauded the "giving presence to what is not present [*Gegenwärtig machen des Nicht Gegenwärtigen*]" effected through the "magic power of *fiction*" (III, 421, # 782). The same pragmatic thrust is apparent in his linking of a symbol with an *a priori* intent for its realization: "The symbolic," he insisted, "causes self-actualization" (III, 693, # 705). Accordingly, as the hero in *Ofterdingen* was to have discovered and plucked the enigmatic blue flower, the androgyne in Novalis' works was also an image calling for its own mimesis. Following the tenets of Novalis' magic idealism, it would exist first of all within a work of art

---

11 There is also in Novalis' insistence on union with a dead partner a similarity to Swedenborg's belief that marriage – that is, the union of sexual polarities into one whole – lasted even after death. See for example Swedenborg's *Conjugial Love*, pp. 55-69.
12 Benz, *Adam*, p. 27.

and then help to shape the empirical world. In his own way Novalis accomplished this goal most successfully in *Ofterdingen*, although it it also achieved in the *Hymnen*, if a bit fanatically. One can concur with Haywood's conclusion concerning Novalis' works, that "all of his poetry is concerned ultimately with revealing and celebrating the poetic spirit,"[13] only if the symbolic potential within that poetry is recognized. The proviso even then must be added that just as the symbols themselves, poetry was for Novalis ultimately a mediator, another stage in the progression to a cosmic paradise.[14]

---

13 Haywood, p. 2.
14 This point is made in the fifth hymn, which contains allusions to poetry as a consolation necessary in the stage preceding the Golden Age. This is especially clear in the earlier handwritten version (I, 142, line 440).

Chapter Five

FRIEDRICH SCHLEGEL'S GREEK PERIOD: THE ANDROGYNE AS A MODEL FOR EQUALITY

Romantic poetry, Friedrich Schlegel once stated, was to be "nothing but ethical poetry" (LN 1336).[1] His theories of literature, intended ultimately to perfect his world, established him in the late 1790's as the seminal thinker of the Jena Romantics. But even before Romanticism coalesced as a movement, and before he could offer a Romantic plan for saving the world, Schlegel was committed to perfecting his society. The impact of Hermetic thinking, which dominated so much of the religion and *Naturphilosophie* around the turn of the century and which had made such inroads in Novalis' thinking, was less important for Schlegel's early development. To be sure, towards the end of *Lucinde* Hermetism asserts a strong claim, but it was a concern which other early Romantics had helped to kindle, especially during the summer of 1798. The practices associated with that philosophy continued to be an absorbing interest for Schlegel even after the demise of the Jena circle. Literary historians have usually seen the Romantic fascination with esoteric thinking as one which Schlegel did not share. But a set of materials discovered only in 1967 and published in the critical edition as the *Tagebuch [über*

---

1 Since the critical edition is incomplete, Schlegel's works will also be quoted from other sources. They will be cited in the text along with the page number, in parentheses, according to the following abbreviations:
LN = Friedrich Schlegel, *Literary Notebooks 1797-1801*, ed. Hans Eichner (Toronto: University of Toronto Press, 1957)
P = Friedrich Schlegel und Novalis, *Biographie einer Romantikerfreundschaft in ihren Briefen*, ed. Max Preitz (Darmstadt: Gentner, 1957).
W = Friedrich Schlegel, *Briefe an seinen Bruder August Wilhelm*, ed. Oskar Walzel (Berlin: Speyer and Peters, 1890).
The *Lyceum* and the *Athenäum* fragments as well as the *Ideen* are included in the second volume of the critical edition and will be referred to in the text by fragment number.

die Magnetische Behandlung der Gräfin Leśniowska 1820-1826] (Volume XXXV) provides ample documentation of this later preoccupation. At the beginning of his career, however, more rational pursuits concerned Schlegel; his ambitions were humanistic rather than metaphysical. More deeply influenced by the spirit of the French Revolution than was Novalis, Schlegel hoped to incorporate freedom and equality -- to say nothing of brotherly love -- into his own societal structure.

The pronouncements he made on art and life during this early period are significant for this study, for when he advocated freedom and equality as necessary to the development of a full human being, he was, at least for a time, taking the virtually revolutionary step of including women as human beings, a step his contemporaries seem never to have taken. And for a short time in the mid 1790's, Schlegel's vision of sexual equality was so comprehensive that, despite very real flaws, it remains unsurpassed by any male writer in Germany to the present. Prefiguring the concept of androgyny advocated by many contemporary feminists, Schlegel's definition emphasized an individual's freedom to develop along a broad continuum without deference to sex roles. This idea was part of his thinking for several years; even in 1798, he stressed in "Über die Philosophie. An Dorothea" that every individual should have the opportunity "to move freely within the entire spectrum of humanity" (KA VIII, 45). But by this time he was involved in the Romantic movement and his earlier preference for sexual equality was all but completely neutralized by his greater need to see the sexes as complementary opposites of an androgynous essence. In *Lucinde*, written soon after, even less remains of his early dream. Although androgynous perfection is no less vital in *Lucinde*, it meant to Schlegel something different than it had only a few years before.

One of the great catalysts of Schlegel's life was Caroline Böhmer. She undoubtedly provided the major inspiration for his early views on sexual equality, but other factors, as well, combined to prepare him for this radical departure from conventional thinking. Schlegel studied law in Leipzig from 1791 to January, 1794. Frustration and unhappiness, even desperation, echo from his letters to his brother, August Wilhelm, the best source available for the development of his thinking during those years. In a letter of 1791 he traced his discontent to the discrepancy between his intelligence and the little that he had already accomplished, and attributed the imbalance to his own lack of harmony (W, 94). For the next few years he continued to feel isolated from society and from himself, encountered financial problems partially because of gambling, was extremely uncomfortable with women and often verged on suicide. At the same time, however, he was diverging from the conservative views of his family and becoming an independent thinker. As he found himself increasingly alienated from the mainstream, he also began to realize that a law career would be too stifling. In June, 1793, he complained to his brother about the incompatibility of a profession which required that he harness himself "into a bourgeois yoke," when his goal was "to live, to live freely" (W, 90). Very shortly thereafter he gave up his law studies to devote himself to Greek literature and philosophy, at which important juncture August Wilhelm asked him to befriend Caroline. He met her in July, 1793, shortly after having thrown off his "bourgeois yoke" and after having made the decision to devote himself to the study of antiquity, but before he had determined the vehicle for his contribution.

Caroline Böhmer was by all accounts a fascinating woman. Years later, after her death, Schelling wrote of her in terms which elucidate her impact upon Schlegel and indicate the distance which separated her from Novalis' Sophie. She was "her own person, a unique being;" she was a woman "of masculine greatness of soul, of the sharpest intellect combined with the gentleness of the most feminine, most tender, most loving heart."[2] That Schlegel perceived her in much the same way can be surmised by the description of Julius' first love in the autobiographical "Lehrjahre" of *Lucinde*. Although we might object to Schelling's attribution of characteristics to sexes, his words hint at an androgynous character. Certainly she was unusual. Late in 1799, Tieck wrote to his sister and her husband of the women in Jena, among them Caroline, in whose company one seemed to be "with an androgyne or . . . hermaphrodite." To Tieck, however, the

2 *Caroline: Briefe aus der Frühromantik*, ed. Erich Schmidt, vol. 2 (Leipzig: Insel, 1913), p. 577-578. The two volumes of her letters provide testimony to her vibrant personality.

term was pejorative; in the same letter he caustically referred to the Schlegel women as "these tasteless whores."[3] Whether Caroline could be called androgynous according to today's definition is not the issue; more important is that her example alerted Schlegel to the perversion inherent in sex role stereotyping. She provided a model of possibility by which he measured, at least for the next few years, the women of Greek antiquity as well as those in his own society.

Most critics have acknowledged Caroline's influence upon Schlegel. Hans Eichner, for example, concluded that she provided him a perspective according to which he could reject his own society's notions of feminine behavior (KA V, XXVII). Kluckhohn has also affirmed her pivotal role in Schlegel's changing view of women; because of her influence, he says, the essence of woman became a "main objective of his contemplation, and a main object of his historical investigations."[4] That Schlegel himself was aware of his debt is also clear. A letter to Caroline in August, 1796, can be offered in proof: "Today it has been three years since I first saw you. Imagine that I were standing in front of you and thanked you silently for everything that you have done for me and to me. What I am and will become I owe to myself; that I am that, in part to you."[5]

Before having met Caroline, Schlegel's attitude toward women was determined by confusion, lack of knowledge and disappointment in their inability to function outside the narrow boundaries of domesticity. The conflicting claims of Christian morality versus his own recognized and repressed sexuality also contributed to his disdain. To his brother he complained of his own incapacity to enjoy contact with "common women" and of his inability to find favor with others; therefore, he wrote, he had determined not to follow this "proclivity," since it seemed beneath one's dignity to become entwined on this level of baseness (W, 10). As to his estimation of women, the same letter is also unambiguous; never had he found in them a trace of the all-important "desire for the infinite," and therefore he had found no one whom he could possibly love. He does make reference to one woman, however, perhaps Caroline, who

---

3 The letter was published by Gotthold Klee in *Euphorion*, Ergänzungsheft 3, 1897, pp. 212-215.
4 Kluckhohn, *Die Auffassung der Liebe*, p. 350.
5 *Caroline: Briefe*, vol. 1, p. 394.

possesses that drive; but, he continues, he does not know whether he values her as a person or is attracted by "her idealized image in the mirror of a noble masculine soul" (W, 47). A few years later, shortly after having met Caroline in person, he began to plan the novel which eventually was to become *Lucinde*, the heroine of which would exhibit a high level of development without the destruction of her femininity (KA V, XVIII).

Caroline's free spirited independence and lack of bourgeois values -- one could even say her anti-bourgeois sentiments -- appealed greatly to Schlegel. That she was an ardent supporter of the French Revolution also had an impact. During the short-lived Mainz Republic, she had stayed in that city with Georg Forster, a sympathizer of the Revolution, and his wife. She had been incarcerated and had escaped only with the help of August Wilhelm Schlegel, who had spirited her off to Lucka, near Leipzig – despite her pregnancy after a liaison with a French soldier. There in Lucka Friedrich Schlegel began his caretaking responsibilities. He had long been aware of Caroline's pro-revolutionary stance, but until they met his attitude toward this involvement was aloof if slightly curious. Only a month before meeting her he confessed to his brother his fear that she "had really enmeshed herself in history" (W, 89); in other letters he wonders casually about her pro-democratic letters (W, 78). Concerning his own response to events in France, a letter in March of that year mentioning a loss sustained by the Revolutionary army is telling because of its neutral tone (W, 79). Yet a few months after meeting Caroline, a change can be detected; his sympathy for the Revolution had been aroused. In October, 1793, he recorded in reference to the Revolution an "enthusiasm for a great public matter" which "makes fools of us and our petty affairs." Therefore, he declares, he has decided to concern himself with the "mighty, enigmatic drift of contemporary events," a decision which has incited in him a "new way of thinking" (W, 127-128).

At no time in his life was Friedrich Schlegel an active political revolutionary. The evidence suggests, however, that he did respond to what he understood to be the spirit of the Revolution with more than merely aesthetic gestures. Of course, it is well known that in the *Athenäum* he published a fragment designating Fichte's philosophy,

Goethe's *Wilhelm Meister* and the French Revolution as the most important influences on his own time (*Ath. Fr.* 216). Little effort, however, has been expended to define the particular appeal which the Revolution held for Schlegel. In fact, the only full length critical study of his involvement with and perception of the Revolution has been done by Werner Weiland, who tends to make a stronger case for Schlegel as political sympathizer than the evidence warrants.[6] Weiland demonstrates quite convincingly, however, that it was the Revolution's embodiment of what Schlegel termed "republicanism" which proved so irresistible. The "public matter [*öffentliche Sache*]" about which Schlegel enthused in the above quoted letter was, as Weiland points out, a direct translation of the Latin *res publica*.[7]

Schlegel's understanding of the term "republicanism" is most clearly discernible in his 1796 essay on Kant, "Versuch über den Begriff des Republikanismus," in which he takes issue with Kant's failure to equate that concept with democracy. In the course of the essay it becomes clear that political activities gain credibility for Schlegel only if based on a "law of equality." "The *will of the majority*," he insists, "should stand as the surrogate for the general will." "Republicanism," he argues in refuting Kant, is thus "necessarily democratic" (KA VII, 17). It alone can lead "to eternal peace" (KA VII, 22). Although his attitude toward the happenings in France went through several metamorphoses, Schlegel continued to equate republicanism with freedom and to call for it if not in a political, then in an aesthetic or personal context. It should be noted, however, that he had only a glorified view of the masses for whom he was advocating democracy.

When Schlegel began his Greek studies, it was initially a search for the spirit of republicanism in that literature which motivated him. It was not, however, an investigation he pursued inductively, but rather one he initiated to elaborate a premise. His admiration for republicanism had merged with his belief in the perfection of Greek culture – an article of faith in the eighteenth century[8] -- to convince

---

6 Werner Weiland, *Der junge Friedrich Schlegel oder die Revolution in der Frühromantik* (Stuttgart: Kohlhammer, 1968).
7 Weiland, p. 7; see also n. 7.
8 For an evaluation of late eighteenth century views of Greece and the tremendous influence these perceptions had not only for that time, but for later ages

him that that same spirit of freedom must have infused Greek society.[9] Although his long-term goal was to write a complete history of the literature of antiquity, his first essays dealt less with literature for its own sake than with the record of Greek society it offered. Schlegel was not in 1794 the aesthete he was later to become — at this point literature was for him a social document, a history — but his trust in that art form is already apparent. In fact, he is unique not only in analyzing a culture and entire society through its literature, but also in offering his reconstruction as a model for emulation.

Because of the zeal with which he propounded his views, Schlegel was criticized during his own time for "Graecomania."[10] If the charge has merit, it can be relativized by countering that he was not a backward looking prophet; rather, his interest in Greek antiquity was motivated by his intense desire to define a model according to which his own imperfect world could be improved. Perhaps it was to fend off criticism in his choice of literature as the tool for effecting that change which prompted his observation to his brother in 1796 that his writings on the ancient Greeks would encounter no threat from the censor; his protection would lie in "the obscurity of abstract metaphysics." When one writes for philosophers, he continued, one can be "incredibly bold" before the censor comprehends one's intent (W, 258).

In the winter of 1793-1794 his belief in republicanism as real freedom for all, his new realization that women were capable of greatness, that is, of a "desire for the infinite," and his own desire to study Greek literature to provide a pattern for his own imperfect time all coalesced. In both "Über die weiblichen Charaktere in den griechischen Dichtern" and "Über die Diotima" he developed his thesis that Greek civilization flourished or decayed in direct pro-

---

as well, see E.M. Butler's *The Tyranny of Greece over Germany* (Boston: Beacon, 1958).

9 Schlegel was not alone in this assessment. Tieck, for example, once wrote to Wackenroder, "I greet with delight the spirit of Greece, which I see soaring over Gaul;" see Wackenroder's *Werke und Briefe*, p. 405. Caroline also saw the similarities; in a letter to Friedrich Schlegel she once equated his "ancient Greeks" with her "New Franks;" See *Caroline: Briefe*, vol. 1, p. 367.

10 This was part of Schiller's attack in the *Xenien* versus Schlegel for the latter's disparagement of "Würde der Frauen." See *Schiller und die Romantiker*, ed. H.H. Borcherdt (Stuttgart: Cotta, 1948), pp. 425-427.

portion to the degree of equality it accorded women. The treatment of women in a given culture became his gauge of true republicanism, and hence of a just society.

As he began to work out his history of Greek literature, Schlegel recorded a sudden inspiration for several projects, envisioned as fragments of "Greek femininity — Diotima — Aspasia — Olympias — Cleopatra, perhaps something about Lesbos and Corinth" (W, 181). The first to be realized was "Über die weiblichen Charaktere in den griechischen Dichtern," which he published in 1794 in two installments in the *Leipziger Monatsschrift*. The function of this essay in his grand design is not muted. Clearly intended for the edification of his readers whose views on women Schlegel found incommensurate with those of the populace in a just society, the essay addresses those readers immediately. Nothing, Schlegel claims, frees the human spirit so well from "one-sidedness of opinion and taste" as contact with the "spirit of other nations and others ages." All those who strive to think "freely and correctly" about themselves and their "nearest and most important relationships" (KA I, 46) are his presumed beneficiaries.

Writing to persuade, Schlegel found it expedient to remind his readers at the outset of the organic nature of Greek culture in which, according to late eighteenth century thought, literature, art and society were all intrinsically related. Poetry for the Greeks was, he assured them, "indigenous;" it was a "part of their character itself" and an "important part of their development [*Bildung*]." Later expounded in "Über das Studium der griechischen Poesie," this claim is here the premise for another important consideration. Literature must therefore be recognized as "a true impression of public customs and public mentality," and as "an abundant source for the history" of the Greek "spirit." Thoroughly immersed in a classical frame of reference, Schlegel further defines the ideal he admits to seeking as "the Beautiful;" within the scheme of his thinking, it is an ideal synonymous with moral perfection and one made possible by freedom; it is "the genuine Good and Beautiful, which is and always will remain everywhere the same" (KA I, 46). Given the broad influence of Winckelmann's assumptions about Greek perfection, such assertions were not likely to amaze, but another did. By isolating the Greek ideal of "beauty" in the feminine figures of its literature, Schlegel felt he could prove the ideal a tenable component of Greek society. Such an approach also promised an evaluation of the various periods of Greek culture, for the ideal of feminine "beauty," like Greek history itself, "gradually developed, attained completion and once again degenerated" (KA I, 47).[11] There follows his analysis of selected women in Greek literature.

Homer represented for Schlegel the beginnings. His objection to the Homeric world -- and a criticism serious enough to warrant his placing Homer's literature at the barbaric beginnings even if such a classification were not chronologically dictated -- was prompted by the inequality of the sexes in that society. On the basis of its literature, Schlegel recognized that the heroic age esteemed only the male, and therefore only the virtues with which it associated maleness: strength, independence, intelligence, courage and a capacity for education and development. Women, on the contrary, as represented by Penelope to whom Ulysses returned, were relegated to the domestic sphere and deemed inferior. Penelope's character consists solely in the "few, simple traits of steadfastness and domesticity;" she can not be separated from the "world of the hearth" (KA I, 54). What was later to become explicit is here implied, for as he laments the impossibility of meaningful heterosexual love in such a culture, Schlegel affirms a belief in love as a relationship of equals. During the Homeric age, we are apprised, a man's love for a woman was nothing but "selfish sensuality and condescension;" women were spoken of "like slaves, like wares." Schlegel's assessment is vehement; his readers are advised never to forget that such a position betrays not only a "crude mentality," but also "depravity" (KA I, 48-49).

Even by our own contemporary standards, Schlegel would be recognized for so judiciously disclaiming biological determination as the source of the role division. He assures his readers that the Homeric imputation did not reflect women's innate inferiority, but rather -- and Homer's record was used to demonstrate the point -- their existence "in less favorable circumstances." This left them "unde-

---

11 This view of history shows Schlegel's indebtedness to Herder's idea of history as organic -- consisting of a beginning, a development to a high point, and a decline -- more so than to the Enlightenment view of history which saw a culmination in perfection. These views changed when Schlegel later became part of the Romantic movement.

veloped [*ungebildet*] and repressed." For the Schlegel who later placed such faith in *Bildung*, the emphasis is on the word "undeveloped." Not because of lesser gifts, but because they lacked the opportunity to develop themselves in a wider sphere was Homer's description of them as "domestic" applicable; it is a term Schlegel obviously uses with distaste. Men, on the other hand, benefitted from having available to them "an incomparably larger field" in which to develop their "intellect" and a "moral sense" (KA I, 47). Because a man was expected to function in a variety of roles, he developed these qualities, for the lack of which women were so harshly condemned. Although Schlegel does not advance an opinion as to why these different roles came into being, or why the one should be prized and the other slighted, he does offer a stringent analysis of the devastating consequences to women: "Repression and condescension" forced them to degenerate as a species until they finally merited their "mistreatment" (KA I, 48).

Although Schlegel can be faulted later for idealizing the feminine personality or character, such is not yet the case. Nor is the emphasis on society secondary, as it so often seemed to be in Novalis' works. In the mid 1790's Schlegel's overriding concern is with society; his interest in individual wholeness is a reflection of eighteenth century thinking in which that perfection is the inducement to a greater harmony. Certainly his sympathy in this essay is not merely for women as victims of injustice, but also for the larger society which suffered from a weighted appreciation of "masculine" virtues. Other qualities so necessary to a culture -- innocence, grace and love -- were not honored during the heroic age because, he believed, they were associated with an allegedly inferior sex. A contemporary thinker, Simone Weil, has also analyzed the *Iliad* as a poem of force; and that, as Heilbrun points out, is certainly a description of a masculine world.[12] Schlegel's concern is thus for all individuals, male and female alike, for whom role stereotyping has an equally detrimental effect. Perspicacious enough to recognize the harm accruing to women from a prescription of domesticity, Schlegel also saw that men, though in a more subtle way, were not allowed to develop

---

12 Heilbrun, p. 4. See Simone Weil, *The Iliad or the Poem of Force*, trans. Mary McCarthy (Wallingford, Pa.: Pendle Hall, 1970).

complete personalities. If positive figures they could only be heroic and, as such, in his judgment, inferior to even Homer's Trojans. Hector's valor was not at the expense of his emotions; he was able to cry and could kiss his son without risk of disparagement. In Greece such a combination of "raw greatness and tender feelings," a synthesis vital for "beauty," was only to be approached in a male friendship, the "noblest fruit of this era" (KA I, 49).

Repeatedly Schlegel admonishes the reader not to blame Homer for this presentation, for Homer, he emphasizes, was describing his society, not providing models. His works reflect not the "personal characteristics of the poet," but instead the "character of the age" (KA I, 48); Homer's poetry did not portray ideal beauty but represented "a genuine copy of nature" (KA I, 49). Although other opinions had wavered by 1798, this had not; in *Athenäums-Fragment* 145 we read that as a poet Homer was "moral" because he was "natural;" as a "teacher of morals," he was to be judged "immoral." As a result of his analysis, Schlegel in 1794 could only conclude that the Greeks of the Homeric age, those "crude favorites of nature," so full of "beautiful potentiality" and possessing their own "small beginnings of development," were, in fact, little more than "lovable savages."

Little was known to Schlegel about the Greeks between the Homeric period and what we call Classical Greece, by which time they had changed quite thoroughly. Among the poets of this period was "the divine Sappho" whose very existence was to him enough to read into history a parallel change in attitudes toward women and, correspondingly, in morality. He presumes an organic development; but his assertion that the "seed of sociability and humanity," which was to be noted in the earlier works, had now in the literature of Classical Greece "unfolded into the most beautiful flower," is a statement of faith rather than a demonstrable fact. Only when the Athenians with their "love for freedom" and their "restless activity of all kinds" (KA I, 55) chose to express their spirit in drama, he believed, did their republicanism reach its zenith.[13] For only then, according to Schlegel, had the Greeks acquired "a higher moral sense," that is, had embraced the spirit of democracy and equality for all, and had thus been able to infuse their own mythology with their

---

13 In "Über das Studium der griechischen Poesie" Schlegel explains his belief that every age in Greek history, at least until decay set in, was perfect within itself and so produced perfect literature: in Homeric Greece the epic, in the Dorian period the lyric, and in Athens the drama.

newly attained morality. In contrast to Homer, who was "completely nature," Greek tragedy was "completely ideal" and in all its aspects reflected "the Beautiful" (KA I, 56). Allowing a slight modification of the classical canon, the reader is to understand that female and male figures in that society were allotted a similar claim to humanness.

The Greek perception of women and of humanity had altered only gradually, however. Schlegel singles out the dramas of Aeschylus, specifically his tragedy of Clytemnestra, to represent the period before Sophocles in which the Greeks were striving for, but had still not acquired, proper morality. Aeschylus' only thorough characterization of a woman -- and therefore according to the frame established by Schlegel the only tragedy capable of yielding a measure of Greek republicanism -- presents a heroine whose "terrible greatness" could not but be unfavorably compared with the tragic heroines of Sophocles. Only in Sophocles did Greek literature reach its pinnacle. The claim is hardly controversial, but Schlegel does not justify it with an aesthetic argument; rather he bases his conviction on evidence that ideal beauty in Sophocles' tragedies is "spread over the entirety of the action and over all the characters." That is, his female figures as well as the males, whether major or minor characters, are "conceived and designed according to the same ideal" (KA I, 57).

One of the characters adduced to illustrate Sophocles' achievement is Antigone. Schlegel's characterization underscores his approbation of androgynous personalities, for he stresses that Antigone has overcome the designations of active and passive to male and female, respectively. She acts; she "desires only the true Good, and accomplishes it without strain" in contrast to her sister Ismene who, more mindful of her feminine role, "suffers in silence." Although Schlegel agrees that the "greatest charm of feminine innocence and gentleness" is distilled in Ismene, she is not his ideal -- as she was not Sophocles' heroine; for she is limited to those qualities. Antigone, on the contrary, by transcending the stereotypes, represents to him a harmonious blending of the most diverse personality traits. Her character, he avows, "is the Divine" (KA I, 58).[14]

---

14 Giese attempts to analyze Schlegel's concept of androgyny from a psychological perspective; he discusses this essay but misses the important distinction between the two sisters, p. 167.

In his discussion of the Homeric age, Schlegel had intimated that a specific type of heterosexual love could have eliminated role division and in some way helped each partner to avoid the extremes which Schlegel himself discerned as either "greatness" or "feeling." Sophocles' characters, however, and Antigone is one example of several, had aspired to completion without the benefits of love. In advancing Antigone as a model for his age, Schlegel was deviating from a pattern which entrapped so many of his contemporaries, and to which he himself would later fall victim. He was, in fact, one of the first thinkers in Germany to avoid Christian demands and to understand the human potential for completion in psychological terms, divorced from the pieties of love. That he later heaped such accolades upon the love union only signals his return to a secularized Christianity and to a more traditional view of fulfillment. In 1794, he was seeking verification for harmonious, that is, androgynous, individuals. Because of Sophocles' portrayal of whole characters — not just because of his female protagonists — his works, according to Schlegel, record the high point of Greek history and represent the standard by which all other Greek works should be measured. Others have reached the same conclusion, even obliterating the national restrictions, but none has valued Sophocles' presentation of sexual equality enough to use it as the sole criterion for that conclusion.

As the dramas before Sophocles were inferior, so those after him participated in a decline. To Schlegel, the works of Alcibiades, for example, lack "moderation, harmony and order" and abound in such "licentiousness" that Alcibiades can be accused of granting "a seductive charm to vice." Euripedes, another example Schlegel chooses to demonstrate the retrogression in values, is praised for his ability to portray passion, for example in his dramas of Medea and Phaedra, but reproved for the lack of harmony and control his characters display. The possibility that a Greek artist could be alienated from his own time is apparently so inconceivable to Schlegel that the "aesthetic extravagance" (KA I, 60) he identifies as the ideal in the works of Alcibiades and Euripedes is understood to have been the ideal of the populace as well. Public opinion in Athens, we are reminded, was so persuasive that no artist could have transcended it.

Schlegel had little to say about the period he calls that of the new Greek comedy, dismissing it as a picture of domestic life which had once again become the domain of women. Its literature boasted few important female characters; the few roles which were written for women were intended for a class which could not garner respect. Lacking a dedication to ideal beauty and to ethical ideals, this literature, according to Schlegel, suffers from "a certain monotony" (KA I, 67). And from such a literature, he deduces that once again society had separated the sexes; the republican spirit had vanished with debilitating consequences for society. After the Greek republics had "left their virtue behind because of ambition and sensuality," he contends, they also lost very quickly their political and moral superiority (KA I, 68). He confesses no surprise that the Greeks were soon thereafter conquered. Thus Schlegel's analysis of Greek history: the strength of the Greek republic during Sophocles' day had been a result of its "virtue" -- its attribution of equality to the sexes. This was Schlegel's message and hope for his own time.

Schlegel's sympathies in "Über die weiblichen Charaktere" were unequivocally with that period of Greek history which had produced Sophoclean tragedy, for there he distinguished what he judged to be the highest ideals of humanity reflected in the ideal characters of tragedy. He had, however, merely presumed an equation between the real and the artistic ideal. In "Über die Diotima" he ventured forth to investigate the correspondence by assessing a real woman of that period. Given the "stream of democracy" (KA I, 84) which he saw flowing through Greek history, the outcome was never in doubt. Appearing in the *Berlinische Monatsschrift* in 1795, again in two installments, this essay, although eventually included in his history of the Greeks and Romans, was initially intended for popular consumption.

The friend and revered teacher of Socrates, Diotima was familiar to most literate Germans of the 1790's from the *Symposium*, the Platonic dialog on love. Contemporary works, especially by Hemsterhuis, had also helped to popularize and further idealize her name. The elusive figure fascinated Schlegel primarily, we can assume, because of the similarities he discerned between her and Caroline, his own "independent Diotima."[15] In Diotima Schlegel

---

15 *Caroline: Briefe*, vol. 1, p. 375.

thought he saw the combination of qualities he had valued in Caroline; his description of Diotima as the image not only of "beautiful femininity," but even more of "completed humanity" (KA I, 71), could just as well have been applied to Caroline. Diotima was, in Schlegel's view, unrestricted by traditional concepts of sexual roles.

What Diotima had been to Socrates, Caroline was to Schlegel: a friend and intellectual companion whom he trusted even to judge his work,[16] and through whom he believed he had become a better person (W, 149). He was also drawn to the figure of Diotima because, by Socrates' own admission in the *Symposium*, it was she who had taught him about love. By that love, Schlegel assures us, was meant "not transitory pleasures," but instead "the pure Goodness of a completed soul" (KA I, 72). Not a physical but an abstract love for humanity and the universe had been the lesson of Diotima. Such a heterosexual friendship had to be admired by the Schlegel of 1795 for whom sexuality was still suspect as incompatible with a striving for higher ideals. His relationship with Caroline had done nothing to dispel this bias, for as his brother's fiancée, she could only exist for him in terms of such a rarified relationship. This essay, in which he is seeking to comprehend and elucidate the nature of a Greek woman of Sophocles' day, can also be seen as an outlet for his awe of and curiosity about Caroline. Eichner's reference to the work as "at least in part . . . an indirect homage to Caroline" is surely no overstatement (KA V, XXVII).

Throughout the essay "Über die Diotima" one is struck with Schlegel's ability to see people and events as he chose. Lacking dependable histories of antiquity, he felt quite free to operate from his assumptions of Greek perfection, which to him dictated androgynous female characters not only in the idealized literature, but also in reality. Diotima, he assumed, was one of many who helped define the circumference of the ideal woman immortalized by Sophocles. Nevertheless, the intensity of his argument leads one to suspect that he above all is attempting to convince himself. Had he been completely sure of the identification between the artistic representation and

---

16 See for example *Caroline: Briefe*, vol. 1, p. 395.

reality, the question which is the basis for the essay would be moot. Schlegel's work is an answer to the question of who and what Diotima really was.

Proceeding boldly, Schlegel first of all refutes the conclusion that Diotima was a hetaera, although public knowledge of the customs in Athens, he admits, would seem to indicate that respectable women did not have intellectual contact with men and that such an opportunity was allowed only to courtesans. However – and here one is granted an unclouded insight into Schlegel's methods – such an explanation, which would deny Diotima respectability, was so distasteful that, he says, "we must completely reject it" (KA I, 73). Although he provides reasoned arguments for removing Diotima from the circle of the hetaerae, the impression remains that subjective motivations were dominant. If she had truly been a courtesan, he contends, her name would have been listed in the books of courtesans; in addition, Plato had referred to Diotima as a priestess, a designation which to Schlegel assumed the freedom not granted a courtesan. Furthermore, the ideal of love she offered Socrates, a dedication "to the eternal and universal Beautiful, in the enjoyment of which life merits being called life" (KA I, 81), is hardly compatible with the type of love honored by a courtesan. The only alternative, according to what was then known of Greek life, identifying her as a wife, was also unthinkable. Marriage at that time, Schlegel argues, was characterized by "selfishness and sensuality, deception and discord" (KA I, 77). Scorning marriage, the philosophers had preferred the company of educated women who were, we are to be convinced, not all hetaerae. Schlegel derides the Greek polarization of women as either courtesans or wives and mothers, but at this point is uninterested in a synthesis, for their sum he would still have rejected as an arbitrary role assignment. A different possibility intrigues him.

To explain Diotima's existence as a free, educated woman, Schlegel resurrects an exegesis of Plato's *Republic* by Proklus which has Socrates embracing equal education for men and women partially because of his knowledge of Pythagorean women, among them someone named Diotima. Associating Diotima with Pythagoras is at first repugnant to Schlegel, because of that thinker's identification in the popular mind with orgiastic happenings; he acknowledges such information, however, as being "uncertain" and "indefinite" (KA I, 82). It can be verified, Schlegel advances cautiously, that Pythagoras' circle included intellectually active men and women. Soon he has convinced himself of Pythagoras' respectability and the corollary: a refutation to the claim that all Greek women but the courtesans were uneducated. The problem then became one of proving the presence of Pythagorean women in Greece during the time of Plato and Socrates. To this problem he devotes the remainder of the essay.

Further examination of the tenets of Pythagorean philosophy soon convinces Schlegel to see that body of thought more positively as "an early, though still crude attempt" to organize society and the state itself according to the "ideas of pure reason." Nevertheless, he can not overlook proof that it was also unfortunately the attempt "to resist the prevailing tendency toward democracy," a trait evidencing a "preference for Egyptian cast separations." Schlegel's disapproval is coupled with his claim that such political tendencies were doomed to failure given the irrevocable "stream of democracy" in Greek history. Since Pythagoras' sense for equality can not be ascribed to his political affiliation, Schlegel suggests it to have been a product of his reliance on reason. Thus follows Schlegel's original conclusion, phrased in what was surely intended as a rhetorical question: "What is then the political philosophy of Plato . . . but the mature, complete development of the Pythagorean seed?" (KA I, 84-85). In fact, he continues, Pythagoras, whom most twentieth century thinkers consider a mystic philosopher, could be seen as the "Father of rational morality and politics" in the Greek world (KA I, 86). And with that he has confirmed his base for identifying Diotima with the Pythagorean women as well as with Plato, for such an influence presupposes, for Schlegel, the existence of Pythagorean schools at Plato's time.

Historical credibility for these claims was difficult to establish, but Schlegel was never intimidated by a lack of documentation. A paucity of direct evidence, he had blithely stated earlier in the essay, merely enabled him and others like him "to take refuge in our suppositions" (KA I, 73). He thus proceeded with indirect proofs by aligning Pythagoras first of all with Doric customs and further with the Spartans, who maintained the purest form of Doric culture known to Schlegel. Carried away by what he considers evidence that the Spartans had overcome the alignment of certain attributes to biological sex, Schlegel posits Pythagorean influence. Working with multiple assumptions, he declares that both they and Plato's Greeks believed that femininity and masculinity "should be subordinated to a higher humanity" (KA I, 87); thus he feels justified in designating the Spartans as the historical mediator between Pythagoras and Plato.[17]

It would seem that Schlegel was laboring under the fear of losing his conventional reader, for, having committed himself to such a claim, he assumes a defensive posture. He is not, he insists, advocating a society without sex differences; he is not proposing the "destruction of femininity." Rather he desires "to subordinate the sex, without eradicating it, to the species" (KA I, 92). But whereas in the earlier essay he had parried the same potential attack by taking refuge in indisputable biological differences which would always distinguish the sexes, his defense now includes a psychological component. Women, he calms his readers, will forever be characterized by their "sincerity and tenderness" and men by their "range and determination." In his attempts at defining human rather than sexually determined behavior, Schlegel had been charting an independent course. Spurred now by his fear of offending the very readers whom he hoped to inspire to new heights of humanness, he betrays an inability to resist traditional thought patterns.

Although such yielding to convention would increase as time passed and does detract even from his present argument, it does not destroy the focus on sexual equality which is the underlying impetus in his search for Diotima's essence. And once having appeased his readers, he attempts to reclaim his former position. Even though experience might seem to dictate a lengthening of the list of eternal sexual attributes, such additions, he cautions, are not verifiable and

---

17 Schlegel's discussion of the Spartan customs includes comments indicating he recognized their glorification of homosexual love, but he makes no judgments; he is unable to find fault with a culture so closely identified with that of the Greeks. He does feel moved, however, to explain the Spartan capacity to appreciate male beauty with the rather spurious argument that female beauty was also appreciated (KA I, 90-91).

would lead to an "absolute absence of character." Denounced also are those characteristics usually identified with gender; "the tyrannical vehemence of the man and the selfless yielding of the woman" must be rejected as "exaggerated and ugly." His summation is again a call for what he considers an androgynous personality. "Only independent femininity, only gentle masculinity," he insists, "is good and beautiful" (KA I, 93).

A sizeable problem still remains to be solved. For Athens, which supported the acme of Greek culture, did not accord to women the legal right to freedom granted men; nevertheless, its society was not the male bastion of the Homeric age. In fact, Schlegel detects the vitality of a "feminine" principle throughout Athenian life. Did not the "essence of femininity and of love, the revelation of enthusiasm and the history of the heart" characterize the literature and language of the Greeks? Answering his own question in the affirmative, he concludes that such qualities were also universally characteristic in all aspects of Greek life (KA I, 101). Thus he is at a loss to explain the blatant inequality in Athenian law, for according to his premises, such a society could only have been possible if founded upon a wide-ranging equality.

With the advantage of a broader historical perspective, Schlegel might have seen that worship of a "feminine" principle — an illusory concept from the beginning — has never been synonymous with sexual equality. It might have allowed him insights which could have mitigated his insistence on Greek superiority and allowed him to maintain his own ideal of equality while recognizing its paucity in ancient Greece. Instead, given his inflexibility, the confrontation between the ideal and the real could only force him to compromise his own stance by positing explanations for the discrepancy which all but negate his argument. He feels impelled to conclude, for example, that Athenian laws restricting women to the home served the common good which required that female passions not be permitted to interfere with the workings of that republic. He even allows himself to suggest that Euripedes' misogyny was not a function of real hatred toward women, but rather of experience which had taught him distrust. Undaunted, Schlegel ultimately concludes that although Plato lived during a time of excesses, Pythagoras' influence was still viable, and thus education was available to women. Whether or not they took advantage of the opportunity depended on the "desire and situation of the individual" (KA I, 96).

To his own satisfaction, then, Schlegel has found a way to rescue Diotima's reputation and affirm her reality in Greece as an independent intellectual, equal to the greatest men of her day. "Über die Diotima" in its entirety, however, is much less convincing than was the earlier essay. Despite much intellectual maneuvering, Schlegel's efforts to establish a connection between the ideal women of Sophocles' tragedies and the real women of Athens were unsuccessful. Such characters had no more been a part of ancient Greece than of Schlegel's own time. The tensions between Schlegel's own ideal and the character of Diotima can not be bridged and one must ultimately conclude that the Diotima he is attempting to describe is not the same Diotima whom Plato portrayed. For Schlegel Diotima is more than a teacher of men, she exists in her own right. The essay is not well argued, includes too much speculation and too many deductive arguments based on intuited premises. But it is ardently presented. It gains considerably if one can sift through the layers, stripping away the faltering attempts at discerning a "feminine" principle and the readiness to compromise with tradition. Although it fails to establish the reality of androgynous women in Greece, the essay stands as testimony to Schlegel's great belief that individuals in a republican state could not be limited by sex roles, but, if they were to become truly human, must be free to combine the best of all attributes commonly associated with feminine and masculine personalities. Schlegel's interpretation of Diotima lends itself to clarification by reference to one of de Beauvoir's theses: what a man "says" about a woman characterizes the man rather than the woman.

Schlegel's obsession with the Greeks did not last. The constellation which had originally motivated him -- the French Revolution, Caroline, his studies of antiquity -- altered significantly. The French Revolution lost its claim to republicanism and, also of great importance for him, Caroline married his brother. Perhaps Schlegel also became aware that his view of Greek society was untenable, that the ancient world was not as perfect as it could have or should have been. As he turned his attention to the literature of his own age, he also adapted a more conventional view of the sexual differences; contact with his contemporaries soon convinced him of the positive value in defining the sexes as opposing entities. But his early ideas on sexual equality should be evaluated apart from his Romantic proclamations. In trying to identify a "hidden river of androgyny" throughout literature, Heilbrun helps to provide a perspective for such a judgment. She refers to Sophocles' Antigone as a prime example of an androgynous character who has never been analyzed in these terms. Whole generations of critics, she says, have spent endless hours arguing Antigone's role without noticing that she fulfills her destiny by being "altogether human rather than merely ladylike."[18] This is what Schlegel knew in the middle years of the 1790's when he was striving to define a model for humanness. Although his later involvement with the Romantic movement persuaded him to adopt a more conventional attitude, his early perspicacity -- as well as the modernity of his thought -- should not remain unrecognized.

---

18 Heilbrun, p. 10.

Chapter Six

FRIEDRICH SCHLEGEL'S ROMANTICISM: EMBRACING METAPHYSICS

By the late 1790's Schlegel no longer believed that Greek culture should provide the model for his own world. But even after his concern with ancient literature abated, his ideal of republicanism remained intact. In 1796 he could still confess to his brother that he valued it even at the expense of poetry. He could not deny, he admitted, that republicanism was closer to his heart than either "divine criticism" or "poetry, the most divine" (W, 278). When he began to direct his attention to the literature of his own era, he sought the spirit of freedom and equality in this new field of interest. There too he felt impelled to criticize much of what he found because of its sexual stereotyping which denied especially to women their free development. In the spirit of truth he criticized Schiller's "Würde der Frauen" in the poet's own *Musenalmanach*. Although his growing interest in literary theory prompted him to ridicule the poem as an entity -- it would improve, he suggests, if one would read it backwards -- his most cutting criticism was directed at Schiller's sexually stereotyped characters. With derision Schlegel asserted that such men should be bound hand and foot, and that to be led around on a leash would befit such women (KA II, 6). Not only Schiller's but the works of others among his contemporaries also incurred Schlegel's disparagement, for too frequently he found a literature infused with Rousseau's contention that women were incapable of greatness. Remembering the examples of Sappho and Diotima, Schlegel felt called upon to polemicize against this error of thinking.

His strongest salvo was directed against Jacobi's novel *Woldemar*. Although Schlegel's essay was in its form a literary critique, and did, in fact, make aesthetic judgments in a way which contributed greatly to the art of literary criticism, it was primarily a forum for his opinions

131

on the relations between the sexes. Schlegel was not a static thinker, and this critique indicates the direction of change. It is a definite advance over his work on Diotima in one respect, for regardless of the fervor with which she and her right to humanity had been defended, Schlegel's Diotima was not a complete human being. True, she had combined what Schlegel considered the most noble traits of male and female; but in his overwhelming desire to disprove her identification as a courtesan, Schlegel had created a woman who was idealized and asexual. Despite his having decried the Homeric division of women into Penelopes or Helenes in "Über die weiblichen Charaktere," and having derided the Greek tendency to see women as either courtesans or wives in "Über die Diotima," he had made no attempt to discover these more earthy roles in his own ideal, Diotima. They were apparently considered roles assigned solely because of biological gender and therefore, consistent with his definition of humanness at that time, had to be avoided.

By 1796 Schlegel was coming to terms with sexuality as a vital component of personality and therefore his model of female completion was more substantial. His criticism rings true when he judges Jacobi harshly for that author's version of a hero. Woldemar lived with two women, with Henriette whom he called his friend and whom he loved, scoffs Schlegel, "just as if she were a man" (KA II, 61), and with Allwine, his sexual partner. Jacobi characterized the latter relationship, Schlegel suggests, when he has Woldemar immodestly claim that he possessed Allwine without the obverse being equally true. Such manipulation in Schlegel's opinion reduces Woldemar to a "course egoist" (KA II, 65). Not because of any moral dilemma on Woldemar's part, but rather because of the one-sidedness imposed upon both Allwine and Henriette is Schlegel launching his attack. From such repression, he insists, it follows that both women must "sooner or later come to ruin" (KA II, 61).

Early in the critique Schlegel had summarily declared the "original sin of modern education" to be the "fragmentation of those human powers which can remain healthy only in a free combination" (KA II, 58). Such a statement could have been included in either of the earlier essays on Greek women, but the "powers" to be united now have different referents. What Jacobi's work does, Schlegel asserts, is to perpetuate this stifling "original sin" by denying women the vital combination of sexuality and spirituality. As the main point of contention he singles out Jacobi's distinction between friendship and love. What Woldemar offers Henriette can not be friendship although it is labeled as such in the novel, because friendship, Schlegel insists, can exist between members of the opposite sexes only if the man is strong enough to harness his erotic desires and his ego and if the woman is strong enough to elevate herself above the common level of home and family. One sees behind this definition Schlegel and Caroline, who apparently had been "strong" enough for such a friendship. Henriette and Woldemar, on the contrary, are completely unsuited. Therefore Schlegel finds especially odious Woldemar's claim that he and Henriette became friends "as persons of the same sex could never become." Even persons of different sexes, Schlegel inserts, do not deserve such a relationship (KA II, 64).

For friendship Henriette is "too much — woman and girl." She is the sort who would thrive in a marriage in which her entire existence could be focused on a man who would define for her her own attitudes and who would grant her unity. Her soul would find complete satisfaction only in the most intimate union with a man. She is, so Schlegel argues, a being capable of a relationship in which two "become and remain a whole" (KA II, 63). Yet she is denied that status as wife which would bring her fulfillment. She is forced to prudery and a consequent denial of self. And this, as Schlegel demonstrates, was Jacobi's intention, for his hero Woldemar admitted without compunction that Henriette had "destroyed a part of herself" in order to fulfill his ideal. As Schlegel adroitly puts it, she was required to be "under the agreeable figure of a woman, sexless." And, he demands: "Whom will she then be able to interest?" (KA II, 62).[1]

Although Schlegel is defending Henriette and thus other women from the severing of their sexual natures, Henriette is not his ideal.

---

1 Kluckhohn, in *Die Auffassung der Liebe*, uses this essay and such quotes to argue that, because Schlegel intends no mixing of the sexes and indeed finds the sexual distinctions very important, the word "androgyny" has no application in his works, pp. 354-355.

Nowhere in the novel is there an indication that she was capable of growth beyond home and marriage, of the "desire for the infinite" still important to Schlegel as a measure of humanness. Adhering to the hierarchy he had evolved in "Über die Diotima," Schlegel judges Henriette's a limited existence; she would never attain the androgynous completion associated with love and life on a higher plane. Schlegel's admiration for the independent woman who would have been capable of an elevated "friendship" is still intact. Giese observes that Schlegel's vehement reaction to Jacobi's novel indicated an assessment of relationships for the first time from the perspective of the woman.[2] In a limited sense Giese is correct; no greater collective good hovered in the background to give import to Henriette's fulfillment and no man was to benefit from her happiness. We could wish, however, that such a position had been motivated by indignation at Henriette's lack of independence and freedom rather than her unrequited passion. It can be noted that Schlegel's Romantic heroine Lucinde, with her sexual nature restored, would be a closer sister to Henriette than to Diotima.

Schlegel's next forum for addressing the relationship between the sexes was the essay "Über die Philosophie. An Dorothea." By 1798, when it appeared, he was completely absorbed in the art and philosophy of his own age and was beginning to develop the tenets which would later be identified with Romanticism.[3] His public defense of Georg Forster and certain aphorisms, such as *Lyceums-Fragment* 106 in which he condemned modern society for having imposed the "servitude of women," indicate a continuing interest in the rights of all individuals, but the Schlegel of 1798 was decidedly unpolitical. Even the republicanism which he had so diligently sought just a few years before was now abstracted into a component of a Romantic art. That art he hailed as the medium for purifying the world.[4] There was, however, a philosophical continuity in his thinking. Eichner, for

---
2   Giese, p. 187.
3   The *Lyceums-Fragmente* and his philosophical notebooks (KA XVIII), which he worked on almost obsessively during this time, provide adequate documentation of Schlegel's development.
4   *Lyceums-Fragment* 65 states: "Poetry is a republican speech;" cf. *Lyceums-Fragment* 16 and *Athenäums-Fragmente* 118, 138.

example, has shown that from 1794 onward all aspects of Schlegel's thought were dominated by the vision of a dialectical synthesis of opposites which would achieve the symmetry thought synonymous with perfection.[5] It is no less true to say that at least until 1800, that vision of perfection was dominated by an androgynous ideal. In his varying interpretations of the dialectical tensions inherent within the androgynous model can be seen analogies to his developing theory of literature and therewith another proof that for Schlegel, art and life were indeed quite inseparable; as his view of the world altered, it was accompanied by parallel changes in his concept of bisexual totality.

Schlegel seemed always to understand the world through his own experiences; a major impetus for "An Dorothea," with its profound changes in the definition of sexual differences, is likewise to be found in his personal life. In 1797, shortly after moving to Berlin, he had met Dorothea Veit, his future wife and a vastly different type from Caroline. With Dorothea he also experienced his first meaningful sexual relationship. Besides effecting the change in Schlegel, himself, which would be detailed in *Lucinde*, this encounter had ramifications for his subsequent artistic theories. It was, in fact, a primary reinforcement for the definition of synthesis operative in his proposals for Romantic literature. Between 1794 and 1795 his program for personal fulfillment had called for an overcoming within an individual of the extremes his society attributed to dichotomous masculine and feminine personalities. He understood this as a way to combat the fragmentation inflexible sexual roles had inflicted upon what should have been harmonious beings, men and women alike. By 1798, these socially induced sexual characteristics had hardened into god-given differences, both of which were thought necessary for a whole. The same concept of wholeness figures in the theories Schlegel advanced for the literature of his age, the uniqueness of which was not in the advocacy of a synthesis, but rather in the nature of the synthesis decreed. Not a shapeless merging to a "harmonious platitudinous" – stated more positively this was, in fact, the type of combination called

---

5   Hans Eichner, *Friedrich Schlegel* (New York: Twayne, 1970), p. 63.

for in the earlier essays – but a radically new type of merger in which the original components are vitally distinct yet enriched by the synthesis.[6] Stated differently, Schlegel by this time saw personal and historical progress as the development from unity to multiplicity to a final all-inclusive universality (KA XVIII, XXXVI-XXXVII). Abrams sees this concept of synthesis, an organized unity in which diversity survives, as one of the distinguishing features of Romantic thinking.[7]

While proclaiming the equality of the sexes during his preoccupation with ancient Greece, Schlegel had never asserted their sameness and instead had agitated only for their equal opportunity to become complete human beings. The intent, however, had been a leveling of sexual differences, for his prescription called for neutralizing what he had identified as the exaggerated gender-related character traits. Both male and female should be, he had insisted, "purified to a higher humanity" (KA I, 92). His repeated assurances that he did not aspire to a "destruction of femininity" had been efforts primarily to combat the inevitable misunderstanding such statements were sure to inspire, to assure his readers that he was not postulating an anatomical hybrid. But the seeds for a different view of the sexes were there.[8] One could argue that even his prescription for "gentle masculinity" and "independent femininity" had been based on a belief in sexual differences. He was not advocating gentleness as the primary quality of men, nor independence of women; rather, those qualities should merge with what he thought to be innate within the sexes, namely male independence and female gentleness. Suddenly in "Über die Philosophie. An Dorothea" a relationship between male and

---

6 *Lyceums-Fragment* 79; I use Eichner's translation in *Friedrich Schlegel*, p. 63.
7 Abrams, p. 185.
8 Even though his intent was to bring the sexes together, he had inadvertently in his early essays betrayed his adherence to stereotypes. See KA I, 50; 51; 56; 59; 86-93. After praising Sappho and using her as refutation for Rousseau's contention that women were incapable of inspiration and art, for example, Schlegel admits that there were no examples of female sculptors or dramatists. Thus he concludes that, just as there are different kinds of art, there are at least two types of inspiration, the dramatic and the lyric (KA I, 97).

female is hailed as the means not for eradicating, but for encompassing their polarized attributes into one all-inclusive whole. Claiming to resemble the old uncle in *Wilhelm Meister*, Schlegel underscores this change; for that character, according to Schlegel, recognized that "balance in human life could be maintained only through oppositions" (KA VIII, 44). And now, emphasizing the whole with the male and female as contributing antipodes, Schlegel turns to love as the means of attaining the goal. In so doing, he, like Novalis, was helping to define the prototypical Romantic view of love. In espousing love as the medium for the necessary exchange of qualities, Schlegel became part of the tradition adhered to by a majority of Romantic thinkers, one clearly rooted in an androgynous definition of wholeness.

Schlegel's new concept of fusion inspired one of his most famous aphorisms, the *Lyceums-Fragment* 115: "Poetry and philosophy," he stated there, "should be united." In its widest sense, this was Schlegel's recommendation for regenerating the fallen world. Not only did it become the basis for the doctrines of early Romanticism he was beginning to formulate, but in "An Dorothea" it was also translated into a regimen for individual perfection. This essay is Schlegel's earliest testimony to the significance of the dialectical structure – clearly inspired by sexual parallels -- for both art and life. No less persistent in his demands for individual wholeness than he had been during his Greek period, that goal is articulated in this essay as the attempt to discover and develop "the most human, the most original, the most holy" in each person (KA VIII, 45). Although a similarity to Novalis' search for the center resonates through the work, there is a rational basis for Schlegel's ideas not found in the works of his friend. Schlegel judges harshly those who resist the challenge; a woman without this desire "educates herself for the herd," among which she will be "fed [*gefüttert*]." Similarly, a man who refuses the search will lose his humanity and become finally a cipher (KA VIII, 49). Such a man or woman is nothing but "a rational oyster." Schlegel's tendency toward the aphoristic continues unabated as he derides such an existence: "Life solely for its own sake is the real source of commonness" (KA VIII, 50). And if his readers need reminding, Schlegel insists that everything is "common" which does not partake of the spirit of philosophy and poetry.

Punctuating the work are numerous variations of the message in *Lyceums-Fragment* 115. "Poetry and philosophy," for example, are labeled "an indivisible whole;" they are "eternally bound" (KA VIII, 52). This is the paradigmatic combination for individual wholeness. Written to clarify -- one suspects, to immortalize -- a previous assertion that philosophy was necessary to the education of women, this essay soon makes clear that poetry is just as vital for the development of a man. The system of complementary opposites he establishes here is based on a distinction Schlegel feels so obvious that, once stated, it requires no further discussion: poetry is of the earth and philosophy is closer to the divine (KA VIII, 53). Thus a woman, who is defined now without denigration as "a domestic being" (KA VIII, 42) and a being linked closely to the earth, is said to express herself instinctively in poetry.[9] Men are still granted activity in public life, but are also defined now as artistic; their proximity to God, which Schlegel understands as self-evident, makes philosophy their natural mode of communication. Since poetry and philosophy, and thus female and male, are halves of a whole, he summarizes that philosophy is for women "the finest source of eternal youth . . . as is poetry for men" (KA VIII, 53).

In "An Dorothea" the concept of the sexes as polarous entities, a view which he had earlier so vehemently rejected, is now just as definitively affirmed. The "feminine organization" he now sees as "directed entirely to the one beautiful purpose of motherhood." Men, with their more diffused purpose, have a tendency toward "indefiniteness" and therefore exhibit a "divine semblance of the infinite" (KA VIII, 46). It seems, however, that Schlegel was not fully conscious of the dimensions of the change in his thinking. As in the earlier essays he assures the reader again here that sex differences, which for the first time are fundamental to the argument, are only an "external aspect of human existence." Similarly stressed is the danger of their exaggeration. "Masculinity and femininity," Schlegel passionately declares in a much quoted statement, "as they are usually understood and lived, are indeed the most dangerous obstacles to humanity, which according to an old legend...can only be

---

9   *Idee* 127 expresses the same identification: women's "essence" is poetry.

a harmonious whole" (KA VIII, 45). Even Kluckhohn must admit this conclusion to have been premised on Plato's story of the androgyne.[10]

That "An Dorothea" is predominantly about women and their right to and need for full humanity, although the same requirement is acknowledged for men, can be explained quite simply: such a mission was not an accepted tenet of late eighteenth century society. Too often, to use Schlegel's words, women were not mindful of "their divine origin and image" (KA VIII, 43). Because men accepted such a status as their right, the attainment of their needs did not require Schlegel's encouragement. Although later in *Lucinde* his sympathies had changed, he is concerned now not just with women, but with human fulfillment. It is "the true essence of *human* existence" which follows from the "totality, completeness and free activity of all powers" (KA VIII, 50) that he is trying to discover.

Although the words recall earlier goals, wholeness no longer requires a neutralization of sexual characteristics. The "gentle masculinity" and the "independent femininity" to which he aspires now define androgynous individuals who have embraced, not overcome, the diversity of the sexual natures through love of a sexual opposite. A woman's interest in such a masculine pursuit as philosophy, Schlegel reassures Dorothea, will not cause her femininity to suffer; quite the contrary, it is the necessary complement to her personality. Adding insight into the change which Schlegel's thinking has undergone is an aphorism of 1798 in which the *Odyssey*, which he had just a few years earlier castigated for its excessive adherence to sexual roles, is now benevolently viewed as the "oldest romantic family idyll" (LN 1440). Thus it is a different kind of androgyny which he proposes in "An Dorothea" than that which he had advanced in the middle 1790's, but one to which he is no less committed. He promises that the very real sexual differences are part of the natural order which he would not eradicate or reverse, but instead "subordinate to reason." Here the rationalist, Schlegel can then outline his program for a kind of *Bildung* which he thinks will bridge and thus embrace the innate sexual differences; it is a *Bildung* which will perfect nature

---

10 Kluckhohn, *Die Auffassung der Liebe*, p. 354.

according to what Schlegel assumes to be the dictates of human reason. Straining credulity, he even attempts to persuade his readers that his definition of perfected humanity is the end point nature intended. No truths exist, he reasons, which nature has not "indicated in her beautiful hieroglyphics" (KA VIII, 45). Allusions to Böhme's works aside, this statement is mired in circuitous thinking, since the "truth" to which he alludes is based upon his assumption that sexual polarities are the universal components of a whole.

As was the case with other early Romantics, a tendency toward pantheism precluded Schlegel's distinguishing clearly between nature worship and religion. Nature with its hieroglyphics interested him only long enough to serve his argument; soon the referent for the absolute which manifests itself by intimating the direction for human progress is God within us. The "destiny" of all individuals, we have been told, is progress along a path indicated by "the voice of God within" (KA VIII, 43). The all-important *Bildung* is consequently to be thought of as "lessons in emulating God" (KA VIII, 44). That these were the years of Schlegel's burgeoning friendship with Schleiermacher is surely no coincidence. The role of poetry, and therefore of women, is "to reconcile spirit and nature" and to entice "the heaven itself . . . down to earth." The goal of philosophy, that is, of men, is the opposite and is intended "to elevate human beings to the divine" (KA VIII, 51). The vehicle for combining the "godliness" of the male with the "humanness" of the female is love. Although it results in religion, love is not in "An Dorothea" the metaphysical absolute it was to become in *Lucinde*; it seems rather to be a rational enterprise based on the assumption that by contact with a member of the opposite sex, each individual will recognize the value of the other and, by embracing the intrinsic qualities of that partner, become whole. Love is truly for Schlegel "the shaping [*bildende*] eros." The man will strive to elevate the woman he loves "above the usual service of small household deities" and she in turn will help him to love, will make him human. She will stir and guard "the holy fire" within his breast (KA VIII, 49). "The living unity of a human being," Schlegel insists, "consists in a friendly reciprocity" (KA VIII, 52).[11]

---

11 Giese's contention that this essay indicates Schlegel's ideal to have been a

The tension between philosophy and poetry which Schlegel believed operative in love had intrigued him for a long time before he was able to claim religion as the result. That he did set up such an equation was acknowledged in December, 1798, in a letter to Novalis in which he wonders whether the synthesis of Goethe and Fichte could yield anything but religion (P, 140). Other aphorisms written that year also indicate the vitality of this newly discovered combination.[12] For many years Schlegel continued to attribute potency to this union; even in the *Ideen* of 1801 it was a major theme. Later when he became convinced of Böhme's value, for example, he praised that thinker because he had in his theosophy overcome the "enmity" of philosophy for poetry so evident in the works of Plato and Fichte (KA XII, 260).

The emphasis on personal wholeness in "An Dorothea" should not be understated; however, Schlegel proves himself a Romantic with expansive goals as well. Individual harmony is subjugated, at least theoretically, to another goal with the unequivocal statement that the universe and its harmony were for him "One and All" (KA VIII, 49). Speaking for himself, Schlegel claims that he could not worship the universe with his whole soul had he not loved a woman. Although the magical potency of the analogy so important to Novalis plays no role here, the same underlying Hermetic world view is obvious. For in typical Romantic thinking, the human has become a microcosm of the world. "Every individual," Schlegel asserted elsewhere, "is indeed a world;" the opposite, he continued, was just as true (KA XVIII, 326, # 22). The combination of philosophy and poetry achieved through heterosexual union is thus the means for perfecting the individual as well as for reinstating the eternal harmony of the universe. It would soon be the basis for a similarly efficacious Romantic literature.

When Schlegel so adamantly recommended to Dorothea that she study philosophy, he described that discipline as the "voice, language

---

"laying aside of sexuality," p. 196, is extreme. Such a judgment would have been applicable to the earlier essays on Greek women, but by the time of this work Schlegel has begun to recognize a value in sexuality.
12 See for example KA XVIII, 192, #787.

141

and grammar for the instinct of the divine" (KA VIII, 42), that is, according to the idiom of the essay, as the medium for logically defining the path to perfection. An ardent faith in philosophy remained a constant throughout Schlegel's life. Dominating that lifelong commitment was a perennial search for a synthesis between the "infinite plenitude" of life verified by experience and the "infinite unity" dictated by reason. Distinguishable as early as 1793 in a letter to August Wilhelm — here the poles for synthesis were termed "system" and "ideal" (W, 111) — the same goal provided the impetus for "An Dorothea" and was undoubtedly, as Ernst Behler summarizes, one of the "guiding themes" of his philosophical notebooks in all stages (KA XVIII, XVI). These philosophical tenets were also the basis for the theories of Romantic literature which Schlegel intended as the tool for perfecting the world.[13] Thus when he praised "educated freedom [*gebildete Willkür*]" (KA II, 134) in his *Wilhelm Meister* essay, he was formulating a literary ideal consisting of both principles: freedom or plenitude — and the last vestiges of his republican ardor are embodied here -- qualified by an adjective reflecting his concern for a stabilizing impulse.[14] In *Gespräch über die Poesie* he described this ideal in such phrases as an "artistically ordered confusion" and a "charming symmetry of contradictions" (KA II, 318-319). The same philosophical exigency was the impetus for the famous directive of *Athenäums-Fragment* 116 according to which Romantic poetry was to be an attempt to unify all poetic genres; it was as well the propellant for his well known dictum in the same fragment that Romantic poetry should be "progressive universal poetry [*progressive Universalpoesie*]."[15]

Schlegel's most detailed, though far from systematic prescription for Romantic literature was presented in *Brief über den Roman*. Written in 1800 and originally intended as a commentary to *Lucinde*,

---

13 Eichner, *Friedrich Schlegel*, pp. 46-83. See also Behler's "Friedrich Schlegels Theorie der Universalpoesie," in *Jahrbuch der deutschen Schillergesellschaft*, ed. Fritz Martini et al. (Stuttgart: Kröner, 1957), pp. 211-252.
14 Eichner reminds us (KA V, XXXVII n. 78) that Schlegel associated *Willkür* with freedom as did both Schelling and Kant.
15 See for example Behler's "Friedrich Schlegels Theorie der Universalpoesie."

the essay addresses the same philosophical quandary, the desire to harmonize a world of plenitude. Romantic literature, Schlegel declared in this commentary, was to be the vehicle for delivering "a sentimental content in a fantastic form" (KA II, 333). With fantastic form Schlegel associated the untrammeled imagination and the fullness of chaos. "In chaos," he had said earlier, "alternate + and -;" in a "system" both are fused (LN 1520). To impose an order upon, to unify this polarized profusion within the universe was the function of content; for "sentimental" Schlegel understood as did Schiller to mean rational, conscious and ordered. Thus with theoretical brilliance Schlegel had discovered a formula for achieving that seemingly paradoxical desideratum of organized chaos. Behler has labeled the dichotomous forces of his theory those of "chaos" and "system."[16]

The *Brief über den Roman* also provides a rationale for Schlegel's continuing interest in the androgyne. In his literary notebooks he had offered further explication of the preferred thematics for Romantic literature when he defined the philosophy of love as "not merely the best, but the only subject of Romantic poetry" (LN 1420). Although the link was not quite so explicit in the discourse on the novel, he did declare there in explaining sentimental content that "the spirit of love" must hover everywhere (KA II, 333-334). From his interpretation of a rather abstruse fragment (LN 735), Eichner has identified the tensions in Schlegel's poetic ideal as eros and chaos, substituting for what Behler identified as "system" the more precise "eros."[17] Examined more closely, this formula places within an androgynous tradition all literature to which the definition applies.

The fascination with the possibilities of eros as a systematizing principle was forecast as far back as 1794. In "Über die Grenzen des Schönen" Schlegel had written that plenitude was a "gift of nature" while all harmony was a "gift of love" (KA I, 43). In neither "Über die weiblichen Charaktere in den griechischen Dichtern" nor "Über

---

16 Ernst Behler, introd., *Friedrich Schlegel: Schriften und Fragmente* (Stuttgart: Kröner, 1956), pp. XXIII-XXIV.
17 Eichner, *Friedrich Schlegel*, pp. 64-69.

die Diotima" was the concept important, but one can assume Schlegel to have been pondering the definition of an antidote to what he even then perceived to be the chaotic condition of modern life. In the latter essay he had merely been able to discern, and then not very convincingly, an organically developed "law" as the principle for ordering "nature in a human being" (KA I, 105). Only in "An Dorothea" did he accord recognition to the structuring power of love. But even there, despite his several assertions that nature must be subordinated to "reason" which in turn demanded a bridging of sexual characteristics through love, he stopped short of labeling love as the sole agent of synthesis. Gradually however – and one can assume this to be a partial result of his relationship with Dorothea – he became convinced that sexual consummation, that is, eros, was the quintessential *Bildungselement*. Before long eros was heralded as the ordering principle, first of all for human nature and then by implication for a world of plenitude. Numerous fragments attest to the discovery;[18] as he recorded in his notebook: "Only in the answer of the You does the I feel its full unity – before that is chaos" (LN 1481).

Schlegel's interpretation of the alliance between chaos and eros is strongly reminiscent of a version of Greek mythological history with which he was undoubtedly familiar. His modification of the myth underscores his own attitude toward love. According to legend, Chaos was the original all-encompassing principle out of which developed all the polarities of the world. To Eros alone was granted the power of recombination.[19] Although to the Greeks of Schlegel's acquaintance, Eros was irresponsible and fickle, the god and the concept with which he was linked occupied in Schlegel's thought a more favorable position. Recalling the basic structure of androgynous union, eros became for Schlegel the single most important systematizing principle for human nature and the world, embodying rationality and order because it united according to a preordained pattern, reconciling what had been previously sundered. Finally, and Behler says it well, Schlegel came to view the whole world as an organism

---

18 See for example *Ideen* 83, 103; LN 1484, 1961, 2097.
19 Graves, vol. 1, pp. 30-34.

through which pulsed the causality of love.[20] For anyone as loath to concede boundaries between life and art as Schlegel, the implications were clear. By 1799 he could unabashedly proclaim: "Chaos and eros is indeed the best explanation of the Romantic" (LN 1760).[21]

The late 1790's were the years during which Schlegel was defining the novel as the form of Romantic expression *par excellence*. The genre which was to effect the grand synthesis of philosophy and poetry, the novel was hailed as uniquely capable of uniting all elements of modern art and life. Since he had already devoted considerable energies to reforming society with other means and with little success, it was perhaps inevitable that Schlegel would address a novel of his own to the cause. The plan for *Lucinde* had first been formulated in 1794 when he was so awed by Caroline's personality and life style. In the years between the ideal and its actualization, however, Schlegel's view of the sexes and of love had gone through many metamorphoses.

In his article on emancipatory tendencies in Schlegel's *Lucinde*, Eugenius Klin identifies an androgynous impulse throughout Schlegel's early work which, he contends, culminates in the novel. He alludes to the function of the ideal in both of the works on Greek women, in "Über die Philosophie. An Dorothea" and in *Lucinde*; he does not, however, note the change in its application.[22] And the differences are quite substantial; Schlegel could hardly have recast his entire outlook on literature and life -- as well as on love – without altering his perception of bisexual perfection. Diotima is simply not to be equated with Lucinde.

In the "Diotima" essay, Schlegel's concept of love had been abstracted into an adulation for the universe and its infinitude.

---

20 Behler, "Friedrich Schlegels Theorie der Universalpoesie," p. 223.
21 The *Literary Notebooks* contain the best record of Schlegel's praise for chaos and eros in Romantic poetry. See LN 27, 30, 1356, 1420, 1518, 1612, 1804, 1996, 2079, 2097.
22 Eugenius Klin, "Das Problem der Emanzipation in Friedrich Schlegels 'Lucinde,' " *Weimarer Beiträge*, 1 (1963), p. 82. Setsuko Shimaya, in "Über die Androgyne beim jungen Friedrich Schlegel," *Doitsu Bungaku*, 53 (1974), pp. 65-75, has also noted the concept in Schlegel's *oeuvre*, but has not distinguished between the various works in which it appears.

Sexuality and sexual love were seemingly bracketed out and androgyny was a factor because such veneration was only possible for those individuals who were no longer limited by sex role identification; only they were deemed able to partake of such elevated love. The *Woldemar* critique was important because there Schlegel came to terms with the demands of sexuality; although the characters made no attempt to attain androgynous completion – in fact, Schlegel considered both Woldemar and Henriette much too ordinary for such a goal – the insistence on a woman's right to sexuality signaled the beginnings of a new interpretation of individual wholeness. Individual *Bildung* was again the focus in the essay Schlegel dedicated to Dorothea; by now he saw the sexes as antipodal forces and had shifted to a definition of completion as a combination of the extremes he associated with, even required in, masculine and feminine personalities. For the first time he proposed love as the concrete medium for the transfer of these vital gender-related qualities. The analogic function of heterosexual love was also a factor, if only incidentally, and personal wholeness itself was equated with religion. Each of these essays contributed to the creation of *Lucinde*, in which sexual love, the prototypical combination of dichotomous entities, was vested with the metaphysical force to symbolize all such unions within the universe and could consequently be proferred as a saving religion.

Not the result of a completely logical development, Schlegel's new perspectives on love show the definite influence of the Jena circle. In *Lucinde*, Schlegel is no longer the rationalist but the metaphysician. And behind this shift can also be seen the influence of Böhme. Tieck had introduced the theosophist's works to his friends, including Novalis and Schlegel, in 1798. Schlegel's *Philosophische Lehrjahre* documents a growing interest in Böhme's thinking and an increased concern for the natural world after this time. The collection of fragments called *"Zur Physik,"* for example, written in Dresden in the summer of 1798, records the appreciation for nature which Novalis had been trying for some time to kindle (P, 80; 109). There in Dresden were Caroline and Fichte as well as Schelling and Novalis. Under their influence he soon accepted Schelling's notion of the entire natural world as a living, pulsating organism exhibiting throughout the polarities whose desire for tension gave the impulse to organic development. This was the summer, according to Behler in the introduction to the critical edition of the *Lehrjahre*, that changed the focus of Schlegel's thinking from the universe to nature, from religious feelings of oneness with the cosmos to a "poetic physics" (KA XVIII, XXIX).

Novalis had written to Schlegel before their meeting in Dresden that he hoped to surpass Schelling with a method for dealing with physics "in the most far-reaching sense simply *symbolically*" (P, 120). Sceptical at first about this attempt to connect religion and physics, Schlegel became a convert during the summer.[23] During those months in Dresden, Schlegel wrote in a fragment that the world in its totality was a plant and added: "Humanity too in its entirety is a plant" (KA XVIII, 151, # 332). Shortly thereafter, he recorded in the same philosophical notebook a fragment linking his high appraisal of plants to their essence as hermaphrodites (KA XVIII, 153, # 362). Not to be understood literally, this thinking reflects his new interest in science as well as the influence of Böhme, both of which helped to strengthen his belief in the concept of a binary world. As he developed his own religion of love, Schlegel believed he had found a way to reunite all the sundered polarities within the world and so bring about universal harmony. His earlier belief that society was responsible for the undesirable polarization of the sexes yielded to a conviction that their opposition was the necessary prerequisite for the perfection occasioned by their reunion.

By the summer of 1800 Schlegel was so convinced of Böhme's message that he recommended to Schleiermacher that he too study the theosophist's particular brand of Christianity. For Böhme, Schlegel suggested, had fused religion with what Schlegel himself believed to be the revolutionary practices of poetry and physics.[24] Although

---

23 See Behler's introduction to the critical edition of the *Philosophische Lehrjahre* (KA XVIII, XXIX-XXXV). Behler connects Schlegel's interests with the scientific discoveries of the late eighteenth century, galvanism and mesmerism among them.

24 Friedrich Schleiermacher, *Aus Schleiermachers Leben: In Briefen*, vol. 3 (Berlin: Reimer, 1861), p. 192. In his notebooks, Schlegel wrote in the same year that the first work of the "new Christianity" was to be the "gospel of nature" (KA XVIII, 374, # 650).

Böhme's influence on Schlegel has been infrequently discussed, there is increasing recognition that Böhme's theosophy and spirit had incorporated itself into early Romanticism. Marshall Brown, for example, reports an essay Brentano wrote in 1799 and read to the Jena circle around 1800; the essay, according to Brown, is only comprehensible through an understanding of Böhme's theosophy.[25] Behler, one of the critics who has singled out Böhme's influence on Schlegel, has also recognized his impact on Schlegel's view of love. He concludes in an article on Schlegel's *Universalpoesie* that the longing for completion, for the lost half operative in Schlegel's encomium of love in *Lucinde*, is prompted by the same memory of an original bisexuality which propelled Böhme's theosophical prescription for religious salvation. Extending these lines to Schlegel's theory of Romantic poetry and to *Lucinde*, he argues that the "tinctures" of male and female become symbols of far-reaching synthesis. Because the novel presents the "symbolic reunion of feminine poetry with masculine philosophy," he judges Schlegel to have accomplished the "integration of soul and mind" so important to his theory. Precisely therefore, Behler continues, *Lucinde* is a "comprehensive document of Romantic universal poetry."[26] Peter Firchow believes that *Lucinde* demonstrates "perhaps more than any other work of fiction to come out of the German Romantic movement, the relation between Romantic theory and practice."[27] Schlegel, himself, was no less enthusiastic when he referred to his novel as a "wondrous growth of freedom [*Willkür*] and love" (KA V, 26).

If *Lucinde* is a creditable representation of Romantic theory, it is also an attempt to substantiate the role of eros in harmonizing the antipathies of the chaotic world. By late 1798 when he began to work on his novel, Schlegel had come to embrace so thoroughly the concept of eros as the unifier of polarities in art and life that his dedication to a woman's equality had abated; an emphasis on maintaining her "feminity" had instead become preemptive. His

---

25 Marshall Brown, pp. 139-141.
26 Behler, "Friedrich Schlegels Theorie der Universalpoesie," p. 244.
27 Peter Firchow, introd., *'Lucinde' and the Fragments* (Minneapolis: University of Minnesota Press, 1971), p. 22.

position has shifted so dramatically since the time of his infatuation with Diotima-Caroline, that at one point in *Lucinde* the narrator, Julius, can answer a resounding "no" when Lucinde questions the possibility of a discussion without attention first of all to the sex of the conversation partner. Such a talk, Julius avers, would resemble addressing "a sexless amphibian" (KA V, 34). Cognizant now of a change in his attitude toward the sexes and of an attendant shift in his view of love, Schlegel in *Lucinde* defines his religion of love in part by comparison with his former ideal. Diotima, he now admits, had only revealed to Socrates half of love; for love should be not only a quiet desire for infinity, but also the "holy enjoyment of a beautiful present" (KA V, 60).

Early in the novel its form is the subject as Schlegel, through Julius, justifies his "right to a charming confusion;" in fact, he argues, we must rid ourselves of that "which we call order" (KA V, 9), that is, strict chronology, and allow the content to impose its own intrinsic form. The resultant "fantastic form" -- the all-embracing chaos -- is manifested in a medley of letters, dialogs, an idyll, allegories, dreams, verse and fantasies. All have ostensibly found their own natural order and thus constitute a "charming symmetry." Schlegel's plans for continuation emphasize the addition of poetry to this assemblage of forms.[28] While early generations of readers faulted Schlegel for the lack of form in his novel, contemporary critics agree that there is a logical arrangement: six short segments which lead to the main middle section, the middle section composed of the *Lehrjahre*, and a final section comprised again of six shorter segments. Although this can be seen as evidence of conscious design, Schlegel would have us believe otherwise. Through Julius he refers to the ordering principle inherent in his material, in this case the lives and love of Julius and Lucinde; that content, according to Julius, is "incessantly progressive" and "inflexibly systematic." As Julius insists, only the harmonies of eros can be a worthy organizing principle. Consequently, he will imitate and even restore the "most beautiful chaos out of exalted harmonies" (KA V, 9).

---

28 These poems plagued him for several years as he tried to work on the second part of the novel; see Eichner's discussion (KA V, LV-LX).

Once the most beautiful chaos is recognized as the final reunion of all antipodal forces and a condition vastly superior to the original chaos, there becomes recognizable a tripartite historical structure. Tributed as the principle which not only "separates the beings" but which also "forms [bildet] the world" (KA V, 61), eros for Schlegel is accorded the role which other philosophers, among them Kant, had allotted to knowledge. Whether the result of direct or indirect influences, parallels to Böhme's thinking are clear. It had been Adam's desire for the female within him, according to Böhme, which had caused the initial division into sexes, and it would be love again which would overcome that separation. Although the divisive function of love plays almost no part in *Lucinde*, it does contribute to the view of history which shapes the work. Certain fragments explicate this role more persuasively: the dual character of love was the basis for a fragment calling love the "spark of the divine through which the universe becomes nature;" only through reason (*Vernunft*), Schlegel continues, can the process be reversed (KA XVIII, 153, # 361). This fragment was written in 1799; "reason" had also been a key concept in "An Dorothea" where Schlegel had interpreted it as calling for combinatory heterosexual love. Now in *Lucinde* that aphorism is modified: "When one loves as we do," declares Julius, "nature within the human being returns to its original divinity" (KA V, 67). The substitution of "love" for "reason" underscores the development in Schlegel's thinking.

Dating from his relationship with Caroline, Schlegel's definition of love and marriage had been mutually exclusive and thus at odds with late eighteenth century values. During those decades, because of the primacy of reason but certainly owing as much to the influences of Christianity, love and passion were tacitly ignored. Even though the emotionally turbulent *Sturm und Drang* helped to reinstate love as a value, spiritual and physical love remained sharply distinguished. A man, from whose perspective love was invariably defined, rarely found a lover and a friend, the highly touted "soul mate [*Seelenfreundin*]," in one woman.[29] The Schlegel who wrote *Lucinde*

---

29 Kluckhohn, *Die Auffassung der Liebe*, pp. 140-227.

eulogized love as a union to be enjoyed both spiritually and physically. Requiring neither religious sanction nor formal ceremony, such true love, a phrase he substituted for marriage, could only exist when there was "love and reciprocated love, both complete" (LN 1522). A conventional marriage, he contemptuously declared to Caroline, was nothing but a "hateful ceremony."[30] Certainly Schlegel's most notorious public comment on the subject was that in *Athenäums-Fragment* 34 where he defined the marriages indulged in by his contemporaries as "concubinage" to which even a "marriage *à quatre*" would be preferable.

Neither Schlegel's loathing nor his terminology, it should be noted, was entirely original. Fichte's influence is most apparent, for he too had denigrated bourgeois marriage with a similar vocabulary.[31] What Schlegel posited as an alternative, however, differed markedly from Fichte's model. By eliminating the old Cartesian dualism of finite versus infinite in his own version of love, Fichte had been influential for many thinkers. But in its place, he had inadvertently set up a new dualism, that of the "I" versus the "non-I." Thus although Fichte had praised love and sexual union as the means of attaining personal fulfillment, the partner who was associated with the "non-I" was necessarily reduced to an antipodal position. Schlegel, on the contrary, was in *Lucinde* positing the recreation of a previously intact monism through erotic love. The monism, however, retained more traces of Fichte's self-importance than Schlegel perhaps realized.

Much of his novel is devoted to defining the unique relationship which Schlegel was so enthusiastically recommending. In the first letter of *Lucinde*, Julius relates to Lucinde a dream of their eternal love which states the theme of androgynous love. The perfection possible in the dream has brought him contentment; he is unassailable for he has found "the one and only eternally beloved." Making much of opposing word pairs, Schlegel subtly reinforces through form the theme of perfection as a result of a combination of antipodes. The

---

30 *Caroline: Briefe*, vol. 1, p. 478.
31 Johann Gottlieb Fichte, *Sämmtliche Werke*, ed. J.H. Fichte, vol. 3 (Leipzig: Mayer and Müller, 1924), p. 336. For his views on marriage see pp. 304-343.

dream, for example, appears to Julius in the middle of his own "thoughts" and "feelings." The source of life is viewed as a mixture of "joy" and "pain" (KA V, 7); with as much "abandonment" as "religion" the lovers embrace. Lucinde's passion is to be "insatiable" while Julius appreciates with "circumspection." Reporting his own appreciation of love, Julius affirms the mingling of conscious and unconscious states: "I not only enjoyed, but I felt and also enjoyed the enjoyment" (KA V, 8). Even time has blended into a state of simultaneous "memories" of things past and "yearnings" for things to come. Finally the love of Julius and Lucinde is described as "spiritual voluptuousness" and "sensual blessedness" (KA V, 7). Such combinations are not to be dismissed as evidence of Schlegel's delight in clever oxymora; rather they underline his belief in the perfection resultant from androgynous union.

The "Dithyrambische Fantasie über die schönste Situation," although following the first two letters of the novel under the pretense of chance, is actually very well placed; for the dichotomous forces are explicit now in the content. The most beautiful situation to which the title of the section alludes is sexual love between Julius and Lucinde, two opposites who are meant for and complete one another. Lucinde has become for Julius a mirror in which he can glimpse his newly harmonious self; a similar development is to be noted in Lucinde, for through their love she has become "one of the figures who eternally remain." Their love, according to Julius who continues to narrate, has made visible "full and complete humanity" in them both; it has beckoned them "into infinity" where time ceases to exist and thus has granted to them a peaceful understanding of their "original harmony" (KA V, 10). These phrases recall Novalis' description of Heinrich's and Mathilde's love. Indeed, Schlegel in Lucinde is also paying homage to an androgynous *Urbild* of perfection. The idea of prototypes had surfaced in fragments (cf. KA XVIII, 26, # 85) and in "An Dorothea" as well, but Schlegel's belief in them is more clearly stated in a paeon to Winckelmann contained in *Idee* 102: "That holy Winckelmann," he insisted, was the first of their age to recognize "the prototype of completed humanity" in the figures of ancient art. Not until *Lucinde* did that belief in original forms become an integral part of Schlegel's work.

In preparation for writing his own novel, Schlegel reports having reread Plato's *Symposium* in the winter of 1798-1799 (W, 410). No longer was it the elusive figure of Diotima who provided the attraction, but rather the vision of primal wholeness he found in Aristophanes' contribution to a definition of love. It can not have escaped Schlegel that Plato, like the Pietists and Böhme, not only posited androgynous original perfection, but also alluded to its reinstatement through a love which was predetermined. Such an idea was compatible to Schlegel, who once remarked in his literary notebooks: "One dies only once, but one also loves only once" (LN 1297). The theme of predestination is important throughout the novel and reinforces the necessity of the androgynous configuration. Love, the agent for reinstating harmony, has been given now a religious frame; it is a god-given instinct to assure androgynous wholeness.

Julius and Lucinde have been meant for each other since the beginning of time, we are told; they existed long ago in harmonious togetherness, were split, and now through sexual love will regain their original state. Their union is so complete that Julius credits Lucinde with knowing his thoughts before they are uttered. When he rhapsodizes about the possibility for each "I" to find its infinite unity only "in the answer of its You" he is repeating the theme. If completed, the second part of the novel would have intensified the predetermined nature of their love. In notes for the continuation, according to Eichner, Julius and Lucinde are said to love each other "because they have always loved one another." And when asking himself how he knew Lucinde loved him, Julius was to reply: "Because she already loved me before she knew me. She must love me; nature has designed her for it" (KA V, XXXI-XXXII). As Schlegel assessed it in his literary notebooks, true love would be impossible without a "systematic history (historical predestination) in life" (LN 1502).

Schlegel's appreciation for the unique individual, an idea which today helps provide a definition of Romantic literature and theory, can also be traced, at least in part, to this belief in a predestined androgynous love. No longer motivated by the same impulse for wholeness which was present in "Über die Diotima," neither should this perspective be confused with the concept of eccentric individuality for which the later Romantics were to be faulted. The criterion for evaluating each man or woman was for Schlegel similar to the method he espoused for a work of literature; each should be judged on its own merits, according to its own eternal laws (LN 1135, 1733). It followed for him that if each of the partners were truly individual, their love would also be unique and eternal according to its own organic law. Thus Schlegel's commitment to individual differences resulted from his even higher estimation of the harmonious entity created through love. Such a bond was to be contrasted to Goethe's presentations of love which Schlegel disparages in his notebooks as "everywhere the same" (LN 2033).

Only with Lucinde could Julius have attained perfection; she is to him "the most tender lover and the best company" as well as a "complete friend" (KA V, 10). Her sensory experiences are "complete and infinite;" she is not "like the others." Since her personality is unfragmented, life and love are for her inseparable. Together they can thus close out the world and experience all the various stages of love from the "most unrestrained sensuality to the most spiritual spirituality" (KA V, 11). In describing their union in this section, the "Dithyrambische Fantasie," Schlegel again employs linguistic opposites. Every separation, we are told, would only bring them closer; a final embrace would elicit tears as well as laughter. Their burning passion must be cooled. The most beautiful of all, however, confides Julius, is when they exchange roles in their lovemaking, when Lucinde attempts to portray the "considerate ardor of the man" while he enacts the "charming surrender of the woman" (KA V, 12). In this game of sex role exchange which will make each whole, that is, androgynous, Julius sees "a wonderful... allegory of the development of male and female to full and complete humanity" (KA V, 13).

Because the novel so unabashedly proclaims the joys of sexual love, Schlegel expected criticism. The two sections "Charakteristik der kleinen Wilhelmine" and "Allegorie von der Frechheit" address themselves to this inevitability. They are attempts to justify what Schlegel feared might be judged his indiscretion at describing the "most beautiful situation." Together the sections amount to a defense of sexuality versus the prudery of the bourgeoisie, which quality, Schlegel insisted, could only hinder true love.[32] For true,

---

32 Schlegel railed frequently against prudery; see for example *Athenäums-Fragment* 31.

and we can read erotic, love alone is the necessary *Bildungselement*, Schlegel goes on to explain, since the sexes are complementary opposites. The most significant difference between them lies in the way they love. Women, Schlegel believes, love naturally and from instinct; there are no particular stages in their development, for in their hearts resides the "holy fire of divine voluptuousness" (KA V, 20). It is a fire which can be awakened only by a man. Men, on the other hand, according to his characterization, only develop gradually an "artful sense for voluptuousness." Three stages are necessary, and even then the goal is attained through a woman's example and her love. Only in the third stage have men surpassed their interest in the "sensation of the flesh" which characterizes the first level, and the irrational "magic" of the second, to attain "the lasting feeling of harmonious warmth," the criterion of the final stage (KA V, 21). Then and only then has a man fulfilled his destiny and become whole.

In the "Idylle über den Müssiggang" Schlegel elaborates upon the capacity of love to make each partner a total human being. Believed to be a sanctioning of sloth, this section earned him much criticism. His own definition of idleness as a "godlike art" did little to obviate the problem for generations of critics. Unequivocally he judges idleness to be a "gospel of genuine pleasure and love" for which he proposes a hymn of praise: "Oh idleness, idleness . . . you holy jewel! solitary fragment of godlikeness which remained to us from paradise" (KA V, 25). No longer concerned with distinguishing between biologically and sociologically determined characteristics, Schlegel attributes his unusual praise of idleness to its association with women. It is, he declares, the specific quality which renders them capable of loving wholly and living harmoniously with themselves and with nature despite the demands of modern life. The restless activity to which he states such an aversion he links with masculinity and labels a "northern incivility" which can lead only to boredom and antipathy toward the world. With something approaching religious fervor he proclaims industriousness and utility to be "the angels of death with the flaming sword" (KA V, 27) who will prevent the return of humanity to paradise. To the active searchers Schlegel contrasts the poets, wise men and saints, all of whom merit the epithet "godlike" because they have chosen to live in solitude and leisure. Only in a state of passivity can one contemplate the self and the universe; it is a condition succinctly defined in his notebooks as the true "school of self-knowledge" (LN 1524). Only idleness, we are to be persuaded, manifests itself in organic striving to realize the Beautiful and the Good which will always exist in the world.

Thus idleness -- and this is the thrust of the segment -- is a virtue which men must adapt into their own nature through the love of a woman. Only then will men's own development and growth, as well as the progress for which they are responsible in the world, be natural and plant-like as, says Schlegel, it has always been in a woman. Idleness should be raised to the level of art for, and Schlegel intends with this final comparison to seal his argument, the holier or more moral a person may be, the closer he or she is to a plant; therefore the most moral life must be "*a pure vegetating*" (KA V, 27). While the formulaic combination of man and nature is not as vital as it was in Novalis' works, it is still operative. Schlegel's acceptance of the eighteenth century connection between women and nature was also intimated in the opening scene of the novel, where Lucinde was introduced in a garden.[33] A unique comparison between Prometheus, who created people by industrious labor, and Hercules, whose creation was natural and in combination with women, buttresses the approbation of idleness. It was not Prometheus, Schlegel reminds us, but Hercules who ascended to the realm of the Olympians. Instead of being rewarded, Prometheus, Schlegel suggests, was punished for having seduced men into a life of work.

The final segment of the first section, "Treue und Scherz," attempts a comprehensive overview of Julius' and Lucinde's love. Including references to all aspects of their relationship, it is meant to demonstrate what Julius articulates: "Everything is present in love: friendship, pleasant company, sensuality and also passion." Commensurate with Schlegel's priorities, however, the section ends with sexual union, the conclusive unifying act. And in that endeavor equality is alleged to reign. Stressing their equal passion, Lucinde

---

33 Women and nature are linked in numerous fragments, see p. 52 above; they are also termed "vegetable-like" (LN 1265, 1487).

questions: "Who is indeed more passionate, Julius! I or you?" (KA V, 35).

The long middle section "Lehrjahre der Männlichkeit" is a narrative of Julius' development to lover and his concommitant attainment of religion. It is the autobiographical section which chronologically precedes the first.[34] Chronicling the various phases of Julius' maturation, the narrator emphasizes his unsuccessful attempts to establish a fulfilling relationship with a woman. We are told that each endeavor and its consequent failure only left him more miserable and lonely until he met and was saved by Lucinde, the priestess in his "religion of love" (KA V, 12). The religious effect of heterosexual love, first established in the essay written to Dorothea, is here more forcefully stated; love, the narrator asserts, is the only way to the perfection Schlegel equated with religion. Schlegel himself called *Lucinde* a "religious book" (KA V, XXXV) and was presumably thinking of his novel when he confided to Novalis in December, 1798, that he planned "to found a new religion" (P, 138). The ethical implications of Schlegel's intended religion are apparent when one compares a similar confession to Schleiermacher in which he declares his aspiration "to provide a moral philosophy."[35]

Nominally the religious state in *Lucinde* is reached by the sexual union of equals; however, the balance between the sexes in the "Lehrjahre" is strained, to say the least. From the beginning it has been clear that they are not equals, but rather polarized entities, each within its own sphere. Even granting Schlegel's view that love would make each androgynously whole and thus equal, the scales in this section are tilted, for the emphasis is almost solely upon Julius' salvation. To be sure, the male viewpoint predominated in the first third as well, but it was not as objectionable because Julius was speaking in the first person. The "Lehrjahre" is related in third person by a narrator from whom one might expect more equity. Instead Lucinde is ensconced in a role very similar to that of the women in Novalis' works. No surprise in view of Schlegel's acknowledgment to

---

34 Biographical parallels are pointed out in the introduction to *Lucinde* in the critical edition (KA V, XLII-XLIII).
35 Schleiermacher, *Aus Schleiermacher's Leben: In Briefen*, vol. 3, p. 80.

Novalis in mid 1798 that he too recognized the necessity for a mediator in religious matters (P, 115), his weighted interest in the male is nevertheless disappointing when one remembers earlier pronouncements. In both "Über die Diotima" and the critique of *Woldemar*, Schlegel had specifically railed against such exploitation. In the former he had caustically disparaged all attempts to portray woman's primary role as one of service to men; such an error, he had insisted, was tantamount to excluding "the Good and the Beautiful from the feminine destiny" (KA I, 100).

The retreat from equality in this middle section is not consciously ordained; in fact, Schlegel assumes that he is preaching a new religion of sexual parity. The narrator, for example, defines the initial impact of Julius and Lucinde upon each other as the result of their "wonderful equality" (KA V, 53). Both were artists, possessed passionate natures, had similar interests such as nature and solitude; both lived freely and were untroubled by societal opinion. That this commitment is superseded by Schlegel's new affinity for complementary opposites becomes overwhelmingly apparent as soon as the discussion turns to Julius' and Lucinde's sexual relationship. In the language and in the description of their attraction, polarities predominate. Even though the narrator promises that these many differences "were grounded . . . only upon a deeper equality" (KA V, 56), we recognize in this deeper equality a reference to their original condition as halves of one whole rather than to any real social equality. There are reciprocal benefits to their love; for example, each can say to the other: "You are the point in which my being finds rest" (KA V, 79); but the gains do not assure equality. Like Novalis' protagonists, Julius will find his divinity within himself through Lucinde's love, and that endeavor is Schlegel's primary focus. The peripheries of equality are narrowed to a mutual involvement in the erotic sphere, but there too the benefit will go to the male.

Further examples attest to the results of Schlegel's viewing the sexes as opposing pairs. Julius and Lucinde met as artists; because their love has granted him contact with the eternal, Julius' paintings are thereafter referred to as unified and harmonious.[36] Because of

---

36 Many fragments praise the power of love as one of discovering or awakening the "center" in an individual. See for example *Ideen* 45, 83, 87.

their love he could at the outset of the novel even introduce himself as "an educated [*gebildeter*] lover and writer" (KA V, 9). Lucinde's artistic pursuits, however, after functioning as proof of the lovers' initial sameness, are no longer relevant. Although Schlegel refrains from labeling her with his earlier condescension as "domestic," the home and, later, motherhood define her sphere. The fulfillment which we are told love has granted her is apparently a restriction to domesticity. One could perhaps judge the imbalance less harshly by placing Schlegel's work into a historical perspective, by which measure he was still far more charitable than the majority of his contemporaries. That he chose to make *Lucinde* an autobiographical story of Julius' salvation also mitigates the criticism somewhat. But that decision is symptomatic of the problem, for such a framework effectively excludes the equality Schlegel thinks he is defending.

In 1797 Schlegel wrote in his notebooks that a complete novel must recognize the "totality of all individuals" (LN 574). It is not his adherence to this position which has changed in *Lucinde*, but instead his apprehension of what constitutes wholeness in a woman. He certainly would not have included *Lucinde* among the novels to which he indicated such antipathy in *Athenäums-Fragment* 118 -- works in which all characters "move around someone like planets around the sun, who is then usually the author's ill-behaved favorite." We, however, must make the association. Even the title of the novel alerts us to the inherent imbalance, although from a certain perspective it is debatable which of the lovers -- Julius or Lucinde -- would be termed the planet and which the sun. Far from originating in a conviction that women were incapable of progress to perfection, the paucity of attention paid to Lucinde's development issues from Schlegel's instinctive idealization of women. Although he tries to convince his readers and himself that Lucinde, as one equal half of the reunited whole, benefits from love, he is doomed to fail because she is depicted from the beginning as integrated. "The shaping [*bildende*] eros" is necessary only to Julius.

As in the works of Novalis, there is in Schlegel's novel an almost schizophrenic perception of women. Seen on the one hand as the complementary opposites of men, embodying the qualities their counterparts lack, they are on the other, complete beings idealized to perfection. This is the same double tracked thinking which made many of the Romantics' pronouncements on nature so incongruous. Nature was a spiritualized, organic whole, but yet was man's complement, the pole from which he had become alienated.[37] As Mathilde in *Heinrich von Ofterdingen* was Heinrich's complement, so was she also alluded to with symbols of wholeness. Conceived in the same mold, Lucinde is not only Julius' opposite, but a complete being from the beginning. Saviors are, after all, perfect unto themselves. Lucinde's wholeness Schlegel describes in terms of an androgynous ideal, for she includes all opposites within her. She is the Priestess of the Night, a realm reverberating with passion and love,[38] yet in the tradition of Böhme, her name links her with the opposing principle, Light. She has, in fact, been identified by Bärbel Becker-Cantarino as a "bringer of light."[39] As such, her existence calls forth a comparison to a fragment which attributes to light both sexual natures (KA XVIII, 186, # 725). As a woman whose affinities are said to be with the natural world and plants, she resembles the plants in another already mentioned aphorism which Schlegel lauds for their hermaphroditic qualities. Further proof of Lucinde's wholeness rests in her name which allies her with the moon; according to the *Symposium*, which was fresh in Schlegel's mind when he made this identification, the moon was the origin of the very powerful androgynous first beings. Firchow not only associates her name with the Latin *lux*, meaning light, but also interprets it as Schlegel's evocation of Lucine, a Roman goddess of childbirth; she is, he reasons, the private redeemer through whom Julius experiences a kind of rebirth.[40] For all her perfection, Lucinde is no less important as Julius' complement. For a reader familiar with Böhme's works, the association of Lucinde with a mirror in the first section is telling. Böhme had frequently praised

---

37 Compare p. 50 in the text above.
38 It is tempting to assume parallels with Novalis' *Hymnen an die Nacht*, although that work had not yet been published. Conversely, there is no indication that Schlegel's association influenced Novalis.
39 Bärbel Becker-Cantarino, "Priesterin und Lichtbringerin: Zur Ideologie des weiblichen Charakters in der Frühromantik," in *Die Frau als Heldin und Autorin*, ed. Wolfgang Paulsen (Bern: Francke, 1979), p. 111.
40 Firchow, p. 24, see also n. 21.

Sophia, the divine Virgin associated with Light, as the mirror through which man could know himself;[41] Julius venerates Lucinde as his long-lost partner, his mirror who reflects self-knowledge and restores the viewer to himself. Perhaps Schlegel's position during the writing of *Lucinde* can be summarized by the following assertion in his notebook: "Love is the art of egoism; only through love does one become an individual" (LN 1549). Apparently he saw no incompatibility between this goal and sexual equality.

There are indications that Schlegel did recognize some imbalance in the "Lehrjahre;" there is even the semblance of an apology in his claim to Caroline that equilibrium would be restored in a soon to be written second part by a long section detailing "feminine views." Written when he still craved Caroline's respect -- in 1799 he wrote to August Wilhelm that he would like to author something that would be "neither forbidden in Austria nor condemned by Caroline" (W, 412) -- he nevertheless confessed to her that no *Lehrjahre* would be contained in the section. He doubted, he said, whether women required such an apprenticeship.[42] In view of his desire to please Caroline and since the second part of the novel was never written, it is difficult to evaluate how seriously Schlegel judged the disparity; it must be noted, however, that the poems which he did compose for the continuation, for example the "Lob der Frauen," maintain the emphasis on a saving feminine principle. It thus seems legitimate to conclude that Schlegel understood the lack of balance as attendant upon the space devoted to each of the sexes.

Although Schlegel had the right impulses, the influences within his culture were simply too strong for his own vision to counteract. When he had been struggling alone during his Greek period, he had followed his own instincts, and had tried to discover a meaningful definition of humanness to apply to men and women alike. Even there, however, convention had interferred. With his turn to religion, he found himself immersed within a tradition in which, instead of an androgyny synonymous with sexual equality, the vague notion of

---

41 The mirror image recurs throughout Böhme's works; see Robert F. Brown, pp. 51, 56, 76, for discussion. The feminine wisdom is also thought of as the "mirror of God" in *Wisdom of Solomon* 7: 25-26.
42 *Caroline: Briefe*, vol. 1, p. 513.

man's original bisexuality to be regained through love of a woman was pervasive. The long tradition of which he found himself a part believed, as has been discussed, that woman's role was to save man. Although Schlegel was more independent than Novalis and although the framework for his thinking was more secular, his attitude toward women and love by the time he wrote *Lucinde* was remarkably similar to that of his friend. The version of love which they extolled can, in fact, be identified as *the* Romantic version.

As far back as 1921 Josef Körner rejected the general direction of research on *Lucinde* because it stressed biographical parallels instead of the "revolutionary intentions of a powerful (if unsuccessful) artistic plan."[43] It remains as difficult now to overlook biographical data as it apparently was before Körner's comment. Perhaps the very recognition of the failed revolutionary intentions demands a search for the cause; and culpability can be readily apportioned to certain events in Schlegel's life. Most pertinent in view of his plan in *Lucinde* — and Klin is correct when he states unequivocally that in his novel Schlegel was aiming at a new ethic based on sexual equality[44] — are the two women who were the models for Schlegel's ideas of femininity. Although Caroline's personality in the few years of their friendship before she married his brother did turn Schlegel's thoughts toward equality, Dorothea's influence did not tend in the same direction. On the contrary, many accounts testify that she was quite willing to sacrifice herself for Friedrich. A telling comment from Achim von Arnim, for example, refers to her as the "worshipper of the Dalai Lama Friedrich Schlegel."[45] Dismissing Schlegel's marriage to Dorothea as banal and bourgeois, Huch declares that relationship as altogether unworthy of Schlegel's earlier ideals.[46] Even though Schlegel himself judged his union with Dorothea far superior to those of his contemporaries, we must conclude that the differences did not

---

43 Josef Körner, "Neues vom Dichter der Lucinde," in *Preussische Jahrbücher*, 183 (1921), p. 309.
44 Klin, p. 79.
45 Quoted in Kluckhohn, *Die Auffassung der Liebe*, p. 381.
46 Ricarda Huch, "Die romantische Ehe," in *Das Ehe-Buch*, ed. Hermann Alexander Keyserling (Celle: Kampmann, 1925), p. 157.

extend far beyond the form; admittedly they did defy conventional standards by not marrying for several years.

As the relationship with Dorothea found its way into the fiction of the "Lehrjahre der Männlichkeit," Julius learns to love the world through a sexual union with Lucinde. If Schlegel has freed women from one stereotype -- to be sure his advocacy of love as a physical as well as a spiritual endeavor for both sexes should not be overlooked – he has burdened them with others. The pattern of active, seeking male versus passive woman, for example, is a dominant chord of the work. When Eichner labels *Lucinde* "a passionate protest against the inequality of the sexes and the condemnation of sensuality,"[47] he is assessing the novel as its author intended. Unfortunately this can not be the final judgment. Lucinde is not sexually repressed, it is true, but neither does she attain a meaningful equality. By 1798 no more independent types such as Antigone peopled Schlegel's imagination.

Certainly it would be unjust to impute Schlegel's failure to attain his revolutionary goals solely to Dorothea. It would also be inaccurate. The Socialist critic Klin has concluded what now seems quite obvious: Schlegel was simply too unrealistic and did not know people and society well enough to understand equality.[48] Even by the time he wrote his fragments for the *Athenäum*, the only "revolutionary desire" motivating him was "to realize God's kingdom" (*Ath. Fr.* 222). Although less troubled by the penetrating mysticism of Novalis which made that poet's claims at a collective effort negligible, Schlegel's work reflects the same lack of attention to empirical reality. Even in his Greek period, his stated intentions of personal equality had fallen victim to his insistence on a contiguous boundary between the real and ideal worlds. Although his dream of balance had been sincere, his ethical goals had been so thoroughly equated with spiritual progress that he had simply ignored their translation into the political or social sphere. Even his studies on Greek culture demonstrated a lack of sensitivity for genuine social parity; when espousing equality most adamantly in the "Diotima" essay, he did

---

47 Eichner, *Friedrich Schlegel*, p. 85.
48 Klin, p. 99.

not find it contradictory, for example, to praise Solon's compassion even though and perhaps because that ruler bought girls as prostitutes rather than merely conscripting them (KA I, 75-76). Despite the homage paid to women and the passionate attempt to persuade his readers of their commensurate abilities, there were flaws in Schlegel's thinking which doomed his ambition. By the time of *Lucinde*, his own claims to the contrary, Schlegel was no longer interested in social parity; that early dream of individual wholeness and freedom had been subsumed into a more spiritual form of salvation.

In 1794 and 1795 when Schlegel thought he was confirming women's right to humanity, he had also felt coerced, for various reasons, into defining sexual differences. The characteristics he assigned to each sex were in no way empirically verifiable, but were restatements of stereotypes trenchant in the 1790's. Nothing in Homeric literature told him women were capable of infusing love, warmth and natural emotion into a culture. More examples could be adduced, all of which would lead to the conclusion that Schlegel was *a priori* conditioned to fail in his goal of establishing a just society. If he had been unable to discover a genuine kind of sexual equality in the early essays when his goal reinforced that finding, such an affirmation became all but impossible when he turned to religion and philosophy and became imbued with the idea of the sexes as symbols of universal polarities. Social equality has never emanated from a society committed to a doctrine of "separate but equal." Instead of realizing a new sexual ethic based on commensurate potential, Schlegel eventually perpetuated myths which have contributed to the historical maintenance of separate and unequal spheres.

The third and final section of the novel underlines the distance Schlegel has come from his singular goal of psychological androgyny for each individual. Although more rambling than the previous two and tending toward restatement, it illustrates that the recreation of a harmonious universe is now an important consideration. The segment "Metamorphosen" assigns to love the same ability to activate a symbolic dimension for which it had been praised by Novalis. Actually the word Schlegel uses in connection with the powers of love is allegory, but that term has been the subject of much discussion. Lieselotte Dieckmann, as well as others, has concluded that in

Lucinde Schlegel made no distinction between allegory and symbol.[49] *Lucinde* thus follows the dictates of the "Brief über den Roman" according to which symbolism must predominate because everything is a hint of something higher. Consequently, an all-encompassing, if symbolic synthesis through erotic union is implied when Schlegel asserts that "the great chaos of quarreling figures" can be harmonized through "the magic of joy" (KA V, 60).

In the other important segment within the third section, "Eine Reflexion," Schlegel extends the vision of an androgynous whole to its symbolic dimension. In its glorification of nature and the entire universe as an entity fueled by the reunion of sexual antipathies, "Eine Reflexion" allies Schlegel with Schelling and other Romantic philosophers of nature. The alignment reflects Schlegel's new view of nature. Up to the time of "An Dorothea" he had seen in nature an imperfect system in need of direction from human reason; along with Fichte he believed that nature was to be overcome and corrected. In the more mystically, even pantheistically inclined *Lucinde*, the Hermetic spirit dominates; with its "eternally immutable symmetry," nature has the innate potential for recombination and perfection. The whole universe, in fact, is proclaimed to be "an interplay of the definite and the indefinite" (KA V, 73), terms which for Schlegel have sexual references. In the language of the novel, the universe has become for Schlegel a "reflection" of sexual union, a macrocosm of sexual love. Thus the striving for the infinite, for absolute harmony in an imperfect world, can be quenched only through the fulfillment of erotic desire. Eros, the "most holy miracle of nature," the "fire of the most noble life force" (KA V, 67), has become for Schlegel part of God's plan for the reunification of all disparities within the universe. "Voluptuousness," he announced in his notebooks, "is nature at its most potent" (LN 1484). In the largest sense, Schlegel's veneration for eros as the necessary antidote to chaos should be understood as his contribution to the attempts at theodicy so wide spread during the eighteenth century.

At one point in the *Gespräch über die Poesie*, Schlegel had called the boldest realism the best, and as an example named the mystery

---

49 Lieselotte Dieckmann, "Friedrich Schlegel and the Romantic Concepts of the Symbol," *Germanic Review*, 34 (1959), pp. 276-283.

cults with their own unique view of nature. This kind of realism and view of the natural world – further defined as an idealization of reality -- was illustrated in an Orphic fragment, Schlegel stated, which spoke of the bisexuality of Zeus. And Zeus, he added in the 1823 version he prepared for his collected works -- presumably to further clarify his notion -- was hailed as the all-embracing expression of life (KA II, 326). It would seem that Schlegel meant life to include the entire world. In fragments he was more specific as to his intentions. "Sexuality," he declared, "must be projected into the elements – the chemical process resembles procreation" (KA XVIII, 157, # 408). Numerous aphorisms indicate that he has done precisely that, and not merely to the elements. In the philosophical journals, a fragment links the female with the earth and the male with air; both are deemed necessary ingredients for the acclaimed "shaping [*Bildung*] of the earth" (KA XVIII, 184, # 702). In *Idee* 19 the feminine is associated with love and the masculine with genius; the Golden Age, Schlegel concludes, must then be a state in which the two coexist. At another time he wrote that a woman was a classical and a man a progressive being, adding: "Both together a historical system" (KA XVIII, 87, # 693). As Behler has pointed out, the latter were the antipodes to be bridged in the "universal poetry" of *Athenäums-Fragment* 116: the classical and the progressive.[50] A combination of fragments yields a distinction between the Occident and the Orient -- termed the historical dualism -- which also accrued sexual designations. The Occident was for Schlegel the masculine and the Orient the feminine (KA XVIII, 358, # 454; 361, # 488).

Convinced that the sexual polarities were important in all forms of totality, Schlegel also tried to restore a feminine principle where he saw it missing. In *Athenäums-Fragment* 235 he noted that if Christ were adduced *a priori*, the same must be done for Mary (cf. LN 1278).[51] Were Christ to come again, he wrote in his literary

---

50 Behler, "Friedrich Schlegels Theorie der Universalpoesie," pp. 237-238.
51 Schlegel's notion prefigures those of more contemporary investigators, including Ernst Robert Curtius who, in *European Literature and the Latin Middle Ages*, trans. Willard R. Trask, Bollingen Series XXXVI (Princeton: Princeton University Press, 1973), pp. 122-123, expresses a similar opinion.

notebooks of 1801, he would be one with Mary (LN 2188). Even Diotima received a fresh evaluation in 1798; she was, Schlegel declared then, as necessary to Socratic philosophy as Mary has been to the Catholic faith (KA XVIII, 207, #123). Physical hermaphrodism seems also to be the object of his veneration in at least two fragments. In 1800 Schlegel referred to Shakespeare's "Venus and Adonis" as that author's pivotal work, and to Adonis, whose essence Schlegel described as "feminine masculinity," as a measure of his creator's genius (LN 2051, 1977). After seeing a da Vinci painting of a madonna, he wrote in 1802 that he glimpsed in her face "the ideal of the divine" because in its features he found united "solemn femininity and youthful masculinity."[52]

As an old man Schlegel characterized his philosophical work as a "constant striving for eternal unity" (KA V, XXXII). For a time he thought he had found that unity in predestined androgynous love which he then proffered as a myth, a new morality, for an age divested of its mythology. But he was a protean thinker; and just as he denied perfection to Romantic literature, he soon recognized that the fulfillment granted through love was only transitory. Only a few years later, in his lectures at Cologne, he voiced the opinion that true philosophy was incompatible with constancy, that the highest reality was to be found in an eternal becoming. Perhaps even while writing *Lucinde* he began to realize that the work was based on a private myth tailored to his own realities, for ultimately even Lucinde and Julius found it expedient to form other relationships. This development has to be seen as a refutation of the most fundamental premise of the novel; because of it, the ending seems quite unfocused. It is even possible that this conflict contributed to the paralysis which inhibited the completion of the second part of the work. The static condition created by androgynous perfection proved unsatisfactory to Schlegel, as it would have for any thinker committed to continual progress. Although occasional references to bisexual wholeness are to be found in Schlegel's writings after *Lucinde*, no longer was it the central symbol for reinstating a perfect world.

---
52 Quoted in Kluckhohn, *Die Auffassung der Liebe*, p. 354.

Conclusion

THE EARLY GERMAN ROMANTIC ANDROGYNE IN RETROSPECT

Because it implies the reunion of the most extreme dichotomies into one harmonious entity, the totality of the androgyne has appealed primarily to individuals or ages believing in the ultimate perfection of humanity. It has been a structuring force in myth and religion and a prevalent motif in the arts when the various disciplines associated under that rubric have focused upon the search for ultimate truth. This quest has, of course, not been limited to the early German Romantics, nor was the androgyne their exclusive property. But with its view of heterosexual love as the catalytic unitive force within the cosmos and its interpretation of androgynous totality as a psychological state, early German Romanticism seems in retrospect to have occupied a central position in the history of the ideal.

There seems to have been no European literary tradition before Romanticism which allotted to the androgyne a pivotal role;[1] only since that era has it become a frequent motif. In both France and Russia an ideal of bisexual totality became a factor in literature during the nineteenth century, a trend which critics are gradually recognizing.[2] While the influence of Böhme can be detected in both traditions,[3] his theosophy was even more formative for the thinking of the English Romantics. Blake and Coleridge, for example, knew his work and to others a more diffuse influence was transmitted through the Inner Light Protestants who, like the German Pietists,

---

1 Individual authors, however, have occasionally entertained a notion of androgynous perfection; an interpretation of Shakespeare from such a perspective would be productive.
2 Busst has demonstrated its importance in France; its appearance in Russian literature is attested to by Olga Matich in "Androgyny and the Russian Silver Age," *Pacific Coast Philology*, 14 (1979), pp. 42-50.
3 See Benz' *Adam*, pp. 16-30, 171-188, 267-294.

169

drew their inspiration from Böhme. The importance of marriage in English Romanticism has been conclusively demonstrated by Abrams;[4] as in the German movement, such a pattern was based upon an androgynous ideal. Resembling many of his German contemporaries, especially Schelling, Blake in *Marriage of Heaven and Hell* depicted the entire natural world as a macrocosm of sexual love in which the tension between opposing forces was itself the driving force for progress. The ideal was also central to his literature; no better example can be cited than his final engraving for *Jerusalem*, which depicts Albion and his female emanation Jerusalem in a conjugal embrace meant to signal a sexual reunion and thus an incipient paradise. Likewise, in Shelley's *Prometheus Bound* paradise ensues from the reuniting of Prometheus with his feminine counterpart Asia. Wordsworth in his Prospectus to *The Recluse* and Coleridge in "Dejection. An Ode" both heralded the new heaven and earth which would result from a marriage, or in Wordsworth's words, from the "great consummation" in which "the discerning intellect of Man" would be "wedded to this goodly universe."[5]

There is, to be sure, an element of the psychological in the works of English Romanticism. Coleridge, for example, even stated quite uncategorically that great minds must be androgynous.[6] Although this concern with psychological wholeness resembles that exhibited in the poetry and philosophy of Jena Romanticism, the preoccupation with psychological self-fulfillment was more pronounced in Germany. While their counterparts in England so often favored works with an epic sweep, the early German Romantics concentrated upon the individual in whom the grand synthesis should take place. Friedrich Schlegel's unique adaptation in 1794 and 1795 as well as

---

4 Abrams, pp. 27-31, 256-264, 273.
5 William Wordsworth, *The Poetical Works*, ed. E. de Selincourt and Helen Darbishire, vol. 5 (Oxford: Clarendon, 1949), p. 3. I quote from the 1814 edition of the preface to *The Excursion*.
6 Samuel Taylor Coleridge, *The Table Talk and Omniana*, ed. T. Ashe (London: Bell, 1888), p. 183. The male is the norm for Coleridge as clearly as it was for the German Romantics: earlier that year he wrote that "something feminine" can be discovered in the countenances "of all men of genius," pp. 150-151.

the pattern common to many of the Jena circle -- the latter clearly the culmination of numerous historical and cultural traditions – both prefigured the major appropriations of the androgyne which followed, and not just in the German speaking world. For both versions — the one assigning to the sexes gender-associated psychological traits, and the other committed to overcoming them -- represent new adaptations of the ancient ideal which at least some contemporary thinkers still consider valid. After the Romantic era, the myth of bisexual perfection was ready for metamorphoses by nineteenth century psychologists and twentieth century feminists.

When Friedrich Schlegel advanced his idea of sexual equality while studying ancient Greek literature, he was defying all tradition, trying without precedents to establish categories for determining general human behavior. Although he certainly did not transcend the idealization of women which marred many previous attempts at defining sexual differences, he did struggle versus the position which treated women as ancillaries important only for a man's development. It could be argued that his insistence on describing female characters betrays a tendency toward glorifying the feminine. But there are different reasons for choosing female heroines, and Schlegel seems to have done so in the mid 1790's because he was trying to reinstate the balance between the sexes. He was attempting to persuade his contemporaries that not only individuals, but society as well would benefit if the character traits usually associated with gender were available to all; and more importantly, that the positive qualities his culture attributed to the opposing sexes should be merged within each human being, male and female alike.

Contemporary feminists have debated the wisdom of just such a program; [7] it is controversial for several reasons. Its susceptibility

---

[7] Alexandra G. Kaplan and Joan P. Bean, in *Beyond Sex-Role Stereotypes: Readings Toward a Psychology of Androgyny* (Boston: Little, Brown and Co., 1976), present a positive appraisal as does June Singer in *Androgyny: Towards a New Theory of Sexuality*; Singer's views, however, are based on Jungian concepts and would be judged harshly by most feminists. For a more sceptical view of androgyny, see Barbara Charlesworth Gelpi's "The Politics of Androgyny," *Women's Studies*, 2 (1974), 2, pp. 151-160; and Daniel A. Harris' "Androgyny: The Sexist Myth in Disguise," in the same issue of *Women's Studies*, pp. 171-184.

to linkage with homosexuality and asexuality and even with the more modern phenomenon of unisex makes it immediately suspect. But beyond that, there are problems inherent in an androgynous model for psychological wholeness which are as ominous today as they were for Friedrich Schlegel. There is no line of influence between Schlegel and those who today use the androgyne as a guide for sexual equality, but perhaps his works can demonstrate a truth which some contemporary thinkers have failed to realize: Schlegel's call for "gentle masculinity" and "independent femininity" is ultimately meaningful only if there is a true referent for maleness and femaleness, if there truly is an essence which can be called feminine or masculine. And since the goal implies a denial of sexually defined behavior, the terms contradict the premise. The ideal of androgyny in the service of equality is perhaps illusory since from the beginning it requires, even in the language used for its definition, a separation of the sexes.

From this perspective, Schlegel's further development was quite logical. From a position espousing humanness as a neutralization of traits falsely assigned to one or the other sex, he very soon began to promulgate the idea that those attributes which society identified with each were, in fact, biologically determined. When he said in *Athenäums-Fragment* 262 that "to become God, to be human, to develop oneself [*sich bilden*]," were all expressions which "mean the same thing," the divine humanity he intended was to result from the combination of very real male and female oppositions. This is the more common Romantic appropriation of the androgyne, one which Novalis' works and Schlegel's *Lucinde* exemplify.

Earlier ages had believed in the same analogy between humanity and the world which was to the Jena Romantics an article of faith, but what the latter did with the analogy differed significantly from anything that had previously been suggested. Deeply influenced by Böhme, but reacting as well to the needs of their own age, the early German Romantics transformed Böhme's emphasis on individual self-consciousness from a religious to a secular context wherein perfection was a psychological state. For the first time psychological traits were rigidly associated with gender in a far-reaching, universal pattern; the entire world was aligned with the sexual polarities and the differences between the two sexes were seen as paradigmatic. Romantic physics and nature philosophy posited polarous forces throughout the world whose recombination would accomplish the return to paradise.

Formulated in terms of an androgynous absolute, the individual wholeness the Romantics desired and which they believed could change the world was a fledgling attempt at achieving psychological wholeness. As such, it anticipated aspects of Jungian psychology by almost one hundred years, and indeed perhaps even helped to shape it. When Jung posited psychological completion for the male in his integration of the feminine "anima," and the obverse for the female – that is, the integration into her psyche of the male "animus"[8] – he was presenting a more sophisticated method for attaining the same wholeness so desired by the early German Romantics. His works resemble those of the Jena group in another way as well. The Romantic belief in the importance of human perfection, based as it was on an androgynous model, theoretically tributed the sexes as equals. In practice, however, such was not the case. Although Böhme's theosophy had posited the "equal tinctures" of male and female, the male was undoubtedly the norm. Adam was the primal androgyne and at the same time the male longing for the female within him. The image usually adhered to in Böhme's works was consequently that of a male speaker longing for the Heavenly Virgin Sophia. And the Romantics accepted and followed this pattern. As de Beauvoir has observed about men throughout history, the early Romantics appraised women primarily as "other." Stated differently, the Jena Romantics idealized women to such an extent that there is in their work a pervasive belief in a saving "feminine" principle. Jung's thinking was in the same way subtly masculist, for the male was the normative principle; women were rigidly assessed as nonrational and men as rational. Although his system was capable in theory of facilitating a reciprocal integration, Jung believed as did the Romantics that women were less in need of such integration

---

8 Jung's conception of the "anima" and "animus" are presented in *Archetypes and the Collective Unconscious*, vol. 9, part 1, 1968, pp. 3-41 and 54-72.

than men. In "Women in Europe" he even warned women of the dangers to society if they were indeed to integrate the "animus."[9] The all-embracing mother world he envisioned -- also prefigured and perhaps influenced by Novalis' merging of mother, virgin, goddess and personal partner -- was the means for achieving male wholeness.

Lacking the tools which the psychologists later developed, the Jena Romantics could see the necessary exchange of sexual qualities only in love. As Novalis once said: "It is because of *love* that magic is possible. Love effects magic" (III, 255, # 79). And more to the point, it was the sexual drive which they honored; it was eros alone which would assure the combination necessary for perfection. But individual wholeness was only a part of the Romantics' program. Ultimately they turned to art to effect their cosmic dreams; and in this they were also forging their own tradition, for more than their predecessors they believed in the symbols they created. Poetry was for the early German Romantics, as Northrop Frye has said about English poetry in the late eighteenth century, "incantatory...and in the original sense of the word, charming."[10]

Thus in their lives and in their works, the myth of the androgyne provided the impetus for the male poets and philosophers of early German Romanticism to become complete human beings, to incorporate into their psyches the "feminine" attributes they thought they lacked. What perhaps began as a pragmatic attempt at wholeness led to a metaphysics of sex, for heterosexual love soon became the way to the Golden Age. Expressed in the Romantic idiom, androgynous love was their prescription for salvation, both for themselves and for what they judged to be their equally fragmented world.

The German adaptations of androgyny discussed here have also been reflected in subsequent German literature. Although it played

---

9 Jung, "Women in Europe," in *Civilization in Transition*, vol. 10, 1970, pp. 113-133.
10 Northrop Frye, "Towards Defining an Age of Sensibility," in *Fables of Identity: Studies in Poetic Mythology* (New York: Harcourt, 1963), p. 133. Werner Vordtriede, in *Novalis und die französischen Symbolisten* (Stuttgart: Kohlhammer, 1963), and Mario Praz, in *The Romantic Agony*, offer quite different analyses of Romantic symbolism.

little part in German literature before that time, the ideal of bisexual perfection has appeared in the works of many writers who followed the Jena group. In selected works of Rilke, Musil, Kafka, Thomas Mann, Hesse, Trakl and Brecht, for example, it is discernible. With the exception perhaps of Brecht, the ideal in the thinking of these writers retains its Romantic trappings; the polarization of the sexes is unquestioned. Others have challenged the verity of those stereotypes as Schlegel did in the mid 1790's. In the literature of certain writers at work today — among them Wolf, de Bruyn and Sarah Kirsch — the androgyne functions as a model for the goal of sexual equality, for overcoming the definition of the sexes as complementary oppositions. When one recognizes the similarities between these nineteenth and twentieth century works and the writings of Friedrich Schlegel and Novalis in the few short years between 1794 and 1800, the significance of the Romantic contribution to the history and understanding of the androgynous ideal becomes ever more obvious.

BIBLIOGRAPHY

Primary Sources

ARNOLD, Gottfried. *Das Geheimnis der göttlichen Sophia*. Part 2. 1700; facsimile rpt. Stuttgart: Frommann, 1963.
—. *Das eheliche und unverehelichte Leben der ersten Christen*. Frankfurt: Fritschen, 1702.

BAADER, Franz v. *Sämmtliche Werke*. Leipzig: Bethmann, 1851-1857.
BERNARD OF CLAIRVAUX. *Saint Bernard on the Love of God*. Trans. Rev. Terence L. Connolly. Techny, Ill.: Mission Press, 1943.
BÖHME, Jakob. *Sämmtliche Werke*. Ed. K.W. Schiebler. Leipzig: Barth, 1922.

Caroline: Briefe aus der Frühromantik. Ed. Erich Schmidt. 2 vols. Leipzig: Insel, 1913.
COLERIDGE, Samuel Taylor. *The Table Talk and Omniana*. Ed. T. Ashe. London: Bell, 1888.

FICHTE, Johann Gottlieb. *Sämmtliche Werke*. Ed. J.H. Fichte. Vol. 3. Leipzig: Mayer and Müller, 1924.

GICHTEL, Johann Georg. *Theosophia Practica*. Vol. 3. Leyden, 1722.
—. *Theosophia Revelata*. Vol. 1. [Holland], 1715.
GOETHE, Johann Wolfgang v. "Faust." In *Berliner Ausgabe*. Vol. 8. Berlin: Aufbau, 1965.
—. *Goethes Gespräche*. Ed. Wolfgang Herwig. Vol. 2. Zürich: Artemis, 1969.

HEGEL, Georg Wilhelm Friedrich. "Love." In *Early Theological Writings*. Trans. and ed. T.M. Knox and Richard Kroner. Chicago: University of Chicago Press, 1948.

Hermetica. Trans. and ed. Walter Scott. 4 vols. Oxford: Clarendon, 1924-1936.
HÖLDERLIN, Friedrich. "Hyperion oder der Eremit in Griechenland." In *Sämtliche Werke*. Ed. Friedrich Beissner. Vol. 3. Stuttgart: Kohlhammer, 1957.
HUMBOLDT, Wilhelm v. "Über die männliche und weibliche Form." In *Gesammelte Schriften*. Ed. Albert Leitzmann. Vol. 1. Berlin: Behr, 1903.

JUNG, C.G. *The Collected Works of Carl G. Jung*. Trans. R.F.C. Hull. Bollingen Series XX. 2nd ed. Princeton: Princeton University Press, 1961-1979.

KANT, Immanuel. *Werke*. Ed. Ernst Cassirer. Vol. 4. Berlin: Cassirer, 1922.
KLEIST, Heinrich v. "Briefe." in *Sämtliche Werke und Briefe*. Ed. Helmut Sembdner. Vol. 5. München: Hanser, 1970.

MECHTHILD v. MAGDEBURG. *Das fliessende Licht der Gottheit*. Ed. Margot Schmidt. Einsiedeln: Benzig, 1955.
The Midrash Rabbah. Genesis. Trans. Harry Freedman. Vol. 1. London: Soncino, 1977.
New Testament Apocrypha. Ed. Edgar Hennecke and Wilhelm Schneemelcher. Trans. A.J.B. Higgins et al. Vol. I. London: Lutterworth, 1963.

NOVALIS. *Schriften*. Ed. Richard Samuel et al. 4 vols. 2nd ed. Stuttgart: Kohlhammer, 1960-1975.

OETINGER, Friedrich Christoph. *Über Jakob Boehmes Adamsspekulation*. 1776; rpt. Stuttgart, 1849.

PARACELSUS. *The Hermetic and Alchemical Writings of Paracelsus*. Ed. and trans. A.E. Waite. Vol. 1. London: Elliot, 1894.
PLATO. *The Symposium*. Trans. W. Hamilton. Harmondsworth, Middlesex: Penguin, 1951.

RITTER, Johann Wilhelm. *Fragmente aus dem Nachlass eines jungen Physikers*. 1810; rpt. Heidelberg: Schneider, 1969.

SCHELLING, Friedrich. *Sämmtliche Werke*. Ed. K.F.A. Schelling. Stuttgart und Augsburg: Cotta, 1856-1861.

SCHILLER, Friedrich. "Über naive und sentimentalische Dichtung." In *Schillers Werke: Nationalausgabe*. Ed. Benno von Wiese. Vol. 20. Weimar: Böhlaus, 1962.

Schiller und die Romantiker. Ed. H.H. Borcherdt. Stuttgart: Cotta, 1948.

SCHLEGEL, August Wilhelm. *Sämmtliche Werke*. Ed. Eduard Böking. Vol. 11. Leipzig: Weidmann, 1847.

SCHLEGEL, Friedrich. *Briefe an seinen Bruder August Wilhelm*. Ed. Oskar Walzel. Berlin: Speyer and Peters, 1890.

—. *Kritische Ausgabe*. Ed. Ernst Behler et al. München: Schöningh, 1958—.

—. *Literary Notebooks 1797-1801*. Ed. Hans Eichner. Toronto: University of Toronto Press, 1957.

SCHLEGEL, Friedrich and Novalis. *Biographie einer Romantikerfreundschaft in ihren Briefen*. Ed. Max Preitz. Darmstadt: Gentner, 1957.

SCHLEIERMACHER, Friedrich. *Aus Schleiermacher's Leben: In Briefen*. Vol. 3. Berlin: Reimer, 1861.

—. *Schleiermachers Werke*. Ed. Otto Braun et al. Leipzig: Meiner, 1911.

SCHUBERT, Gotthilf Heinrich. "Von der Liebe der Geschlechter und der Zeugung." In *Die Geschichte der Seele*. Vol. 1. 1877; rpt. Hildesheim: Olms, 1961.

SILESIUS, Angelius. "Der cherubinische Wandersmann." In *Sämtliche poetische Werke*. Ed. Hans Ludwig Held. Vol. 3. 3rd ed. München: Hanser, 1949.

SWEDENBORG, Emanuel. *Conjugial Love*. Trans. Samuel M. Warren. New York: Swedenborg Foundation, 1928.

TIECK, Ludwig. Letter published by Gotthold Klee. *Euphorion*. Ergänzungsheft 3, 1897, pp. 212-215.

WACKENRODER, Wilhelm Heinrich. *Werke und Briefe*. Heidelberg: Schneider, 1967.

WORDSWORTH, William. *The Poetical Works.* Ed. E. de Selincourt and Helen Darbishire. Vol. 5. Oxford: Clarendon, 1949.

ZINZENDORF, Count Nikolaus Ludwig v. In *Das Zeitalter des Pietismus.* Ed. Martin Schmidt and Wilhelm Jannasch. Bremen: Schünemann, 1965, pp. 255-416.

Secondary Sources

ABRAMS, M.H. *Natural Supernaturalism: Tradition and Revolution in Romantic Literature.* New York: Norton, 1971.

BAUMANN, Hermann. *Das doppelte Geschlecht: Ethnologische Studien zur Bisexualität in Ritus und Mythos.* Berlin: Reimer, 1955.
BAUMGARDT, David. *Franz von Baader und die philosophische Romantik.* Halle: Niemeyer, 1927.
BECK, Lewis White, introd. *On History: Immanuel Kant.* New York: Bobbs-Merrill, 1963, pp. vii-xxvi.
BECKER-CANTARINO, Bärbel. "Priesterin und Lichtbringerin: Zur Ideologie des weiblichen Charakters in der Frühromantik." In *Die Frau als Heldin und Autorin.* Ed. Wolfgang Paulsen. Bern: Francke, 1979, pp. 111-124.
BEHLER, Ernst, introd. *Friedrich Schlegel: Schriften und Fragmente.* Stuttgart: Kröner, 1956.
—. "Friedrich Schlegels Theorie der Universalpoesie." In *Jahrbuch der deutschen Schillergesellschaft.* Ed. Fritz Martini et al. Stuttgart: Kröner, 1957, pp. 211-252.
BENZ, Ernst. *Adam: Der Mythus vom Urmenschen.* München: Otto-Wilhelm-Barth, 1955.
—. "Immanuel Swedenborg als geistiger Wegbahner des deutschen Idealismus und der deutschen Romantik." *Deutsche Vierteljahrsschrift für Literaturwissenschaft und Geistesgeschichte,* 19 (1941), 1, pp. 1-32.
—. "Johann Albrecht Bengel und die Philosophie des deutschen Idealismus." *Deutsche Vierteljahrsschrift für Literaturwissenschaft und Geistesgeschichte,* 27 (1953), 4, pp. 528-554.

BERTHOLET, Alfred. *Das Geschlecht der Gottheit.* Tübingen: Mohr, 1934.
BRINTON, Howard H. *The Mystic Will: Based on a Study of the Philosophy of Jacob Boehme.* London: Allen and Unwin, 1931.
BROWN, Marshall. *The Shape of German Romanticism.* London: Cornell University Press, 1979.
BROWN, Robert F. *The Later Philosophy of Schelling: The Influence of Boehme on the Works of 1809-1815.* Lewisburg: Bucknell University Press, 1977.
BRUFORD, W.H. *Culture and Society in Classical Weimar: 1775-1806.* Cambridge: Cambridge University Press, 1962.
—. *The German Tradition of Self-Cultivation.* Cambridge: Cambridge University Press, 1975.
BUSST, A.J.L. "The Image of the Androgyne in the Nineteenth Century." In *Romantic Mythologies.* Ed. Ian Fletcher. London: Routledge and Paul, 1967, pp. 1-95.
BUTLER, E.M. *The Tyranny of Greece over Germany.* Boston: Beacon, 1958.

CAMPBELL, Joseph. *The Masks of God: Occidental Mythology.* New York: Viking, 1964.
—. *The Masks of God: Primitive Mythology.* New York: Viking, 1959.
CURTIUS, Ernst Robert. *European Literature and the Latin Middle Ages.* Trans. Willard R. Trask. Bollingen Series XXXVI. Princeton: Princeton University Press, 1973.

DALY, Mary. *Beyond God the Father.* Boston: Beacon, 1973.
DELCOURT, Marie. *Hermaphrodite: Myths and Rites of the Bisexual Figure in Classical Antiquity.* Trans. Jennifer Nicholson. London: Studio Books, 1961.
DIECKMANN, Lieselotte. "Friedrich Schlegel and the Romantic Concepts of the Symbol." *Germanic Review*, 34 (1959), pp. 276-283.
DIETRICH, Ernst Ludwig. "Der Urmensch als Androgyn." *Zeitschrift für Kirchengeschichte*, 3. Folge IX, Vol. 58 (1939), 3/4, pp. 297-345.
DIJKSTRA, Bram. "The Androgyne in Nineteenth Century Art and Literature." *Comparative Literature*, 26 (1974), pp. 62-73.

EDERHEIMER, Edgar. *Jakob Boehme und die Romantiker.* Heidelberg: Winter, 1904.
EICHNER, Hans. *Friedrich Schlegel.* New York: Twayne, 1970.
—. "Friedrich Schlegel's Theory of Romantic Poetry." *PMLA*, 7 (1956), pp. 1018-1041.
ELIADE, Mircea. *Mephistopheles and the Androgyne.* Trans. J.M. Cohen. New York: Sheed and Ward, 1965.
—. *Patterns in Comparative Religion.* Trans. Rosemary Sheed. New York: New American Library, 1958.
EXNER, Richard. "Androgynie und Preussischer Staat. Themen, Probleme und das Beispiel Heinrich von Kleist." *Aurora*, 39 (1979), pp. 51-78.

FABER, Richard. "Apokalyptische Mythologie: Zur Religionsdichtung des Novalis." In *Romantische Utopie, Utopische Romantik.* Ed. Gisela Dischner and Richard Faber. Hildesheim: Gerstenberg, 1979, pp. 66-92.
FEILCHENFELD, Walther. *Der Einfluss Jacob Böhmes auf Novalis.* Berlin: Ebering, 1922.
FIRCHOW, Peter, introd. *Friedrich Schlegel's 'Lucinde' and the Fragments.* Minneapolis: University of Minnesota Press, 1971.
FRAZER, James. *The Golden Bough: A Study in Magic and Religion.* Vol. 1. New York: Macmillan, 1940.
—. *Folklore in the Old Testament.* New York: Macmillan, 1923.
FRYE, Northrop. "Towards Defining an Age of Sensibility." In *Fables of Identity: Studies in Poetic Mythology.* New York: Harcourt, 1963, pp. 130-137.
FURNESS, Raymond. "The Androgynous Ideal: Its Significance in German Literature." *Modern Language Review*, 60 (1965), pp. 58-64.

GELPI, Barbara Charlesworth. "The Politics of Androgyny." *Women's Studies*, 2 (1974), 2, pp. 151-160.
GIESE, Fritz. *Der romantische Charakter I: Die Entwicklung des Androgynenproblems in der Frühromantik.* Langensalza: Wendt and Klauwell, 1919.
GINZBERG, Louis. *The Legends of the Jews.* Trans. Henrietta Szold. Vol. 1. Philadelphia: Jewish Publication Society of America, 1909.

GODE-VON AESCH, Alexander. *Natural Science in German Romanticism*. Columbia University Germanic Studies 11. Morningside Heights, N.Y.: Columbia University Press, 1941.
GRAVES, Robert. *The Greek Myths*. Vol.1. New York: Braziller, 1959.
GRAY, Ronald. *Goethe the Alchemist: A Study of Alchemical Symbolism in Goethe's Literary and Scientific Works*. Cambridge: Cambridge University Press, 1952.

HARRIS, Daniel A. "Androgyny: The Sexist Myth in Disguise." *Women's Studies*, 2 (1974), 2, pp. 171-184.
HAYWOOD, Bruce. *Novalis: The Veil of Imagery*. Harvard Germanic Studies I. 'S-Gravenhage: Mouton, 1959.
HEILBRUN, Carolyn G. *Toward a Recognition of Androgyny*. New York: Harper and Row, 1973.
HUCH, Ricarda. *Die Romantik I: Blütezeit der Romantik*. 13th ed. Leipzig: Haessel, 1924.
—. "Die romantische Ehe." In *Das Ehe-Buch*. Ed. Hermann Alexander Keyserling. Celle: Kampmann, 1925, pp. 147-169.

IMLE, Fanny. *Novalis: Seine philosophische Weltanschauung*. Paderborn: Schöningh, 1928.

JAMES, William. *The Varieties of Religious Experience*. New York: Longmanns, Green and Co., 1912.

KANTZENBACH, Friedrich Wilhelm. *Orthodoxie und Pietismus*. Evangelische Enzyklopädie, No. 11/12. Gütersloh: Mohn, 1966.
KAPLAN, Alexandra G. and Joan P. Bean. *Beyond Sex-Role Stereotypes: Readings Toward a Psychology of Androgyny*. Boston: Little, Brown and Co., 1976.
KIRK, G.S. and J.E. Raven. *The Presocratic Philosophers*. Cambridge: Cambridge University Press, 1957.
KLIN, Eugenius. "Das Problem der Emanzipation in Friedrich Schlegels 'Lucinde.'" *Weimarer Beiträge*, 1 (1963), pp. 76-99.
KLUCKHOHN, Paul. *Die Auffassung der Liebe in der Literatur des 18. Jahrhunderts und in der deutschen Romantik*. 2nd ed. Halle: Niemeyer, 1931.

KLUCKHOHN, Paul. *Das Ideengut der deutschen Romantik*. 3rd ed. Tübingen: Niemeyer, 1953.
KÖRNER, Josef. "Neues vom Dichter der Lucinde." In *Preussische Jahrbücher*, 183 (1921), pp. 309-330.
KORFF, Hermann August. *Geist der Goethezeit*. Vol. 3. Leipzig: Weber, 1940.

LANGEN, August. *Der Wortschatz des deutschen Pietismus*. Tübingen: Niemeyer, 1954.
LITTLEJOHN, Richard. "The 'Bekenntnisse eines Ungeschickten.' A Re-examination of Emancipatory Ideas in Friedrich Schlegel's 'Lucinde.' " *Modern Language Review*, 72 (1977), pp. 605-614.
LOVEJOY, Arthur. O. *Essays in the History of Ideas*. Baltimore: Johns Hopkins University Press, 1948.
—. *The Great Chain of Being*. Cambridge: Harvard University Press, 1961.

MÄHL, Hans-Joachim. *Die Idee des goldenen Zeitalters im Werk des Novalis*. Heidelberg: Winter, 1965.
—. "Novalis und Plotin." In *Novalis: Beiträge zu Werk und Persönlichkeit Friedrich von Hardenbergs*. Ed. Gerhard Schulz. Darmstadt: Wissenschaftliche Buchgesellschaft, 1970, pp. 361-375.
MATICH, Olga. "Androgyny and the Russian Silver Age." *Pacific Coast Philology*, 14 (1979), pp. 42-50.
MAY, Rollo, ed. *Symbolism in Religion and Literature*. New York: Braziller, 1960.
MCFARLAND, Thomas. "A Complex Dialogue: Coleridge's Doctrine of Polarity and Its European Contexts." In *Reading Coleridge: Approaches and Applications*. Ed. Walter B. Crawford. London: Cornell University Press, 1979, pp. 56-115.
MEEKS, Wayne. "The Image of the Androgyne: Some Uses of a Symbol in Earliest Christianity." *History of Religions*, 13 (1974), 3, pp. 165-208.

NEUMANN, Erich. *The Origins and History of Human Consciousness*. Trans. R.F.C. Hull. New York: Pantheon, 1954.
NICOLSON, Marjorie Hope. *The Breaking of the Circle*. 2nd ed. New York: Columbia University Press, 1962.

PAGELS, Elaine. *The Gnostic Gospels*. New York: Random, 1979.
PASCHEK, Carl. *Der Einfluss Jacob Böhmes auf das Werk Friedrich von Hardenbergs*. Diss. Bonn, 1967. Bonn: Rheinische Friedrich-Wilhelms-Universität, 1967.
PASSMORE, John. *The Perfectibility of Man*. London: Duckworth, 1970.
PECKHAM, Morse. "Towards a Theory of Romanticism: II. Reconsiderations." In *The Triumph of Romanticism*. Columbia, S.C.: University of South Carolina Press, 1970, pp. 27-35.
PRAZ, Mario. *The Romantic Agony*. Trans. Angus Davidson. London: Oxford University Press, 1970.

REIK, Theodore. *The Creation of Woman: A Psychoanalytic Inquiry into the Myth of Eve*. New York: McGraw-Hill, 1973.
RITSCHL, Albrecht. *Geschichte des Pietismus in der lutherischen Kirche des 17. und 18. Jahrhunderts*. 3 vols. Bonn: Marcus, 1880-1886.
RITTER, Heinz. *Novalis' Hymnen an die Nacht*. Heidelberg: Winter, 1974.
—. *Der unbekannte Novalis: Friedrich von Hardenberg im Spiegel seiner Dichtung*. Göttingen: Sachse and Pohl, 1967.

SCHABER, Steven C. "Novalis' Theory of the Work of Art as Hieroglyph." *Germanic Review*, 48 (1973), pp. 35-43.
SCHMIDT, Martin. *Wiedergeburt und neuer Mensch*. Witton: Luther, 1969.
—. *Pietismus*. Stuttgart: Kohlhammer, 1972.
SCHOLEM, Gershom G. *Major Trends in Jewish Mysticism*. 3rd ed. New York: Schocken, 1954.
SCHULZE, W. *Das androgyne Ideal und der christliche Glaube*. Lahr-Dinglingen: St-Johannes, 1940.
SHIMAYA, Setsuko. "Über die Androgyne beim jungen Friedrich Schlegel." *Doitsu Bungaku*, 53 (1974), pp. 65-75.
SILBERER, Herbert. *Problems of Mysticism and its Symbolism*. Trans. Smith Ely Jelliffe. New York: Weiser, 1970.
SINGER, June. *Androgyny: Towards a New Theory of Sexuality*. Garden City, N.Y.: Anchor/Doubleday, 1976.

STACE, Walter T. *The Teachings of the Mystics*. New York: New American Library, 1960.

TATAR, Maria M. *Spellbound: Studies on Mesmerism and Literature*. Princeton: Princeton University Press, 1978.
TAYLOR, Anya. *Magic and English Romanticism*. Athens: University of Georgia Press, 1979.
THOMAS, Keith. *Religion and the Decline of Magic*. London: Weidenfeld and Nicolson, 1971.
TUVESON, Ernest. *Millennium and Utopia: A Study in the Background of the Idea of Progress*. Berkeley: University of California Press, 1949.

UNDERHILL, Evelyn. *Mysticism: A Study in the Nature and Development of Man's Spiritual Consciousness*. 12th ed. New York: Dutton, 1930.

VORDTRIEDE, Werner. *Novalis und die französischen Symbolisten*. Stuttgart: Kohlhammer, 1963.

WAITE, A.E. *The Occult Sciences*. 1891; rpt. Secaucus, N.J.: University Books, 1974.
WALZEL, Oskar. "Ricarda Huchs Romantik." In *Vom Geistesleben alter und neuer Zeit*. Leipzig: Insel, 1922, pp. 337-365.
WATTS, Alan. *The Two Hands of God: The Myths of Polarity*. New York: Collier: 1969.
WEIL, Simone. *The Iliad or the Poem of Force*. Trans. Mary McCarthy. Wallingford, Pa.: Pendle Hall, 1970.
WEILAND, Werner. *Der junge Friedrich Schlegel oder Die Revolution in der Frühromantik*. Stuttgart: Kohlhammer, 1968.
WETZELS, Walter D. "Aspects of Natural Science in German Romanticism." *Studies in Romanticism*, 10 (1971), 1, pp. 44-59.

YATES, Frances A. *Giordano Bruno and the Hermetic Tradition*. Chicago: University of Chicago Press, 1964.

INDEX OF NAMES

Abrams, M.H. 20n., 21n., 27, 27n., 28n., 43, 43n., 46, 48n., 57n., 65, 68, 68n., 76, 136, 170
Aeschylus 11, 120
Alcibiades 121
Aristophanes 15-16, 16n., 153
Arnim, Achim v. 162
Arnold, Gottfried 33-34, 34n., 85n.

Baader, Franz v. 58-60, 87
Baumann, Hermann 11n.
Baumgardt, David 43n., 59, 60n., 87n.
Bean, Joan P. 171n.
Beauvoir, Simone de 128, 173
Beck, Lewis White 44n.
Becker-Cantarino, Bärbel 160
Behler, Ernst 142, 143, 144, 147, 147n., 148, 166
Bengel, Johann Albrecht 43
Benz, Ernst 32, 36n., 37, 43, 102n., 106, 169n.
Bernard of Clairvaux 28
Bertholet, Alfred 11n.
Blake, William 169, 170
Böhme, Jakob 29-37, 40, 44, 46, 48, 48n., 53, 56, 58, 59, 60, 65, 68, 73, 78, 81, 86-87, 88, 89n., 93n., 97-98, 103, 140, 141, 146, 147, 148, 150, 153, 160-161, 169, 170, 172, 173
Böhmer, Caroline 110, 111-113, 115n., 122-123, 128, 133, 135, 145, 146, 149, 150, 151, 161, 162
Böttiger, K.A. 40
Brecht, Bertolt 175
Brentano, Clemens 148
Brinton, Howard H. 29
Brown, Marshall 37, 148

187

Brown, Robert F. 48n., 56n., 161n.
Bruford, W.H. 49, 49n.
Bruyn, Günter de 175
Busst, A.J.L. 40n., 61-62, 102n., 169n.
Butler, E.M. 114-115n.

Campbell, Joseph 10, 11n., 13n., 14, 89n.
Carlyle, Thomas 46
Claudius, Matthias 37
Coleridge, Samuel Taylor 169, 170, 170n.
Creuzer, Friedrich 40
Curtius, Ernst Robert 166n.

Daly, Mary 17n.
Delcourt, Marie 12, 13n.
Dieckmann, Lieselotte 164-165
Dietrich, Ernst Ludwig 22

Ederheimer, Edgar 32n., 75, 86n.
Eichner, Hans 112, 123, 134-135, 136n., 142n., 143, 149n., 153, 163
Eliade, Mircea 9n., 10, 11, 12n., 13, 14, 18n., 19n., 55-56, 57
Euripides 11, 121, 127
Exner, Richard 40n., 61, 102n.

Faber, Richard 104n.
Father Festugière 21
Feilchenfeld, Walther 86n., 89n.
Fichte, Johann Gottlieb 46, 47, 51, 72, 87, 105, 113, 114, 141, 146, 151, 151n., 165
Firchow, Peter 148, 160
Forster, Georg 113, 134
Frazer, James 12, 17n.
Frye, Northrop 174
Furness, Raymond 102n.

Gelpi, Barbara Charlesworth 171n.

188

Gichtel, Johann Georg 32, 33, 34
Giese, Fritz 39, 39n., 40n., 83n., 102n., 120n., 134, 140-141n.
Ginzberg, Louis 17n., 18
Gode-Von Aesch, Alexander 82, 85n.
Goethe, Johann Wolfgang v. 22n., 26, 34, 36, 45, 49, 55-56, 57, 59, 61, 78, 85, 114, 141, 154
Gottfried v. Strassburg 39
Graves, Robert 11-12, 12n., 144n.
Gray, Ronald 22n., 23n., 24, 58, 85n.

Harris, Daniel A. 171n.
Haywood, Bruce 72, 75, 75n., 76, 80n., 91, 107
Hegel, Georg Wilhelm Friedrich 37, 45, 56-57, 60
Heilbrun, Carolyn G. 14n., 118, 129
Hemsterhuis, Franz 122
Heraclitus 14
Herder, Johann Gottfried 44, 117n.
Hermes Trismegistus 20-21
Hesse, Hermann 175
Hölderlin, Friedrich 11, 37, 45, 62, 76
Homer 117, 118, 119, 120
Huch, Ricarda 39, 39n., 102n., 162
Humboldt, Wilhelm v. 58

Imle, Fanny 67n.

Jacobi, Friedrich Heinrich 131, 132, 133, 134
James, William 26
Jung, C.G. 10, 23-24, 25n., 26n., 90, 173-174
Jung-Stilling, Heinrich 36

Kafka, Franz 175
Kant, Immanuel 36, 37, 42, 43, 44-45, 56, 114, 150
Kantzenbach, Friedrich Wilhelm 33, 35n.
Kaplan, Alexandra 171n.
Kirk, G.S. 14n.
Kirsch, Sarah 175

Kleist, Heinrich v. 45, 54, 62
Klin, Eugenius 145, 162, 163
Kluckhohn, Paul 22n., 29n., 33n., 40, 53n., 62, 73n., 86, 89n., 90, 91, 92, 92n., 102, 103, 104-105, 112, 133n., 139, 150n.
Körner, Josef 162
Korff, Hermann August 102-103
Kühn, Sophie v. 67-68, 91-92, 96, 98, 99, 111

Lavater, Johann Kaspar 36
Lessing, Gotthold Ephraim 43
Lovejoy, Arthur O. 44n., 45n., 85n.

Mähl, Hans-Joachim 42-43, 43n., 66, 68n., 72n., 75, 85n., 88n., 89n., 90, 103, 103n.
Mann, Thomas 175
Marx, Karl 49
Matich, Olga 169n.
May, Rollo 54-55
McFarland, Thomas 56n.
Mechthild v. Magdeburg 29
Meeks, Wayne 19-20
Musil, Robert 175

Neumann, Erich 24
Nicolson, Marjorie Hope 64
Nietzsche, Friedrich 11

Oetinger, Friedrich Christoph 34-35, 36, 86

Pagels, Elaine 19, 81
Paracelsus 29
Paschek, Carl 32n., 73n., 86, 86n.
Passmore, John 26n.
Peckham, Morse 41, 72
Plato 15-16, 15n., 16n., 18, 41, 124, 125, 126, 127, 128, 139, 141, 153
Plotinus 41, 66

Praz, Mario 61, 174n.
Proklus 124
Pythagoras 124, 125, 126, 127

Reik, Theodore 17-18
Rilke, Rainer Maria 175
Ritschl, Albrecht 33n.
Ritter, Heinz 68n., 92n.
Ritter, Johann Wilhelm 49, 57-58, 66
Rousseau, Jean Jacques 44, 50, 131, 136n.

Saint-Martin, Louis Claude de 32, 37
Samuel, Richard 73n., 89n., 92, 92n.
Sappho 119, 131, 136n.
Schaber, Steven C. 65n.
Schelling, Friedrich 37, 47-48, 47n., 48n., 50, 51, 54, 58, 66, 81-82, 87, 111, 146-147, 165, 170
Schiller, Friedrich 37, 44, 45, 46, 49, 51-52, 52n., 58, 75n., 115n., 131, 143
Schlegel, August Wilhelm 58, 62, 110, 111, 113, 142, 161
Schlegel, Caroline (later Schelling), see Caroline Böhmer
Schleiermacher, Friedrich 37, 50-51, 53n., 82, 85, 140, 147, 157
Schmidt, Martin 33n., 35n.
Scholem, Gershom G. 18-19, 19n.
Schopenhauer, Arthur 8, 60
Schubert, Gotthilf Heinrich 37, 49, 57-58, 88n.
Schulze, W. 22
Shaftesbury, Earl of 50
Shakespeare, William 167, 169n.
Shelley, Percy Bysshe 170
Shimaya, Setsuko 145n.
Silberer, Herbert 23n.
Silesius, Angelius 25
Singer, June 11n., 171n.
Socrates 122, 123, 124, 125, 149
Sophocles 120, 121, 122, 128, 129
Spinoza, Baruch 50

St. Augustine 28, 80, 101
Stace, Walter T. 25n.
Staël, Mme. de 49
Swedenborg, Emanuel 32, 36, 36n., 106n.

Tatar, Maria M. 67, 81n.
Taylor, Anya 65
Thomas, Keith 65n.
Tieck, Ludwig 37, 60-61, 73, 77, 111-112, 115n., 146
Trakl, Georg 175
Tuveson, Ernest 44n., 47

Underhill, Evelyn 24n., 25n., 27n.

Veit, Dorothea 135, 144, 157, 162, 163
Vordtriede, Werner 174n.
Voss, Johann Heinrich 53

Wackenroder, Wilhelm Heinrich 61, 115n.
Waite, A.E. 23n., 81, 81n.
Walzel, Oskar 40, 40n.
Watts, Alan 11n.
Weil, Simone 118
Weiland, Werner 114
Welcker, Friedrich 40
Wetzels, Walter D. 58n.
Wieland, Christoph Martin 49
Winckelmann, Johann Joachim 11, 13, 40, 116, 152
Wolf, Christa 175
Wolfram v. Eschenbach 80
Wordsworth, William 170

Yates, Frances A. 20n., 21n.

Zinzendorf, Count Nikolaus Ludwig v. 35, 66, 68n.